Alan Ayckbourn

PLAYS FIVE

Ayckbourn was born in London in 1939 to a
st father and a mother who was a writer. He left
at seventeen with two 'A' levels and went straight
e theatre. Two years in regional theatre as an actor
ge manager led in 1959 to the writing of his first
he Square Cat, for Scarborough's Theatre in the
at the instigation of his then employer and subse-
mentor, Stephen Joseph. Some 75 plays later, his
as been translated into over 35 languages, is per-
on stage and television throughout the world and
n countless awards. There have been English and
screen adaptations, the most notable being Alain
s' fine film of *Private Fears in Public Places*.

successes include *Relatively Speaking*, *How the
Half Loves*, *Absurd Person Singular*, *Bedroom Farce*,
rus of Disapproval, *The Norman Conquests*, *A
Family Business*, *Henceforward . . .*, *Comic Potential*,
* We Do for Love*, and, most recently, *Life of Riley*.
009, he retired as Artistic Director of the Stephen
Theatre, where almost all his plays have been and
e to be first staged, after 37 years in the post. He
d the 2010 Critics' Circle Award for Services to the
d became the first British playwright to receive both
vier and Tony Special Lifetime Achievement Awards.
He was knighted in 1997 for services to the theatre.

by the same author

WOMAN IN MIND (DECEMBER BEE)
MR A'S AMAZING MAZE PLAYS
INVISIBLE FRIENDS
TIME OF MY LIFE
WILDEST DREAMS
COMMUNICATING DOORS
COMIC POTENTIAL
THE BOY WHO FELL INTO A BOOK
WHENEVER
DAMSELS IN DISTRESS
THE JOLLIES
MY SISTER SADIE
SEASON'S GREETINGS

ALAN AYCKBOURN: PLAYS ONE
(*A Chorus of Disapproval, A Small Family Business,
Henceforward . . . , Man of the Moment*)

ALAN AYCKBOURN: PLAYS TWO
(*Ernie's Incredible Illucinations, Invisible Friends,
This Is Where We Came In, My Very Own Story,
The Champion of Paribanou*)

ALAN AYCKBOURN: PLAYS THREE
(*Haunting Julia, Sugar Daddies,
Drowning on Dry Land, Private Fears in Public Places*)

ALAN AYCKBOURN: PLAYS FOUR
(*The Revengers' Comedies, Things We Do for Love,
House & Garden*)

adaptations
THE FOREST by Alexander Ostrovsky

theatre books
THE CRAFTY ART OF PLAYMAKING

ALAN AYCKBOURN

Plays Five

Snake in the Grass
If I Were You
Life and Beth
My Wonderful Day
Life of Riley

with an introduction
by the author

faber and faber

First published in 2011
by Faber and Faber Limited
74–77 Great Russell Street, London WC1B 3DA

Typeset by Country Setting, Kingsdown, Kent CT14 8ES
Printed in England by CPI Group (UK) Ltd, Croydon CR0 4YY

A CIP record for this book
is available from the British Library

ISBN 978–0–571–27462–8

2 4 6 8 10 9 7 5 3 1

Contents

Introduction, vii

Snake in the Grass, 1
If I Were You, 87
Life and Beth, 201
My Wonderful Day, 289
Life of Riley, 375

Introduction

In 1994 I wrote *Haunting Julia*, which I had originally intended to be performed as an end-stage production to christen our company's eagerly awaited, soon to open, 'second' auditorium of our new Scarborough home, the 160-seat McCarthy Theatre. In the event, building schedules being what they are, the move was delayed and the production was performed in the round in our old building, but that's another chapter.

Haunting Julia was unusual for me in two other ways. First it was a ghost story, and second it had an all-male cast.

Ghost stories, especially theatrical ones, had always fascinated me ever since seeing as a child (far too young!) a stage adaptation of the W.W. Jacobs classic short story, *The Monkey's Paw*. It gave me sleepless nights for months. My interest in the genre of 'small-scale frighteners' had recently been rekindled following my Associate Director, Robin Herford's terrifying studio production of Susan Hill's *The Woman in Black* in an ingenious stage adaptation by the late Stephen Mallatratt.

Eight years later, in 2002, now securely installed in the splendid new Stephen Joseph Theatre, I resolved to set right the casting imbalance by writing a piece to complement *Julia* for three women. Finances being somewhat limited (but then whenever have they not been in theatre?), the play needed to occupy our larger, round auditorium. It also needed to utilise a previously existing set, in this case for the production of *Joking Apart*, which was in rep at the time. It also, rather cheekily, even took its title from a line in *Joking Apart – Snake in the Grass*. Three women in a garden, then, with a glimpse of a tennis court. I based it loosely on the H.G. Clouzot classic movie *Les Diaboliques*, which wasn't set in a garden with three women, but a boys' private school and featured two women and a man and several others besides.

In the event, as soon as I started writing *Snake in the Grass*, the 'ghostly' subject matter was soon overtaken with other darker, deeper lying themes, like the lasting damaging effects left on two sisters by previous parental and marital abuse. As with *Julia*, the troubled, tormented child genius of misguided, over-protective parents, the haunting shades in *Snake* grew from all too solid human origins.

The plays are grey pathways, occasionally illuminated by comedy but whose light ultimately only serves to lead to darker places.

The next play, *If I Were You* (2006), grew from an idea which had been in my creative bottom drawer for some time. Indeed, I had previously made attempts to start it and given up. Like all simple ideas, it proved the very devil to write. The simple idea? What if a husband and wife, Mal and Jill, dissatisfied with their existing stereotypical gender roles, were to wake up one morning and discover they had exchanged bodies? To all outward appearance they looked unchanged, their family perceived them to be the same people they were before – only their inner selves, their egos, their spirits, had changed. As both found themselves inhabiting a different, alien shell, an unfamiliar external carcass, how would they cope, both perceiving the world through the eyes of the other? And more interestingly, both being perceived as the other.

Dramatically, dealing with the question of explaining how this state of affairs came about, I chose a course I had taken previously in earlier plays with inexplicable scientific phenomena – two women waking up in hospital with each other's head in *Body Language*; mysterious portals in hotel rooms that induce time travel in *Communicating*

Doors, and others – by ignoring what caused it altogether, leaving this to conjecture. The alternative of attempting to explain the impossible leading to endless pseudo-scientific mumbo-jumbo really doesn't appeal to me at all. My experience with children's plays is they either accept that the prince has suddenly become invisible or they don't.

Years ago, as a young director, I once made suggestions to clarify an old and wise Irish dramatist's play which I felt needed explaining. He looked at me reproachfully and shook his head. 'Now, Alan, please don't start getting logical.'

If the switch was going to take place, I felt it was important to make the two central characters positively 'male' and 'female'. Mal, the husband, decidedly alpha male and Jill whatever the female equivalent is to that – omega female?

Once the basic characters and situation were established, the unexplained exchange happens at the halfway point. Any doubters in the audience would have the interval at least to swallow their disbelief with a drink. In the first act we largely see the two of them as they were. In the second act we see them coping, post-change, as they have become.

Needless to say, the acting challenge the roles present for an actor and actress truthfully and convincingly to play each other without hint of caricature is considerable. On that, the play rises or falls. And here, though, as with most of the best things in the theatre, it was also a lot of fun to rehearse, as you can imagine.

My history of scheduling a middle-scale regional producing repertory company like the SJT has been a continuing struggle with under-finance, presenting an annual challenge to invent novel, ingenious ways to shave valuable pennies from slim production budgets.

On occasions this has produced – as pressure on the artist occasionally does – some pleasant surprises. Ever since the seventies I found solutions with projects such as *The Norman Conquests* (three plays, one cast, same costumes) through the eighties with *Intimate Exchanges* (two actors playing sixteen roles in eight variations in the same setting), then the nineties with *House & Garden* (two plays performed simultaneously in two separate theatres with the same casts) and finally the 'noughties' (surely there's a better word for them?) with *Damsels in Distress* (three separate plays with the same cast in the identical set), I feel as a dramatist that I will own up to many things but lack of ingenuity certainly isn't one of them.

In my final year as Artistic Director before retiring, I had planned a small-scale season with a revival of the two linked plays previously mentioned here, namely *Haunting Julia* and *Snake in the Grass*, the two separate companies playing in and out of rep with each other. In order to utilise the two companies, who would otherwise be in terms of performance numbers considerably under-used, I came up with the solution of combining both, the three men from *Julia* and the three women from *Snake*, for a third six-handed companion piece, *Life and Beth*.

I sensed, given the dark nature of its two predecessors that *Beth* should be an altogether lighter-hearted ghost story. It's about completion, saying a final goodbye, in this case after a long marriage together. Recently widowed, Beth has loyally enjoyed and then latterly we suspect endured her long and rather dull, humdrum marriage. Initially the departure of Gordon, a pernickety, overbearing former Health and Safety Officer, has left a considerable gap in her life. After all, especially for the past few years, her life has been his life as his nurse, his foil and domestic skivvy. As the play opens, Beth is facing her first Christmas alone without Gordon. Her friends and family rally round assuming Beth, having been little more than a glorified extra limb for her husband, will be lost without him. But on the contrary. Beth is on the brink of coming to terms with her new life. Until a well-meaning prayer by a sympathetic clergyman brings Gordon back for a final time . . . Secretly I dedicated the play to all those ('oh, she'll be lost without him') widows I have known, who have, in the words of the song, picked themselves up, dusted themelves down and started all over again.

The fourth play in this volume, *My Wonderful Day*, is the story of a child who spends a day off school with her mother, a domestic cleaner. Bound by a promise of good behaviour to write her school essay and practise her French, the intelligent eight-year-old sits alone, silent and largely unnoticed, while increasingly frenetic domestic activity occurs around her – a solemn, grown-up child, surrounded by adults behaving childishly, recording her 'wonderful day' as she sees it.

This play, more than most, can be traced autobiographically to my own experience of early single-parent childhood. And although I changed both the sex (and indeed the colour!) to distance myself, I was often as a child in similar situations to my heroine, with my mother, a professional short story writer for women's magazines, dragging me in tow whilst she wheeled and dealt in Fleet Street editorial offices. Like the fly-on-the-wall child, Winnie Barnstairs, I spent much of my time overhearing the secrets and indiscretions of adults. Just before I wrote the play – and probably, if truth be told, what triggered me to write it – was catching sight of my solemn eight-year-old grandson on the edge of a boisterous family gathering, behaving in similar fashion.

I prefaced the original play script by stressing the importance of trying to avoid entrusting this crucial central role to a child actress. Quite apart from the demand on their attention span and concentration – she never leaves the stage throughout – there is also a practical consideration: in the event of a heavy professional performance schedule, rules and regulations being as they are, the requirement to find a second young actress to spread the workload. Hard enough finding one prodigious eight-year-old to fill such a role, but two . . .

Finally, from a play in which the central character, although onstage, is seldom noticed by the other characters, to a play where the central character never appears at all. In *Life of Riley*, written and first performed in 2009, we gradually learn everything about the terminally ill George Riley through his friends and loved ones. Naturally, each has a different take on a varied, sometimes very different George. For Katherine, he was her first love that she romantically remembers, her view of him flatteringly misted by time. For Monica, his more recently estranged wife, who bore the day-to-day brunt of George's volatile, eccentric behaviour until she could no longer bear it, and for Tamsin, the neglected wife of George's best friend Jack, the temptation of a retaliatory extra-marital fling.

From all this, we are left to draw our own picture of George, charismatic or just plain infuriating, romantic or impetuously childish, deeply loved or downright infuriating. There is little doubt that the departure of such a positive person will mean that the lives of those he leaves behind will never be quite the same again.

The group are linked by a common interest in amateur theatricals – not the first time I have strayed into this area, but the first time they have been rehearsing a play of my own, the forty-five-year-old *Relatively Speaking*. Incestuous? Possibly. But then *Riley* was after all my seventy-fourth play, so I hope I can be forgiven.

Alan Ayckbourn,
April 2011

SNAKE IN THE GRASS

Snake in the Grass was first performed at the Stephen Joseph Theatre, Scarborough, on 5 June 2002. The cast was as follows:

Annabel Chester Fiona Mollison
Alice Moody Rachel Atkins
Miriam Chester Susie Blake

Director Alan Ayckbourn
Designed by Roger Glossop
Lighting by Mick Hughes
Costumes by Christine Wall
Music by John Pattison

The first London production was at The Print Room, Notting Hill, on 14 February 2011. The cast was as follows:

Annabel Chester Susan Wooldridge
Alice Moody Mossie Smith
Miriam Chester Sarah Woodward

Director Lucy Bailey
Designed by William Dudley

Characters

Annabel Chester
fifty

Miriam Chester
her younger sister, forty-four

Alice Moody
a nurse, forties

Setting

The garden of the Chesters' house.
Two days in August.

Act One

A garden.
  We see part of a tennis court which, although in evident disrepair, has solid enough fencing and a door that is in working order. The rest of the court extends offstage. There is a bench alongside the court. At the other side, a small summerhouse/pavilion, very weathered and derelict. This contains a solitary piece of furniture, an old, weather-worn but solid and still serviceable rocking chair. From the roof hangs a rusty outdoor wind chime. It is far too calm a day, though, for this to sound.
  Elsewhere, rough grass underfoot. Bushes and trees.
  It is a late afternoon in August. Annabel, a rather gaunt, tense middle-aged woman is standing staring round the garden. Despite the bright afternoon sunshine, the cheerful birdsong and the general air of peace and tranquillity, her memories of this place appear to be disturbing ones. She moves to the summerhouse and can't resist brushing the wind chime with her finger. It chimes sweetly. But does little to reassure her.
  As she does this, Alice enters. Annabel doesn't see her at first. Alice studies her.

Alice (*eventually, with a slight northern accent*) Mrs Morton?

Annabel (*starting, slightly*) Oh! (*Seeing Alice at last, slightly abruptly*) Yes?

Alice Alice Moody.

Annabel Oh, yes?

Alice You'll be Mrs Morton?

Annabel No. I was.

Alice Ah.

Annabel Not any more.

Alice Oh.

Annabel I'm Annabel Chester.

Alice How do you do.

Annabel Who did you say you were?

Alice Alice Moody.

Annabel Do I know you?

Alice I'm –

Annabel Ought I to know you?

Alice I'm – I was your father's nurse. At one time. I don't know if your sister mentioned me at all . . .?

Annabel Oh, yes. Alice. Of course. Yes. Miriam did mention you. In her letters. Yes. Alice Moody?

Alice That's right.

Annabel Yes. (*Slight pause*) Alice *Moody*. Just a moment, aren't you the one my sister got rid of?

Alice Technically speaking, yes.

Annabel Hardly technically. She fired you, didn't she?

Alice She chose to dispense with my nursing services, yes.

Annabel Then what are you still doing here?

Alice I needed to have a –

Annabel Not back to nurse my father, I trust?

Alice No, of course not, I was –

Annabel Because I've bad news if you have, he died three weeks ago.

She laughs. Annabel's humour is an acquired taste.

Alice Yes, I'm well aware that your father's deceased, Miss Chester.

Annabel Then why are you here? If my sister got rid of you, there was obviously –

Alice If you'd allow me to explain, Miss Chester, I –

Annabel Where is my sister, anyway? I arrive to find the house all locked up. Where's Miriam?

Alice I believe she's presently at the shops.

Annabel The shops?

Alice Shopping. She doesn't know I'm here, you see.

Annabel She doesn't?

Alice No, I came to see you, Miss Chester.

Annabel Me?

Alice It's a delicate matter. I needed to speak to you privately.

Annabel How did you know I'd even be here?

Alice I was – I was aware you would be . . .

Annabel Did you now? I've only just got off the plane and here you are lying in wait for me.

Alice I knew you'd be home sooner or later, Miss Chester. I was familiar with the terms of your father's final will, you see. I felt certain you'd be here.

Annabel How do you know about my father's will? Who told you about that?

Alice Your father and I became quite close friends by the end, before I was – forced to leave.

Annabel Did you?

Alice I was rather expecting to see you here for the funeral, as a matter of fact.

Annabel Were you? Well, I wasn't.

Alice Seeing it was your own father's.

Annabel What exactly do you want, Miss Moody?

Alice I've said. I'd like a word with you, Miss Chester, if I may.

Annabel If you're claiming you were wrongfully dismissed or some such, I should take it up with the Royal College of Nursing or whatever –

Alice (*calmly*) No, it's not about that.

Annabel – because there is no point in talking to me about it. If I remember correctly, according to my sister, she dismissed you because you were unpunctual, neglectful, unreliable and unprofessional.

Alice Is that what she called me?

Annabel So far as I remember. I may have them in the wrong order and there may have been a few more reasons, I can't recall. Now I suggest you leave at once, please.

Alice I don't know why you're being quite so hostile, Miss Chester.

Annabel Because, I've had an extremely long flight, I'm very jet-lagged and from what I've learnt from my sister you're not someone whom she'd particularly welcome in her garden, Miss Moody.

Alice Your garden.

Annabel What?

Alice Your garden, surely? I understood this garden belongs to you now. Since your father's departure. Surely?

Annabel What business is that of yours?

Alice I mean, if we're being strictly accurate – technically – I understood that under the terms of the will you own, or will shortly own, the house, this garden and all the contents.

Annabel Possibly. What of it?

Alice Plus the bulk of the estate.

Annabel I don't know how you obtained this information . . .

Alice I obtained it because your father wrote to me and told me that was what he was doing.

Annabel He did?

Alice Altering his will. In your favour. Just a few days before he died.

Annabel I see.

Alice But that's not all he wrote to tell me. He also wrote to say he was almost certain your sister was trying to kill him.

Pause.

Annabel I beg your pardon?

Alice That's what he believed.

Annabel What rubbish!

Alice I've got the letter.

Annabel This is complete nonsense. *Miriam?* My sister *Miriam?*

Alice Would you care to see it? (*Producing a sheet of paper from her bag*) Here. It's alright, you can keep it. It's a photocopy.

She hands the paper to Annabel. After a second, Annabel takes it and starts to read it. Alice watches her.

(*As Annabel reads*) I have shown the original to your sister. It's perfectly genuine, isn't it? Definitely your father's handwriting. A little bit shaky, but then he was very ill. He must have dragged himself all the way to the post box. On his own. While your sister was out. That must have taken a bit of doing. He was very weak, even when I was still here to care for him. After I went, with the dosages your sister was giving him, God knows what sort of state he must have been in. Amazing he could stand up at all, really.

Annabel (*finishing the letter*) This is no sort of proof at all.

Alice No? Don't you think so?

Annabel This is clearly written by a man who hardly knew what he was doing. He was probably not even thinking straight. Look at the state of the handwriting. He was obviously delirious. Fantasising.

Alice Oh, but he wasn't, you see.

Annabel How do you know? You weren't even here.

Alice I know because when I confronted your sister with it a few days ago, she admitted it.

Annabel Admitted what?

Alice That she'd been doubling his doses. Tripling them some days.

Annabel She admitted it?

Alice Evidently one night he got up to answer a call of nature, hardly knowing where he was at all, blundering about in the dark – he wandered on to the landing looking for the – little boys' room – and she shoved him down the stairs.

Annabel She pushed him?

Alice The poor man never stood a chance. It was pitch dark, you see. She'd taken all the light bulbs out as well, just to make sure.

Annabel This is unbelievable. I'm sorry. I simply do not believe you. You're talking about my sister Miriam. She would never do anything like that to a living soul. Let alone her own father. She's – she's the gentlest, most – harmless person in the world . . .

Alice You haven't seen her for a bit, though, have you?

Annabel No. But we've corresponded regularly. I –

Alice I think you might be a little bit surprised when you see her. She's probably changed a lot since you last saw her. Someone who spends fifteen years of their life, virtually a prisoner, looking after a sick old man – no social life to speak of – no – sex life – no nothing – well, you might undergo a few changes yourself. But you were alright, weren't you? Safe and sound in Australia.

Annabel Tasmania, if you must know.

Alice Well out of it there, weren't you?

Annabel That is absolutely none of your business.

Pause.

If you must know, my father and I – never saw eye to eye.

Alice I see.

Annabel I was forced to stay away. We simply didn't agree on things.

Alice He liked you enough to leave you everything, anyway.

Annabel Well. People do that. When people realise they're dying they often – want to try and put things straight, don't they? That's all that was.

Alice Just in case, eh?

Annabel If you like.

Pause.

Anyway, assuming there's a single grain of truth in all this –

Alice Oh, there's more than a grain, believe me –

Annabel – what do you hope to get out of it?

Alice Why should I want anything?

Annabel Obviously you do. Or you'd have done your proper duty as a nurse and reported all this in the first place.

Alice Yes, I probably should have done that.

Annabel Then don't stand there pretending you don't want anything.

Alice I'm not pretending.

Annabel Well, then.

Alice I want a considerable amount, as a matter of fact, Miss Chester. I think I'm entitled to that for wrongful dismissal, don't you? Despite what your sister said to you, I was a good nurse to your father. I was very fond of him and all – he was a wicked old boy, he used to make me laugh like a drain – and I took good care of him. Too much care, as it happens. If I'd been working here now, he'd have still been alive, wouldn't he? Only your sister chose to get shot of me in order that she could get rid of him. Calling me incompetent. Tarnishing my professional reputation. I think I'm entitled to something for that, don't you?

Pause.

Annabel I see. What is it you want, then?

Alice I've already told your sister what I want.

Annabel Then why are you talking to me?

Alice Because I thought, as her sister, you ought to be aware of the situation. And I wasn't sure how much she'd tell you.

Annabel I see.

Alice Besides, I thought the least you were entitled to was the truth, seeing as you're the one who now has all the money.

Annabel Ah.

Alice No point in asking her for anything. Poor cow hasn't even got a decent coat to her back.

Annabel Would you kindly not refer to my sister like that!

Alice I have to say he kept her on a short chain, your father. Just enough to get her to the village shop and back. Hardly what you'd call a generous allowance . . .

Annabel Now you listen to me. I want you to leave now, do you hear? I will talk to my sister –

Alice Yes, you'll need to talk to her –

Annabel – I say, I will talk to my sister and get to the bottom of all this. But I must tell you that my instinct at present, Miss Moody, is to call the police and have you charged with extortion and blackmail.

Alice You could give it a go if you like. It'll all have to come out then, won't it? Depends how much you care for your sister, I suppose. Tell you what, I'll come back tomorrow around about this same time, shall I? Then we can all sit down and discuss it properly. I'll leave you a night to sleep on it. Get over your jet-lag.

Annabel You will come back when we call you back.

Alice You don't know where I live though, these days, do you? But I know where you live. Good afternoon, Miss Chester. Or may I call you Annabel?

Annabel You most certainly may not. Good afternoon, Miss Moody.

Alice (*impervious*) I'll go out the back way. I'll see you later.

Alice goes out past the tennis court.
Annabel stands for a moment.

Annabel (*shaking her head in disbelief, to herself*) Oh, my God. Miriam!

Suddenly, the mesh of the tennis court fencing resonates as if something or someone has knocked against it.

(*Startled, calling*) Who's that?

No reply.

Who's there? Is there someone there?

Miriam, her younger sister, appears at the mesh. In contrast with Annabel she is a rounded, soft, rather vulnerable figure.

Miriam (*rather tearful*) Annabel . . .?

Annabel (*only half recognising her*) Miriam . . .?

Miriam comes out of the court and embraces Annabel passionately.

Miriam Oh, Annie, it's good to see you! I'm so glad you're here!

Annabel (*rather taken aback by this effusiveness*) Miriam, what are you doing? How long have you been there?

Miriam I came back from the village – I saw you talking to her – I just had to hide – (*Going totally to pieces*) Oh, Annie, she's a terrible woman – you've no idea . . . it's been a nightmare, it's just been a nightmare . . .

Annabel Miriam! Miriam, calm down, now. Just calm down. My God, woman, look at you. Look at the state of you . . .

Miriam I'm sorry. I'm sorry. I'm such a mess.

Annabel Sit down, now. Come along. Sit down.

She seats Miriam on the bench.

Miriam I'm such a terrible mess. Oh, Annie, I'm so happy to see you, you've no idea . . .

Annabel Miriam, is all this true? All the things that woman's told me? Are they really true?

Miriam Oh, God! I'm such a mess . . .

Annabel Miriam . . .

Miriam . . . such an awful mess . . .

Annabel Yes, I can see you are.

Miriam . . . just look at me . . .

Annabel Yes, I've looked, I've said. Now, Miriam, what that woman told me just now – is any of it true? Is there any truth in it?

Miriam You don't know what it was like, Annie, those last months, you don't know. He was getting worse and worse.

Annabel Father?

Miriam He was just terrible to me. So cruel and unkind, I couldn't do anything right for him . . . (*Weeping afresh*) Everything I did, he . . . he shouted . . . and threw things and threw his food . . . I just couldn't take any more . . .

Annabel Miriam, calmly, now. Calm down, dear. Take a few breaths.

Miriam does this.

That's it. Deep breaths.

Miriam (*a little calmer*) Sorry. I'm sorry. God, I'm such a mess.

Annabel Yes, yes, we've established that. (*Locating a tissue*) Here . . . Wipe yourself a bit.

Miriam Thank you . . . I'm sorry . . . I never even asked. How are you? Did you have a good flight?

Annabel Yes, I had a perfectly wonderful flight. Apart from being seated next to a woman with a screaming baby all the way from Singapore, absolutely perfect – now never mind about me. Miriam, tell me something. I need to know. How much of our conversation, me and that woman's, did you hear just now?

Miriam (*snuffling*) A little bit, just a little bit . . .

Annabel (*talking to her like a child*) Then tell me, honestly. Now you have to be honest with me, Miriam . . . do you hear me? Honest?

Miriam (*weakly*) Yes.

Annabel Promise?

Miriam Yes . . .

Annabel Tell me, did you deliberately dismiss that woman?

Miriam Yes.

Annabel Why?

A little wail from Miriam.

Don't start again! That isn't helpful.

Miriam Sorry.

Annabel Did you dismiss her so that you could start – altering father's medicine?

Another wail.

Miriam, was that the reason? Was it or wasn't it?

Miriam (*faintly*) Yes . . .

Annabel Did you deliberately increase his dosage?

Miriam (*nodding*) A little bit . . .

Annabel A little bit?

Miriam I thought it might make him sleep more. So he wouldn't shout at me.

Annabel What do you mean by a little bit?

Miriam shakes her head.

Did you double the dose?

Miriam shakes her head again.

Triple the dose?

Miriam Maybe a little bit more.

Annabel Oh, God in heaven! And did you really push him down the stairs?

Miriam Only a little push . . .

Annabel (*agitatedly moving from her*) Oh, dear Lord! Oh, dear heavens! And did you also remove the light bulbs as well . . .?

Miriam Just one or two . . .

Annabel Miriam! You murdered him. You murdered Father. Do you understand that?

Miriam I didn't mean to . . .

Annabel What do you mean, you didn't mean to?

Miriam It was an accident . . .

Annabel Miriam, I've never heard anything less like an accident . . . You deliberately give him quadruple doses of medicine, you take out all the light bulbs and push him down the stairs . . . No one in the world's going to believe that was an accident, Miriam, are they?

Miriam starts crying afresh.

And you've confessed all that to this woman?

Miriam She had the letter. She showed me the letter from father.

Annabel I see. And it seemed perfectly genuine to you?

Miriam Oh yes . . . It was on his writing paper . . .

Annabel Yes, well, that's not necessarily – And what did she say to you?

Miriam She said unless we – you gave her an awful lot of money she'd show the letter to the authorities – and then they – they'd dig up Daddy and have a post –

Annabel A post? You mean an autopsy?

Miriam Yes.

Annabel Would they be able to tell, after all this time?

Miriam Oh, yes. She's a nurse, she said they'd be able to tell, once they started looking for it . . . Then I'd have to go to prison. I don't want to go to prison, Annie . . .

Annabel Don't be silly. You wouldn't go to prison . . .

Miriam She said I would.

Annabel She's just trying to frighten you, that's all . . . You're not going to go to prison . . .

Miriam You just said I deliberately murdered Father. Don't they send you to prison for that? For deliberately murdering your father.

Annabel Yes, well – sometimes maybe they probably do, yes. Sometimes. It depends if there are any extenuating . . . (*Giving this up*) Listen, Miriam, what does she want from us, that woman? Did she tell you what she wanted in order to keep quiet?

Miriam Yes.

Annabel Money, she wanted money, you say?

Miriam Yes.

Annabel How much money, Miriam?

Miriam hesitates.

Miriam, how much does she want?

Miriam A hundred thousand pounds.

Silence. Even the birds have stopped singing.

Annabel (*at last*) I don't have a hundred thousand pounds. I don't have that much money in the world.

Miriam You don't?

Annabel Of course I don't. Not at all. I have practically nothing left of my own. A tiny little bit set aside to live on. Invested. A few stocks and shares, that's it. I don't have that sort of money.

Miriam What are we going to do then? What am I going to do? What do we say to her?

Annabel We'll tell her she's – she's going to have to whistle for it. We simply don't have it.

Miriam What about from your business?

Annabel Miriam, I wrote and told you my business folded. You know it did. . . .

Miriam Oh, yes.

Annabel I no longer have a business, any more than I still have a husband, thank God. Practically all I have in the world is in those three suitcases outside the back door there.

Miriam Then what am I going to do?

Annabel I don't know. I really don't.

Miriam If we don't pay her what she wants, she'll go to the police.

Annabel Then she'll have to. She needs to understand we simply cannot pay her that sort of money.

Miriam What about what Father left you?

Annabel According to the lawyer's letter, that amounts to considerably less than a hundred thousand pounds, I can promise you that. And after death duties . . .

Miriam What about the house?

Annabel Yes, I planned to sell this, anyway. But we'll need that money in order to buy somewhere else for ourselves, won't we? Somewhere smaller. For us both. In, say, Fulham perhaps. I rather fancied Fulham.

Miriam Fulham?

Annabel Well, somewhere – like Fulham. I don't know. Something with two bedrooms, you know. Nothing too grand but . . . With both of us working – we should just about manage. I had it all planned out. I can go back to secretarial work – temporarily. Until I find something more challenging.

Miriam You're alright to work again, now?

Annabel Oh yes, of course I am. Providing I'm sensible. I'm perfectly fit.

Miriam What about me, then? What shall I do? If I'm not in prison?

Annabel You? Well, you can – you can – we'll find you something, don't worry . . . You can go back to teaching, surely?

Miriam I haven't been in a classroom for ten years –

Annabel That doesn't matter – the children aren't going to know the difference. Most of them are so stupid these days, anyway. And besides you were a drama teacher, weren't you? That's not going to have changed. It'll be the same old waving and shouting, surely?

Annabel laughs. It's another of her jokes.

Miriam (*gloomily*) What am I going to do, Annie? Seriously . . .

Annabel Oh come on, Miriam. We'll sort it out, don't worry. At least if you go to prison that'll save us some money, anyway. (*She laughs again*) No, the point is we're not giving that woman a hundred thousand pounds, I can tell you that. Even if I had it, that would go completely against the grain.

Miriam Then I will go to prison.

Annabel Listen, we'll meet her here tomorrow afternoon as she suggests and I'll offer her – a – a compromise sum. I'll have to do some calculations this evening to see how much I can afford to give her. And she'll have to be content with that, won't she?

Miriam What if she isn't?

Annabel She'll have to be. She won't get any more. There'll certainly be no negotiation.

Miriam But what if she – says no?

Annabel That won't happen.

Miriam You don't know her. You don't know Alice.

Annabel Then we'll – we'll face that if it comes, won't we? Come on, I'm desperate for a cup of tea. Then I need to go to bed and sleep. I'll unpack in the morning. I hope you've given me my old room?

Miriam Yes. I'm afraid it's all a bit – run down, though . . .

Annabel It certainly looks it from the outside. When on earth was it last painted – ?

Miriam Oh, God knows . . . Not in my lifetime . . .

Annabel (*moving off*) Come along, Miriam, brighten up now. We'll think of something, don't worry. We're bound to think of something, aren't we?

Annabel strides off towards the house.

Miriam (*as she follows her*) Yes, we're sure to think of something.

As she goes the lights fade to: –

Blackout.

SCENE TWO

The same.
The following afternoon. Again, it is very warm and sunny.
Annabel is waiting. She again seems to be drawn towards the tennis court. She stares through the fence.
In a moment, Miriam enters with a small folding table and an upright garden chair. She goes to the summerhouse and during the next sets up the table in front of the rocking chair and then positions the garden chair. The atmosphere seems a little cooler between the two women.

Annabel (*watching Miriam*) I don't know why we're bothering with this, I really don't.

Miriam does not reply.

We're treating the woman like some honoured guest.

Miriam (*coolly*) No, we're not.

Annabel It's all cut and dried. I've been over all my accounts this morning. I'm offering her five thousand and that's it. She can take it or leave it. No negotiation. Nothing. That is final.

Miriam Yes, you said.

Annabel That's all I can afford. And I have to say yet again, I begrudge every penny.

Miriam And if she refuses to accept that?

Annabel Too bad. That's all. Too bad.

Miriam is silent.

Frankly, Miriam, I don't believe that we have that many other options. If she refuses to accept the five thousand – and I'm fully prepared to give her cash in hand – if she refuses – then the chances are, if she's the type of woman you say she is, that she will go to the police and show them Father's letter. And should they choose to follow it up, which I presume they will, then they will probably exhume Father's body – why on earth you didn't have him cremated . . .

Miriam He didn't want to be. He didn't like it.

Annabel Right – they will probably exhume Father's body and, if she's right and they do detect evidence of the overdose – then that will establish a *prima facie* case and the result of that will be – that you'll probably be arrested, prosecuted and go to prison for a considerable time. I mean, that's it in a nutshell.

Silence.

Miriam That's your alternative scheme, is it?

Annabel As I see it. I'm sorry, Miriam, but you really have behaved extremely stupidly. I mean, I have every sympathy with you pushing Father downstairs – I'd probably have done much the same in your place – but to involve a woman like that and then to confess it all to her . . .

Miriam (*quietly*) Alright.

Miriam has started to walk towards the house. She appears to have come to some sort of decision.

Annabel Where are you going now?

Miriam I'm fetching some wine.

Annabel Wine? We're offering that woman wine?

Miriam We can at least try to get her on our side, can't we?

Annabel Listen, all I'm offering is the money and saying, take it or leave it. That's it. Goodbye. This is not a social occasion. It's bad enough offering her a chair –

Miriam (*angrily*) Look, it's alright for you, isn't it? I'm the one that has to –

Annabel (*responding*) What do you mean, it's alright for me –?

Miriam – I'm the one that has to –

Annabel – it is certainly not alright for me –

Miriam (*shouting*) – I'm the one that has to go to prison if she refuses to –

Annabel (*shouting*) – and I'm the one who has to find all the money in the first place, aren't I?

Silence. They stand glaring at each other.

Miriam (*calming down*) We're arguing again.

Annabel Well. Honestly.

Miriam That's the third argument we've had since you came back.

Annabel (*drily*) Really?

Miriam You've only been back a day.

Annabel Well, you're an extremely irritating person sometimes.

Miriam First you were on about your bedroom curtains ...

Annabel They clash with the bedspread. What was wrong with the old ones?

Miriam They were forty years old and falling to pieces.

Annabel Because they'd been hand washed. I told you, if they'd been properly dry-cleaned like they were supposed to be –

Miriam (*shouting*) Don't start again!

Silence.

Annabel (*muttering*) – they'd have lasted a lifetime. (*Slight pause*) What was the other one, anyway?

Miriam (*through clenched teeth*) I'd bought the wrong sized eggs for breakfast. Need I say more? I rest my case.

Annabel I've told you, they're too much for me, I can't eat large eggs.

Miriam (*muttering*) I don't know why not. Your mouth's big enough.

Annabel What?

Miriam I'll fetch the wine.

Miriam goes off to the house.

Annabel (*calling after her*) Not for me! (*Muttering to herself*) Wasting wine on that – woman.

She stands looking around her.

I can't possibly eat large eggs. They don't even taste the same. They put something in them, I know they do.

She moves back again to the tennis court and presses her face to the mesh fence.

28

Quite suddenly she gives a little cry, half in anguish, half in pain. She clutches her chest and moves with difficulty to retrieve her handbag. She takes out a strip of tablets, pops two out of their foil and swallows them.

She sits in one of the chairs to recover, trying to control her breathing.

As she does this, Miriam returns with a tray with a bottle of quite decent white wine already opened and three glasses. It appears that Miriam has already poured herself a glass. The bottle is depleted and one of the glasses is already filled.

Miriam (*as she puts the tray on the table*) What's left from the cellar. Might as well use it up. Father never got round to it. (*Noticing Annabel*) You alright?

Annabel Yes, just a – I'm fine.

Miriam Another one –?

Annabel Just a mild one . . . It's not serious.

Miriam You had one this morning.

Annabel It's not a problem. It's probably still the jet-lag.

Miriam You should see someone.

Annabel I already have. I know what it is, I have the medication and it's not a problem. Now forget it. Is one of those glasses intended for me?

Miriam Yes, I thought you might like a –

Annabel I told you, I don't. I told you that. Not any more.

Miriam I thought maybe a small one . . .

Annabel Miriam, if you're someone like me, there's no such thing as a small drink. It's all or nothing.

Miriam Right. (*She takes her own glass and sips it*)

Annabel And you'd better watch it, as well.

Miriam How do you mean?

Annabel You were knocking them back last night, too, weren't you?

Miriam I may have had a glass or two. It was only wine.

Annabel Hah! Only wine, she says.

Miriam God, is there anything more boring than a reformed alcoholic?

Annabel I know what I'm talking about, that's all –

Miriam A born-again non-smoker, perhaps?

Annabel I've never smoked.

Miriam Thank God for that! We'd never have heard the end of it.

Pause.

We never got on, did we? Even in the early days. You were always shouting at me. My big sister. You were meant to take care of me. All you ever did was shout at me. Or ignore me completely when it suited you.

Annabel You were a spoilt little brat. Daddy's little girl.

Miriam Some days you'd look straight through me. Like I wasn't even there.

Annabel You were also a congenital liar and extremely irritating . . .

Miriam Maybe I was just trying to get some attention . . .

Annabel Well, you succeeded.

Pause.

By the way, you haven't changed a bit, you're still extremely irritating . . .

Miriam Thank you so much.

Pause.

Annabel I'm sorry. That wasn't very nice.

Miriam It wasn't.

Annabel I'm sorry.

Pause.

Miriam You just say things, don't you? You just say things without thinking sometimes, don't you? So clever. And yet so hurtful. Born with all the brains and you never even bother to think half the time.

Annabel Maybe you're right. Don't worry, I've paid for it in my time. Don't worry.

Miriam Then perhaps you should have learnt from experience.

Annabel Do we ever? Any of us? We're what we are, aren't we? I'm thoughtless and you're stupid.

Miriam There you go again!

Annabel I'm sorry. And I'm sorry if I gave you a rotten childhood. I had a pretty rotten one myself . . .

Miriam I'm sure you did. I know you did. Some of it, anyway. From what I can remember – what I could understand of it.

Slight pause.

Nevertheless, it was extremely hurtful to me. That's all I'm saying. When Mother died it was so lonely. Once you'd gone – run off. Just me, Father and Auntie Gwen . . .

Annabel Auntie Gwen. My God. It's amazing you survived at all, really. (*She laughs, one of her laughs*) It's certainly amazing you have anything left to drink in the wine cellar, anyway.

Miriam Auntie Gwen only drank vodka.

Annabel So she did.

Miriam Lots and lots of vodka. I needed a big sister. You should have been here, Annabel. You shouldn't have gone away.

Annabel Well, I couldn't stay. And I've told you before, don't call me Annabel. Annie or Anna if you have to, please.

Miriam Sorry!

Annabel The only person who called me Annabel was Father.

Miriam How could I forget? The last few days that was practically all he said. 'Annabel, Annabel! Where's Annabel? Go away, you, I want Annabel! Annabel, Annabel, Annabel!'

Annabel I don't believe that.

Miriam 'She's not here, you stupid man. She ran off thirty-five years ago.'

Slight pause.

It's true.

Annabel Well, don't call me it again, please.

Miriam I'll try and remember.

Annabel It always makes me feel I've done something terribly wrong.

Miriam finishes her wine and immediately pours herself another from the bottle.

You're not having another one, surely?

Miriam Just a minute. I'll fetch the other chair. She should be here soon.

Miriam walks back towards the house, carrying her glass. She pauses and looks back at Annabel, still seated at the table.

That summerhouse hasn't been used for years, you know. When you're on your own you don't really bother, do you?

Annabel I can't remember us ever using it, actually. He only had it built because of the well, didn't he?

Miriam Oh yes, the well. I'd forgotten the well.

Annabel To stop either of us falling down it. Is it still there?

Miriam Probably. The trap door is, certainly.

Annabel Where?

Miriam Where you're sitting, I think.

Annabel (*rising hastily*) Oh, yes.

Miriam It's OK. It hasn't been opened for years (*Moving off*) Won't be a second.

Miriam goes back to the house. Annabel picks up the bottle and examines the label and the contents. She frowns and puts down the bottle.
Suddenly the tennis court fencing gives another twang as if something or someone has knocked against it. Annabel starts rather nervously.

Annabel (*approaching the court, cautiously*) Who's that? Is someone there?

She listens.

Who is that? Miss Moody? I can see you, you know.

Pause.

Hallo?

Miriam returns with her glass and carrying a second folding chair.

Miriam What's wrong?

Annabel I think there's someone in there.

Miriam (*putting down the chair and joining her*) Where?

Annabel I heard them just now. Banging against the fencing.

Miriam (*looking through the mesh*) Well, there's no one in there now. God, it's overgrown. Couldn't play in here now, could you?

Annabel Even if you wanted to. Maybe they're round the side. Look round the side.

Miriam investigates.

Anything?

Miriam Not a soul.

Annabel I heard something.

Miriam Probably a bird. They're always flying into that fence. Stupid things.

Miriam returns to the chair and puts it up. Annabel stays by the court.

Annabel I've always hated this place.

Miriam What, the tennis court?

Annabel Don't you remember? No, you would have been too young. I was seven, eight years old. Every single day of the holidays. When I wasn't trapped in that bloody awful boarding school. He used to drag me out here each afternoon, determined to teach me.

Miriam Father did?

Annabel God, he was relentless. 'Come along, Annabel. Hit it, girl! Hit the damn thing! What's the matter with you, girl?' Firing these bloody tennis balls at me, hour after hour, ball after ball. In the end I was crying so much, I could no longer see them anyway. Faster and faster – used to hit me, a lot of them. Couldn't get out of the way quick enough. But then he was – so strong. And I was always, a little – uncoordinated. Like human target practice. Black and blue. 'Come on, Annabel, shift your fat arse!' I used to fall over, my knees were skinned, my elbows were grazed . . . It suddenly all came back to me just now. God, how I loathe sport. I could never watch Wimbledon.

Miriam (*sipping her wine*) Still, it's a lovely garden. I'll miss it. If we move to Fulham.

Annabel I only said – Fulham. Could be somewhere else. Battersea, even.

Miriam Ah. (*She reflects*) Couldn't we just stay here?

Annabel I don't want to stay here. It's full of the most awful memories. Isn't it for you? It must be.

Miriam Well . . . It's just I've lived here for ever, that's all.

Annabel Time for a change, then, surely. Anyway. There's no work round here. We'd both have to commute. We can't start all that at our age.

Miriam A lot of people do.

Annabel Well, I'm not one of them. (*Looking at Miriam with displeasure*) Do you drink a lot on your own?

Miriam Oh, don't get at me again!

Annabel No, do you? I'm asking.

Miriam I have the occasional glass, yes. In the evening. Why not? I think I'm entitled to some pleasures.

Annabel Fine. Do what you like. It's just – it's never good to drink on your own. That's the start of the slippery slope.

Miriam What happens if you don't have the option?

Pause.

Annabel Anyway, it looks corked.

Miriam What does?

Annabel The wine. It's slightly cloudy. It looks corked to me.

Miriam Tastes alright.

Pause.

She's late.

Annabel Stringing us along, probably.

Miriam Possibly.

Pause.

I did try, you know. I didn't just sit here vegetating. At one time, I went to night class. Every Wednesday.

Annabel Really? What were you studying? Something useful?

Miriam Plumbing.

Annabel Plumbing?

Miriam There was a Plumbing for Women course. But I didn't get on very well with that. So I switched to Elementary Electrics for a bit, but that was even more boring. I had this great idea that I could put in an extra bathroom and rewire the house, you see. But then Father got worse and I had to give it all up, anyway.

Annabel Tell me, is there no one else in your life? No one at all?

Miriam No. Not now dear Father's gone, there isn't. No one at all. Just this lonely old maid. Spinster of this parish. Do you take this woman –? No, we don't. Frightfully sorry.

Annabel What about – whoever it was –?

Miriam Oh. You mean Lewis? Lewis went away. I wrote and told you.

Annabel Did you, I . . .

Miriam Didn't you ever read any of my letters?

Annabel Of course.

Miriam You don't appear to have done. You don't seem to know anything about me. I read everything about you and your blessed Brad. Pages and pages of it.

Annabel I needed to write to someone.

Miriam I could tell.

   Pause.

Why did you put up with it for so long? I thought you were the strong one.

37

Annabel It's never that simple.

Pause.

I don't want to talk about it. It's over.

Miriam I don't know how you ever live with someone who hits you.

Annabel Please, I don't want to talk about it, Miriam.

Miriam Punches you in the face. How could you possibly stay with someone after that?

Annabel I didn't. I left him.

Miriam After eighteen months. You put up with it for a year, didn't you?

Annabel I've said, it's never that simple. I'm sorry, I don't want to talk about it. It's forgotten. He's gone. Out of my life. Making someone else's life a misery, no doubt. (*She laughs*)

Slight pause.

(*In a rush*) And, as a result of all that, I started drinking more and more, had a mild heart attack, my business collapsed, I dried out, my sister's just killed my father and here I am home again. It's been a great life so far, hasn't it?

Pause.

Maybe I'm a born loser. I don't know.

Miriam (*solemnly*) I hate people who say that. I really despise them.

Annabel (*a little startled*) What?

Miriam No one's a born loser.

Miriam drinks in silence.

Annabel I take it that – Lewis wasn't abusive?

Miriam No. Far from that.

Annabel You broke up for other reasons?

Miriam We broke up because Father didn't approve of him. He didn't like Lewis, not at all. God knows why not. But there you are. I defied him for a bit – which incidentally is probably one of the reasons I got cut out of the will . . . I kept on asking Lewis round despite. We never made it as far as the bedroom but at least he came round to see me. But, in the end, life was just too short. He had a very strong personality did Father.

Annabel Tell me.

Miriam Right to the end.

Annabel Why on earth didn't he like Lewis? You'd think he'd have been happy that you'd found –

Miriam Father didn't give a reason. He said he thought he was a bad influence, he didn't trust him and he didn't want him to come to the house again. It was his house, after all, what could we both do? I was tied here, we couldn't meet anywhere else much –

Annabel You could have found a way, surely?

Miriam It's never that simple.

Annabel You could always have threatened to walk out and leave him, I suppose.

Miriam (*looking at her*) We couldn't both of us do that, Annabel, could we?

Annabel (*muted*) No.

Miriam Someone has to be responsible, I think. I know you feel you were fully justified but he probably treated us both equally badly in different ways and in the end he was still our father, wasn't he?

Annabel Did he treat you badly?

Miriam Oh, you've no idea, Annabel. You really have no idea.

Annabel (*softly*) Annie.

Miriam Annie.

Pause.

I think that's my greatest regret, you know. That I could so easily go to my grave having never experienced love – real love – neither having had a chance to give it nor to receive it from another human being. I can put up with all the rest of it really. No real, proper close friends, no wild social life, no nice clothes, exotic holidays, no children – I can just about cope with all that. But never to have known – never to have been able to wallow in the knowledge that you were loved by someone. Even for a second . . . That makes me feel very sad sometimes.

Annabel (*moved*) Oh, Miriam . . .

Annabel goes to embrace Miriam, who pulls away from her sharply and instinctively.

Miriam Don't do that, please. That's thirty years too late, Annie. Really it is. I'm sorry.

Annabel, hurt, stares at Miriam.

Annabel She was right about you, that woman. You're very different. You've changed a lot.

Miriam Yes.

Another silence between them. Alice enters from the side of the tennis court. Smartly dressed for their

*meeting, around her neck she wears a distinctive
lightweight summer scarf. She watches them for a
second.*

Alice Afternoon.

Annabel (*coolly*) Good afternoon.

Miriam (*likewise*) Hallo.

Alice Another lovely day. Sitting out here then, are we?
Might as well, eh? Take advantage of it. While we can.
While it lasts. Don't often get the chance to, do we?

Miriam Do you want to sit down?

Alice Thank you.

Alice sits. They all sit.

Miriam Would you care for a glass of wine?

Alice Oh. How nice. I hope you don't think you're going
to get round me that way, though.

Miriam Sorry?

Alice (*amused*) You're wasting your time there, Miriam,
I warn you.

*Miriam pours Alice a glass of wine. Her own glass is
still half full.*

Ta. (*To Annabel*) You not having one?

Annabel I don't drink.

Alice Really? Doesn't know what she's missing, does she?

Annabel Yes, I do.

Alice Good health, then.

*She raises her glass to Miriam.
Miriam drinks.*

Alice drinks.

Right. Lovely. Ready for our chat, are we?

Annabel Quite ready.

A silence.

Alice Do I take it we have a deal, then?

Annabel That depends.

Alice On what?

Annabel On whether you're prepared to accept our offer.

Alice *Your* offer?

Annabel Yes.

Alice I don't think you've quite understood this. Your offer? I'm the one who's made the offer, surely. All you have to do is pay the asking price. Or not. That's the only choice.

Annabel We both feel that your – asking price is totally unreasonable.

Alice I see. (*A glance at Miriam*) Your sister agrees with that, does she?

Miriam – er . . .

Annabel Yes, she does. What you're asking is quite out of the question.

Alice I don't agree at all. I'd have thought a hundred thousand pounds is not unreasonable in return for, say, probably ten years of someone's life. Ten thousand a year – not a lot to spend for your own sister's freedom, surely?

Annabel The point is, I don't even have a hundred thousand pounds.

Alice Then you'd better find it, hadn't you?

Annabel (*irritably*) Don't be so ridiculous. Where am I going to get hold of that sort of money?

Alice I don't know. That's not my problem. You could always sell this house, I suppose. You'd get at least that much for it. Even if it is half falling down.

Annabel When I choose to sell this house, it will not be in order to give the money to you.

Miriam Yes, where are we both supposed to live, if we did that?

Alice Oh, I dare say there'd be enough change out of a hundred grand to get yourselves a nice little mobile home. Even a caravan, who knows?

Annabel A caravan?

Alice Only a small one.

Miriam We're not living in a caravan, what are you saying?

Alice Lots of people do, love.

Annabel No doubt they do. Maybe they choose to –

Alice Maybe they don't have the choice.

Silence.

(*Rising impatiently*) Come on now. A hundred thousand, that's my final offer. Take it or leave it.

Alice moves away slightly.

Miriam (*sotto to Annabel*) We can't both live in a caravan.

Annabel (*sotto*) Certainly not.

Miriam (*sotto*) We'd murder each other in a fortnight.

Annabel (*sotto*) Very probably.

Miriam (*sotto*) I mean, you've only been here twenty-four hours and you're already driving me crazy.

Annabel (*sotto*) I know precisely how you feel.

Alice stands near the tennis court sipping her wine.

(*Trying another tack*) Listen – er . . . Miss –

Miriam Alice.

Annabel Alice.

Alice Made up your minds, have you?

Annabel I should tell you – I do have a heart condition.

Alice (*solicitous*) Oh, dear.

Annabel It's quite serious. I have to be – extremely careful.

Alice Well, you would, yes.

Annabel I mean, any sort of strain, you understand –

Alice (*returning to the table, sympathetically*) Yes . . . yes . . .

Annabel – could prove fatal. You see?

Alice 'Dear.

Miriam refills both her own and Alice's empty glasses. Alice continues to sip hers during the next but Miriam drinks no more.

Annabel And this is not – you know . . . All this isn't . . . For me. Not at all.

Alice Yes, I see.

Pause.

Maybe you should try for a bungalow, then?

44

Annabel A what?

Alice A bungalow. A little house with no stairs, you know.

Annabel (*impatiently*) Yes, I know what a bungalow is.

Alice I mean if that's a problem for you. I do see. Even climbing in and out of a camper van could bring on palpitations, couldn't it?

Annabel (*staring at her*) I don't think you're taking me seriously, are you?

Alice (*evenly*) I don't think you're taking me seriously, either.

> Silence. Annabel searches for another tack. Alice sits back at the table again.

Come on then, let's hear it. How much are you prepared to offer?

Annabel (*after a slight hesitation*) Five thousand pounds.

Alice Sorry. I don't think I quite heard you.

Annabel Five thousand pounds.

Alice For the letter?

Annabel And for your promise of silence.

> Pause.

Alice Thanks for the wine.

> Alice drains her glass and makes to get up.

Annabel What are you doing?

Alice I'm going to the police.

Miriam (*getting up as well, still clutching her glass*) No, wait!

Alice What I should have done in the first place.

Annabel Listen, two can play at that game. I can just as easily go to the police as well, you know . . .

Alice I should.

Annabel I'll tell them what you've been up to –

Alice Do that. I should take your sister with you. It'll save them having to come and find her.

Annabel (*angrily*) Now, look here –

Alice (*suddenly getting tough*) No, you look here, Annabel. You come up with that money or this batty little bitch of a sister of yours is going away for a very long time, alright?

> *Miriam's still full wine glass drops from her hand on to the grass.*

Miriam Oh!

Alice Whoops!

Miriam (*retrieving her glass*) Sorry . . .

Alice So what's your final answer going to be then, eh?

Annabel My final answer is that you're going to have to whistle, aren't you?

Alice Oh, I will don't worry. I'll whistle. I'll whistle good and loud, I promise you that.

> *Alice makes as if to leave again.*

Miriam Just a moment.

Alice Yes?

Miriam Please. If – we were to find the money – from somewhere – somehow – how long would you give us to raise it? How much time would you allow us?

Alice Depends, doesn't it? You're saying you think you could raise it?

Miriam Possibly.

Annabel Miriam . . .

Alice A hundred thousand pounds we're talking about here.

Miriam Oh, yes . . .

Alice And you can lay your hands on that, can you?

Miriam Probably.

Annabel Miriam, what is all this?

Alice Then what have we all been arguing about, then?

Annabel My sister doesn't know what she's saying . . . This is all nonsense.

Miriam (*pouring herself a fresh glass of wine*) I happen to have a friend who might be able to – lend me that much. He might – if I asked him very nicely. He's very – very fond of me. At least I think he is.

She pours Alice a fresh glass as well.

Annabel Who are you talking about? You don't know anyone with that sort of money. Who is this person?

Miriam His name's Lewis. You remember I mentioned him.

Annabel *Lewis*?

Miriam Lewis.

Annabel Lewis has that sort of money?

Miriam Oh, yes.

Annabel And you're saying Father didn't approve of him?

Alice Who's this you're talking about?

Miriam It's a good friend of mine called Lewis.

Alice What, him? Is this the same one who used to come round to see you when I worked here?

Miriam That's right.

Alice On his moped?

Miriam That's the one.

Alice Balding at the front with the funny haircut at the back?

Miriam That's the one.

Alice Him? He wasn't worth a fiver. He used to steal food out of your larder.

Miriam He didn't.

Alice I caught him at it. Stuffing tins of beans up his jacket.

Miriam Well, perhaps he did, occasionally. He was very eccentric.

Alice He was a bloody lunatic. No wonder your dad sent him packing. Listen, love, I'm not buying that. I'm sorry. The most you'd get out of Lewis is twenty-five quid and that's only if he sold his moped, which was probably nicked in the first place. No, I think we can safely assume that negotiations are now at an end, yes? (*To Annabel*) Am I correct?

Annabel doesn't answer.

Yes?

Miriam (*anxiously*) Annabel?

Annabel (*stiffly*) Quite correct.

Alice (*draining her glass again*) Good day to you, then. See you in court, shall I?

Alice puts her glass down on the table and makes to leave round the side of the tennis court.
The others watch her, motionless.

(*Turning as she goes*) I'll just say one thing, though, before I go. (*She sways slightly and slurs her speech slightly*) You've got – You've got yourself one hell of a sister there, Miriam, I have to say. When the chips are down, it's always good to feel your family's behind you, isn't it? Pres— presonally, if I had a sister like – (*Swaying again*) – a sister like – a sis— what's the matter with me – a sis— is – sssss . . . sssss . . . sssss . . .

Alice grabs the tennis fence in an attempt to keep upright but finally buckles at the knees and falls in a heap on the ground.
The others watch her.

Annabel What's the matter with her? What's wrong?

Miriam I think she may have had too much wine.

Annabel But she's only had – what? – three glasses . . .

Miriam (*moving to Alice*) Yes, but she may have had an allergy – to the – to the sediment.

Annabel It never affected you . . .

Miriam Oh, but I didn't drink from that one. My bottle's in the kitchen.

Annabel (*with slow realisation*) Miriam! For heaven's sake – You haven't –? You didn't –?

Miriam Just some pills of Father's – sedatives – (*Moving to Alice*) Help me with her, would you . . . ?

She begins to tug at Alice's body, trying to drag it along the ground.

Annabel Miriam, what do you think you're doing? This is not a solution . . .

Miriam (*still tugging*) Help me, Annie! Are you going to help me?

Annabel All this is doing is putting off the inevitable . . .

Miriam Help me, please!

Annabel (*moving reluctantly over*) You can't just drug people like this, it's totally illegal . . .

Miriam (*slightly frenzied*) I'm not going to prison, Annie! I don't want to go to prison! I'm not going to prison. Will you help me, please!

Annabel What are we doing with her?

Miriam Over to the – over to the summerhouse . . .

Annabel Right. Yes, that's a good idea. Then we can sit her in a chair until she recovers. Sensible idea.

Miriam Pull!

Annabel I'm pulling. (*Breathlessly*) Dear God, she's a weight –

They both begin to drag Alice towards the summerhouse. Annabel is finding it heavy going. She is having increasing difficulty in breathing.

Miriam Keep pulling!

Annabel (*breathlessly*) What on earth came over you? What did you hope to achieve, for heaven's sake?

Miriam Pull!

Annabel I can't do much more of this, Miriam, I really can't . . .

Miriam Nearly there . . .

Annabel No, I have to stop, I'm sorry.

Annabel stands panting, her hand on her chest, in some pain.
Miriam has reached the summerhouse with Alice's body.

Miriam (*triumphantly*) There! (*Seeing Annabel*) You alright?

Annabel (*weakly*) My bag! Would you pass my bag, please . . .?

Miriam Oh. Yes. (*Bringing it to Annabel*) Here!

She hands the bag to Annabel, who locates her tablets and tears off another couple. Miriam removes one of the chairs from the summerhouse and places it by Annabel on the grass.

There. You'd better sit down.

Annabel Thank you. I'll be fine. Don't worry about me. You take care of her. (*She sits*)

Miriam I will.

Annabel sits, a little apart from the summerhouse, hardly noticing Miriam. She breathes deeply, taking a moment to recover from her spasm.
Miriam meanwhile is folding away the table and the garden chair to clear the trap door.

I mean, what was the point of drugging the woman? She's clearly quite determined. The minute she recovers, she's going to go straight to the police, isn't she? All

you've succeeded in doing is to delay things. That's all
you've managed to do.

*During the next, Miriam pulls up the ring on the
trapdoor and, with difficulty, manages to get it open.
Beneath is a seemingly bottomless darkness.*

(*Unaware of all this*) No, I've decided what we'll do. The
best course of action is to go to the police voluntarily
ourselves, both of us together. Before she does. Make a
full confession, we needn't mention the light bulbs –
that's only her word against ours –

*Miriam begins to drag the body towards the open trap
door.*

– and we tell them that you were in a very distressed state
as a result of nursing him day and night – with very little
sleep – frayed nerves – and as a result of that you totally
miscalculated – (*Seeing what Miriam is up to*) MIRIAM!
WHAT ARE YOU DOING?

Miriam Help me!

Annabel (*rising, somewhat hysterical*) What are you
doing? What are you doing? What are you doing?

Annabel moves across to Miriam.

Miriam (*heaving at the body*) Help me with her, please!

Annabel (*trying to pull the body the other way*) No!

Miriam Help me!

Annabel No!

*They have a silent tug of war over Alice for a moment
or two. Annabel eventually is forced to give up. She
totters back. Miriam carries on, on her own.*

(*With difficulty*) I'm going . . . I'm going . . . to call for
help . . . I'm going to phone the police . . . we can't do

this, Miriam . . . it's not right . . . it's very wrong . . . you see . . . you must see that . . .

Miriam (*dragging Alice closer to the trap*) She wants me to go to prison. I'm not going to prison, Annie . . .

Annabel Listen, Miriam, they probably won't send you to prison at all. All they'll do, they'll probably just send you to hospital for a little bit, that's all . . .

Miriam Hospital? I'm not going to hospital!

Annabel Well, maybe not even hospital . . . Miriam, just think about what you're doing before you do it. Think very carefully. If you drop her – if you drop Alice down that well, then there is no going back, there really isn't. They certainly will put you in prison, for a very long time indeed . . .

Miriam now has Alice poised on the edge of the trap opening.

Miriam . . . think carefully. Just think very carefully now . . .

Miriam appears to be gathering her strength for a final effort. Alice appears suddenly to be regaining consciousness.

Alice (*blearily*) What's . . .? What are you –? What are you? What's –?

Miriam Hyaaah!

She topples Alice into the well. As this happens:

Annabel Miriam, no!

Alice (*as she disappears, receding*) Waaaahhh!

Miriam immediately slams shut the trap and stands on it.

Miriam (*triumphantly*) There!

Annabel (*weakly*) Oh, no. No, no, no, no . . .

A moment's stillness.
   Annabel sits back in her chair.
   Miriam starts to tip away the wine glasses. She also empties the remains from the bottle into the grass.

(*Incredulously*) Have you killed her?

Miriam (*quite matter-of-factly*) I imagine so. It's about thirty feet down to the water, at least. You can't even see the bottom.

Annabel Oh, God!

Miriam It was the only way, Annie. It's better this way. We're free now, you see. Both of us.

Annabel They'll find out. They're bound to find out.

Miriam How will they do that?

Annabel Because she'll be missing. Someone will miss her, Miriam. They'll come looking for her, won't they?

Miriam No, they won't. Why should they? No one even knows she's here. She won't have told anyone. And we haven't seen her, have we? Besides, why should she want to come here, for goodness sake?

Miriam finds Alice's bag. She now empties its contents on to the table.

Annabel What about the letter? Father's letter?

Miriam (*sifting*) I'm just checking . . . to see if she was stupid enough – or over-confident enough – to bring it with her . . .? No. She wasn't that stupid. But – aha – what we do have – (*She holds up an envelope*) – is her address. Not so clever. And what's the betting the letter's there?

Annabel What if it is?

Miriam We go round later on tonight, and we let ourselves in – (*She holds up some door keys*) – with her keys, and we find that original letter and then we bring it back here and we burn it.

Annabel We?

Miriam We both need to go.

Annabel Why? Why both of us?

Miriam Because you'll have to be the one that goes in there, Annie. To look for the letter. Someone might recognise me. I'm her ex-employer. It has to be you. You're unknown. A stranger.

Annabel I'm not breaking into someone's flat –

Miriam (*holding up the keys*) You don't have to. You'll have the keys. Listen, nobody knows you – and even if they saw you, you could pretend to be a friend . . .

Annabel I can't do that, Miriam. I'm sorry, I can't do something like that.

Miriam You're not going to help me at all, then?

Annabel Not that way. I'm sorry.

Miriam OK. You know, I believed for a moment that I might have found my sister again. But it wasn't to be, was it?

Annabel I'm sorry.

Miriam So am I.

Miriam tosses the keys down on the table and moves away towards the house. It is nearly dusk now.

Annabel Wait!

Miriam stops.
A pause.

Whereabouts is this place?

Miriam Not far. I know the area. A ten-minute drive, if that.

Annabel We could drive round there, I suppose.

Miriam Alright.

Miriam moves back to the table and begins to scoop the contents back into Alice's handbag.

Annabel That's if the place is not too overlooked. Then we could – I could – possibly . . . If it doesn't appear to be too big a risk.

Miriam (*glancing at the envelope*) It looks like a flat. From the address. Should be safe enough. (*Smiling at Annabel*) Thank you.

Annabel I haven't said I would. Yet. I said I'd take a look, that's all. Case the place. (*She laughs*)

Miriam Well, thank you, anyway.

Miriam gathers up the bottle and the glasses.

I'm going to rinse these out. You coming in? It's getting dark.

Annabel In a minute.

Miriam We'll have some supper first, shall we? Go round there about eleven. Late enough to avoid most people and not so late as to look suspicious. See you in a minute.

Miriam goes off to the house. She carries the bottle and glasses and has Alice's bag slung over her shoulder.
    Annabel, after a second, stands up again with difficulty. She takes one or two deep breaths to calm

*herself. She looks to the house, then moves to the trap
door. She grasps the ring and tries to open it. She
struggles for some time to get it open but it is
apparently too heavy for her. She stops, exhausted
again.*

*She checks in the direction of the house once more
and then kneels on the floor. She knocks on the hatch.*

Annabel (*calling tentatively*) Hallo . . . hallo . . . are you
alright down there? Are you still alive? Hallo . . . Hallo . . .

*She listens for a moment but there is no reply. She gets
to her feet, moves back into the garden. She folds and
tidies the chair on which she has been sitting back into
the summerhouse.*

*She is still very tense and keeps listening, as if she
was hearing something.*

*She moves towards the tennis court and looks
inside. It is now sufficiently dark that she has difficulty
making things out inside the court. She half turns
away, as if to go to the house. As she does so, a tennis
ball, violently and abruptly smashes into the fencing,
inches from her face.*

Annabel screams.

*She backs away from the court. At the last minute
she turns and rushes off towards the house.*

The lights fade to:

Blackout.

Act Two

SCENE ONE

The same night. Around midnight.

The garden is very dark. There is a moon, but it appears to come and go.

The garden chairs, the rocker and the folding table are all there as before.

After a moment, from the direction of the house, two storm lanterns bob into view. These will provide the main sources of light for the remainder of the scene.

The lanterns are carried by first Miriam and then, a little way behind, by Annabel.

Miriam has Alice's handbag slung over her shoulder. She also swings an open bottle of wine. Both are wearing their coats.

Miriam Come on then. If you're coming.

Annabel I'm coming. I'm coming. I'm not sitting up there on my own in the dark. Why are none of the lights working all of a sudden?

Miriam I don't know. It's always happening. I told you, the whole place needs rewiring. I had a man round to look. It'll cost a fortune. I thought of doing it myself only . . . Something to do with phases and fuses, I don't know. All of a sudden they'll all go out. I'll just get rid of her bag. Now we've finished with it. Then we'll go back in and I'll light some candles.

Annabel Well, please hurry up.

Miriam Won't be long.

Annabel What about the lights out here? Don't they work either?

Miriam No, when they go, they all go off. The summerhouse – even the tennis court. Amazingly, a couple of the lights in there still work as a rule.

Miriam clicks the switch on and off a couple of times on the summerhouse column.

No. Nothing. Completely dead.

Miriam snaps the handle of her lantern on to a screw eye in the summerhouse wall and begins struggling to open the trap.

Annabel sits on the bench to wait. She pulls an envelope from her pocket and removing the letter inside, begins to scrutinise it by the light of her own lantern.

(*As she struggles, noticing Annabel*) Last bits of evidence. Then we can relax. Nice work you, Annie. Finding that letter. We'll burn that out here, shall we? Scatter the ashes.

Annabel (*as she studies the letter*) I tell you, I was terrified. Rummaging about in someone else's flat. I was convinced that at any minute someone was going to walk in on me.

Miriam Never mind. You did well. You kept your cool.

Annabel Apart from when her phone rang. Then I nearly dropped dead on the spot. Hearing the wretched woman's voice on her answering machine.

Annabel frowns over the letter. Miriam has the hatch open now. She holds the bag over the hole and then drops it, watching it fall.

Miriam There you go. Down, down, down, down . . .

Annabel Is there any –?

Miriam What?

Annabel Sign, you know?

Miriam Of her? Not unless she's a bat with webbed feet. She'll have drowned, don't worry. She was unconscious, she won't have known a thing about it. (*About to close the trap*) Right. That's that! Unless you want a final look, yourself.

Annabel No, I do not.

Miriam Fair enough.

> *Miriam slams the trap shut and then picks up the wine bottle from the table and swigs from it.*

Good night's work, eh?

Annabel (*putting away the letter*) Miriam, it has not been a good night's work. Not at all. It has been the most terrible twenty-four hours of my life. How can you say that? I don't know what it is about you. You're utterly cold-blooded.

Miriam Annie, with all the strain, the fear, the dread I've been under for the past two weeks – ever since Daddy died – ever since the accident –

Annabel Accident?

Miriam – the pressure from that woman. Her threats. This is a blessed relief, Annie. I tell you. To be free of her. Free of him. You know something? I might actually have a lie-in one morning. I might actually cook a meal when *I* want to have a meal, eat what *I* want to eat, go to bed when *I* want to go to bed. Listen to the music *I* want to listen to. Fart and swear and flush the lavatory in the middle of the night, and sing in the bath and do all the things I was meant to do but was never, never allowed to do.

60

Annabel If you don't mind my saying so, Miriam, those seem curiously limited ambitions.

Miriam When you've been locked in a cupboard all your life, I tell you everything can seem enormous.

Slight pause.

Annabel (*coming to a decision*) Miriam, I have to tell you something.

Miriam Yes.

Annabel I don't want to alarm you, but I don't think this letter's even genuine.

Slight pause.

Miriam What?

Annabel I'm sure it's almost certainly a forgery. I should have noticed it immediately but having only seen a photocopy I stupidly didn't think –

Miriam A forgery?

Annabel It's not Father's handwriting. Looking at it just now, I'm sure it isn't. Not a bad copy but even allowing for the fact that he was ill . . . I mean, seeing the original, it's just not his writing. I can see it now because my writing's rather similar. It's his notepaper certainly, same colour ink he used . . . But she would have access to all that, wouldn't she? Alice. Plenty of examples of Father's writing around for her to copy from.

Miriam (*still stunned*) It can't be. It can't be a forgery?

Annabel See for yourself.

Annabel hands her the envelope. Miriam stands by the summerhouse and studies the letter by the light of

61

her lantern. Eventually, she replaces the letter in the envelope and looks at Annabel.

Well?

Miriam (*softly*) We killed her for nothing.

Annabel What are you talking about? You killed her for nothing, you mean. (*Angrily*) For God's sake, Miriam, why didn't you study that letter more closely in the first place? When the woman first showed it to you? You saw that original, didn't you? Surely you could have noticed then?

Miriam I didn't . . . I didn't . . . I panicked.

Annabel Clearly.

Miriam What are we going to do, Annie? What are we going to do?

Annabel Well, it's too late now. As you said, unless she has wings and webbed feet . . .

Miriam She might be still alive.

Annabel What are you talking about?

Miriam There's just a chance . . .

Annabel She's thirty feet down a well, Miriam.

Miriam Wait . . .

Miriam kneels by the trap and pulls it up a fraction by the ring.

Annabel She's been there for eight hours. What are you doing?

Miriam slides her fingers under the rim of the door and gently prises it open a fraction.

Miriam. It's too late! What is the point?

Miriam Shh!

Annabel What?

They listen.

Miriam (*in a whisper*) I can hear her. I think I can hear her.

Annabel (*whispering too, despite herself*) What?

Miriam I can hear her breathing down there. She's still alive. Help me!

Annabel (*gently*) Miriam, it's too late.

Miriam (*prising the trap door further open*) Help me, Annie! Help me!

But Annabel hangs back.
    Miriam eventually, unaided, cautiously opens the trap door. She gazes down into the emptiness. By which time even Annabel is half expecting something or someone to emerge.
    Miriam, after a second, allows the trap to close again.

(*Dead*) Nothing.

Annabel It's too late, Miriam.

Silence.

Miriam (*eventually*) Are you really going to sell the house? This garden?

Annabel Yes, I've said.

Miriam Why?

Annabel Because it's – impractical. I've told you.

Miriam Because it gives you the willies?

Annabel Partly that. But more important . . . it's just not sensible.

Miriam And you say you saw something? In the tennis court?

Annabel I – it was stupid. Probably a – probably a village boy or some such. Someone just hurled a tennis ball at me. It – it hit the fencing just near my face. Gave me a start, that's all.

Miriam You were outside the court?

Annabel You bet I was.

Miriam It really is a phobia for you.

Annabel It's – just I'd prefer not to go in there, that's all.

Miriam What if I came with you?

Annabel How do you mean?

Miriam Came with you and stood in the tennis court.

Annabel Don't be so silly . . .

Miriam I'd hold your hand. If you wanted.

Annabel What would be the point?

Miriam It's a fear. You're frightened. You need to be free from your fear, Annie. Like we all do.

Annabel I'm not frightened. I just prefer not to –

Miriam No, you're frightened.

Annabel I'm not.

Miriam Yes, you are. Don't be ashamed of it, Annie. We're all frightened of something. We all have our secret fears. That's what sisters are for. To help each other with their fears. You've helped me. Now I want to help you.

Pause.

Go on. Say it. I'm afraid. I'm afraid.

Annabel Very well. I'm afraid. Alright? Satisfied? Even though I'm aware of the cause of it, it's still a completely irrational fear, I accept that, but –

Miriam They always are. Fears. Irrational. It's because it's often to do with things you don't know enough about. The future. Death. What's waiting for you in the shadows? What you'll see if you open your eyes suddenly in the night. Who it is who's standing at the foot of your bed. Who it is that's woken you up from a deep sleep, bending over you breathing on your cheek. Who is it moving about downstairs in that big dark empty house? Who is it who's coming up the stairs to kiss you goodnight?

Annabel I wish you wouldn't talk like this. It's very childish.

Miriam That's because we're both still children, Annie. I'll tell you a scary ghost story, shall I?

Annabel No, thank you.

Miriam This is really frightening. You'd left home –

Annabel Miriam, will you stop this?

Miriam You'd left home. Run off and left us all. Daddy, Auntie Gwen and me. I was still at school, of course. Twelve years old, I must have been. And one night there was this disco, down in the village. One or two of the kids had – got it together. Everyone was talking about it at school. And Daddy said no. 'No, no, no, Miriam. You can't go. You're far too young. No daughter of mine is going down there, half naked and consorting with unsavoury village children.' His actual words. 'Unsavoury village children.' I wonder if he'd have objected if they'd

65

been savoury ones? Anyway, that evening I went up to my bedroom straight after dinner, pretending I wanted to do my homework and have an early night – but instead, I put on my glitzy-ritzy party frock – what there was of it – lots of silver, I remember – mostly silver – and I tossed my big party shoes out of the window on to the grass, climbed down the drainpipe, being ever so careful not to ladder my very naff shimmery tights and off I went to the village. Where I danced my cares away. And I remember I was propositioned by three different boys, all much older than me, one of whom, I recall, managed a quick grope of my then virtually non-existent, late-developing left breast – and since none of them I fancied in the least – I said, 'No thank you, that's very nice of you but I have to go to school in the morning.' And I crept back from the village. Through there, past your dreaded tennis court, a gleaming silver apparition in the moonlight, my by this time agonisingly unwearable shoes in my hand – and I saw him sitting there in that chair – (*She points to the rocking chair in the summerhouse*) Father – waiting for me. And I knew then, I was in deep trouble. And he said, 'You've disobeyed me, haven't you, Miriam?' And I said yes. And he said, 'Then I shall have to punish you, shan't I? You know that?' And I said yes. And he said, 'Would you prefer to be punished here and now?' And I said – I don't know what I said – I just knew it was all – wrong. Suddenly most terribly, awfully wrong. Mother should have been here, you see. You should have been here. But you weren't. Either of you. And he put me over his knee and he lifted my dress and I waited for the slap, for the sting of the pain . . . but it never came. It was worse than the pain. It was worse than anything. Ever. In my whole life.

Silence.

Annabel (*appalled*) Oh. Oh, Miriam.

Pause.

Miriam There. Wasn't that a scary ghost story?

Annabel I had no idea.

Miriam Why should you? Just thank your lucky stars he wanted you to be a boy, that's all. All he did was hit balls at you. You got off pretty lightly, really.

Annabel Why did you never write and tell me?

Miriam I don't know. It's not something you necessarily put in a letter, is it? (*Holding out her hand*) Come on, then.

Annabel What?

Miriam Come with me.

Annabel Where are we going?

Miriam Where do you think? To face your fear. I shared mine with you. Now I want to share yours. This way.

Miriam pulls Annabel one-handedly towards the tennis court. In the other hand she holds her own lantern.

Annabel (*struggling*) No, I don't want – I don't want to, Miriam . . .

Miriam (*gripping her fiercely*) Come on. Don't fight it now, Annie, don't fight it! Time to face your fear. Come on.

Annabel Will you let go of me, please?

Miriam Listen. You're not all that well, are you? I'm much stronger than you are. But then I've been lifting old men in and out of bed, on and off commodes, so I've built up my strength, you see. You're rather weak.

Annabel Why are you doing this?

Miriam I said, I want to share your fear, Annie. I want to feel your fear with you. Come on now, come on. Nothing's going to hurt you. It's all in your head, you see. This way.

Miriam opens the door of the tennis court and slowly draws the reluctant Annabel inside. Annabel's breathing grows heavier.

There we are. There. You see. Nothing to be frightened of, is there, Annie? There.

A brief pause. Then abruptly the raucous shriek of a night bird as it flies away, startled by their presence.
Annabel screams and runs from the court back to the safety of her lantern.
Miriam laughs.

It's only a bird, silly.

Annabel (*steadying herself with difficulty*) I'm getting very cold. Can we go indoors now, please, Miriam?

Miriam Not yet.

Annabel Please, Miriam, I need to lie down now –

Miriam Sit down . . .

Annabel No, I need to rest . . . I'm not feeling at all . . .

Miriam Then sit down. It's your turn.

Annabel My turn?

Miriam To tell a ghost story. It's your turn you see. To scare me.

Annabel Oh, don't be ridiculous. I'm going indoors. I've had enough of this.

Miriam (*stepping aside*) Alright.

Annabel hesitates.

Off you go.

Annabel You're not coming?

Miriam In a minute I might.

Annabel Just as you like. Suit yourself.

She takes up her lantern and with some decisiveness marches off towards the house.

Miriam (*as Annabel does so, calling*) Mind your step, won't you? It's a bit treacherous in places, that path.

Annabel (*huffily*) I can manage.

Annabel goes off. Miriam picks up her wine bottle, takes a swig and then fetches one of the chairs down on to the grass. She stops, suddenly listening. She seems to hear something out in the darkness.
In the silence, the wind chime sounds for the first time as if something had brushed past it.
Miriam turns, startled.

Miriam What?

The sound of Annabel returning.

Annabel (*off, in some pain*) Oh, shit! Oh, bugger it!

Annabel enters angrily, limping slightly.

It's locked, isn't it?

Miriam You alright?

Annabel The back door's locked.

Miriam You didn't hurt yourself?

Annabel Why didn't you tell me the bloody door was locked?

Miriam Is it? (*Vaguely*) Oh, yes. So it is.

Annabel More to the point, I found this.

She holds out Alice's crumpled scarf.

Miriam What is it?

Annabel What does it look like? It's hers, isn't it? It's her scarf. The woman's scarf.

Miriam (*taking it*) It can't be.

Annabel It's identical.

Miriam Where was it?

Annabel It was looped round the door handle.

Miriam It's soaking wet still. She is alive.

Annabel No, that's impossible. It's just not possible.

Miriam (*with a sudden giggle*) Maybe she does have webbed feet after all . . .

Annabel (*impatiently*) Miriam! If she is alive. And I suppose on this evidence we have to presume she . . . she was certainly wearing that scarf when you – when she – went down there. So she's . . .

Miriam She could be out there. Somewhere. Possibly.

Annabel No. I can't accept that.

Miriam What do we do?

Annabel is having what appears to be the start of another attack.

Annabel (*her breathing quickening*) Nevertheless, we – we would still be better off in the house, I think. She – she doesn't pose any real threat. Not any more. We know now she forged that letter so she has no hold over you in that way whatsoever. Even if she is alive. But – but all the same . . .

Miriam We did drop her down a well.

Annabel No – no, let's get this straight once and for all, Miriam. You dropped her down a well. If she has a grievance at all, ration— rationally it will be with you. Not with me.

Miriam Providing she's still rational.

Slight pause.

Annabel Just give me the back-door key, please.

Miriam Sit down a minute. You don't look well.

Annabel I'm fine. Give me the key.

Miriam I don't want to go up there yet.

Annabel Miriam . . .

Miriam I heard something, just now. She may be waiting for us.

Annabel Heard? What did you hear?

Miriam She's nearby. I know she is.

Annabel Please, Miriam, come back indoors . . .

Miriam There's no lights there . . .

Annabel It's still safer than staying out here. Please.

Miriam moves to the summerhouse and brings out the other garden chair.

Miriam Sit down. You need to sit down a second. Look at you. (*She sets down the chair*)

Annabel I banged my leg just now, that's all. It's made me feel a bit dizzy.

Miriam Sit down then . . .

Annabel (*giving in*) Well, just for a second, then. (*She sits*)

Miriam Do you need your tablets?

Annabel I'll – I'll try to do without them. I'm not supposed to take too many. Since I've been here I've been swallowing them like cough sweets. I'll be alright in a second.

Miriam sits facing her in the other chair. She swigs from her bottle.

Do you think she's really out there?

Miriam I have a feeling she is. Could even be watching us.

Annabel You think so?

Miriam Maybe.

A pause. Unexpectedly, Annabel starts to cry. She does so for a moment or two while Miriam stares at her.

Annabel (*sniffing*) Sorry. Not like me to do this.

Annabel cries some more. Miriam is motionless.

I never cry. You know that. Whatever he did to me, I never cried, you know.

Miriam You mean Brad? Or Father?

Annabel Brad. Never. Maybe I should have done.

Miriam pulls a pack of tissues from her pocket and tosses them to Annabel.

Miriam Here. Blow your nose, you look a mess.

Annabel Thank you. (*She blows her nose*) Sorry about that. We can go back in the house now, if you like.

Miriam (*not moving*) Alright.

Annabel (*rising*) Well?

Miriam After you've told me your ghost story.

Annabel What?

Miriam I want to hear your ghost story first. (*She takes a swig from her bottle*)

Annabel What ghost story? What on earth are you talking about?

Miriam I told you mine. I want to hear yours.

Annabel Miriam, why are you doing this to me?

Miriam Sit down.

Annabel What have I done to you?

Miriam I said, sit down.

Annabel sits.

That's better.

Annabel I don't understand this. Why are you being so horrible? I've done nothing to you, have I?

A fractional pause.

Miriam (*softly*) What did you say?

Annabel I said – I've done nothing to you . . . (*She sniffs*)

Miriam That's what I thought you said. Now blow your nose and tell me a ghost story.

Annabel I don't know any bloody ghost stories. Don't be so silly . . .

Miriam What about Brad?

Annabel Brad?

Miriam The man who beat you. Doesn't he count as a ghost?

Annabel Hardly. He was an extremely solid one, if he was. (*She manages a laugh*)

Miriam How did you meet?

Annabel I told you.

Miriam Tell me again.

Annabel I told you everything there was to know. In my letters.

Miriam You can't have done. Tell me again.

Annabel Alright. We met – at a conference. Well, one of these sales fairs, you know. I was – just starting up my business at the time, trying to get it started, and he was on the next stand. His firm had the adjoining stand.

Miriam Baby clothes?

Annabel Yes. I was acting as the agent for this firm in Singapore. And Brad was – well, his firm was vast, of course. Enormous . . . I don't really want to go through all this again, I really don't –

Miriam Go on. You met at the sales fair. And you got talking babywear, did you?

Annabel I think – very briefly we may have done – I think we soon got on to rather more interesting subjects by day three . . . (*She laughs again*)

Miriam What did you talk about, then?

Annabel Oh, I can't remember . . .

Miriam Try and remember . . .

Annabel Why on earth do you want to know? It's not important now, is it?

Miriam I need to know. I don't know you at all, you see, Annie. You walked out when I was nine and I've never seen you till now. I want to know you. I want to know about my sister. Everything.

Annabel Well, I expect you will, in due course. We're going to be talking to each other all the time, aren't we? From now on. Living together –

Miriam In Fulham . . .

Annabel Well, as I say, possibly Fulham. We'll be sick to death of each other, I expect. Can't it wait?

Miriam I need to know now.

Annabel It's the middle of the night.

Miriam This is the best time, isn't it? The middle of the night? When it's dark. This is the time when you can let loose all those secrets you never dare normally tell. Let loose the darkness in you, so it merges with the darkness out there. This way, it never feels so bad. It's only in the daytime we're made to feel ashamed of our own darkness. Come on, Annie, tell me. What did you talk about with Brad?

Annabel We – well, we found we had things in common, of course. As people do. We enjoyed food. We used to go to restaurants a lot, I remember . . .

Miriam That's nice.

Annabel And, yes, we enjoyed a drink, certainly . . . And music. We both loved jazz. We used to go to this club, sometimes. The usual cellar, you know. I don't know why all jazz has to be played in damp cellars but there you are. And movies. We loved going to movies. The usual stuff.

Miriam What movies?

Annabel Oh. Everything. I preferred classics, you know – older movies – black and white. Brad was more for the modern blockbusters – all those explosions – people continually shooting each other – (*She laughs*)

Miriam But you sat through them with him?

Annabel Oh, yes, well, you do, don't you? If you love someone. You put up with all sorts of appalling rubbish so as not to hurt their feelings. And sooner or later – well, sooner actually – we, you know, started – sleeping together and that seemed to work out rather satisfactorily and so we –

Annabel laughs again. It is an increasingly nervous laugh.

Miriam At your place?

Annabel What?

Miriam Did you sleep together at your place or his?

Annabel Oh, mostly mine. I had an impossibly small bed but at least the place was clean – his flat was quite disgusting.

Miriam Disgusting?

Annabel Well. Untidy, you know. The way men are. Usually. Most men.

Miriam Father wasn't untidy. He'd always punish you if your room was untidy.

Annabel Yes. Well, as I say, most men. Anyway, then Brad and I both decided to put things on a regular footing and we – got somewhere together. A flat. And – then got married – register office, nothing elaborate – he'd been married before, of course and – it was all fine. We were very happy. (*Slight pause*) Until one day, we both came home from work – and – he'd gone out slightly later than me that morning and he'd left the place in a bit of a mess – you know, dirty washing up, unmade beds – and I said something quite mild I think and – we were both rather tired, you understand, but he suddenly pushed me – you know – quite hard and I fell over. And that's how it started. I mean, he was terribly apologetic. Said he didn't know what had come over him – couldn't apologise enough actually – bought me flowers next day, and all that sort of thing. But it went on from there.

Miriam He would hit you?

Annabel Yes. You see the sex had gone rather – you know – as it tends to do after a bit. He started to lose interest, I think. And I began – you see this is the stupid thing – I began to try and make him notice me more. Because I still loved him, I still wanted him, you see. That way. And when he'd turn away from me in the night – I just felt so incredibly hurt. And I began to say things just to get some reaction from him – any reaction, really. But I knew – I knew exactly what I was doing, how he'd react. To the things I said. Occasionally I'd deliberately say something – quite deliberately, you know – and eventually he'd lash out – and . . . You see I did it deliberately. I brought it on myself. I was partly responsible for his behaviour. At least, that's how I felt at the time. And because afterwards, after he'd – hit me – he was always so remorseful, so needful for me to forgive him, so – almost loving. Just for a while, anyway. But then even that went . . . And then there was nothing. So I ran away. Again. Just another pathetic battered wife.

Miriam Why didn't you go to someone? You could have had him arrested.

Annabel Very probably.

Miriam Why didn't you?

Annabel Miriam, I was a young – youngish – dynamic businesswoman with a suite of offices, twelve full-time employees and my own PA. Do you realise how much pride I would have to have swallowed? I was prepared to risk getting slapped round the face occasionally, but I wasn't brave enough to let the world know about it. To face all those – sympathetic looks. I was far too proud. God, I'm embarrassed enough telling you now. You're right. Thank God, it's dark.

Miriam Did you ever enjoy it?

Annabel What?

Miriam Being hit?

Annabel What a question. Of course not. I've said, it was just part of a vicious cycle. I certainly didn't enjoy it. Nobody likes being hit.

A slight pause.

Don't tell me you did? I mean when Father punished you, you didn't enjoy that, surely?

Miriam I don't know now. Sometimes anything is better than being left alone, isn't it?

Slight pause.

When you think about it. It's all tied in with love really, isn't it? Love's at the root of everything. Or what we believe to be love. What we understand as love. Father – he used to shout at us, he used to smack us, because he loved us. Or that's what he believed. 'I'm doing this for your own good,' he used to say. 'Because I love you, Miriam.' And Brad, he probably hit you because he loved you.

Annabel Yes?

Miriam Yes, because he cared. He cared what you thought about him. If he didn't care about you at all, he would never have touched you, would he? I mean, he didn't go around slapping strangers in the street, did he? Did he ever pick fights in pubs?

Annabel Not as far as I know.

Miriam Of course not. Only you. He only hit you. You were the only one that mattered enough. Unless we're mad or deranged those are the only people we ever try to hurt. The people we love. The people we need to love us. People who've somehow taken their love away from us. Spurned our love. Left us on our own. Those are the ones we want to hurt.

Annabel (*uneasily*) Yes. Well, was that enough of a ghost story for you? Can we go inside now, please?

Miriam It was a terrific ghost story, Annie. Thank you. But the point is, do you feel better for telling it?

Annabel I – Maybe. Maybe, maybe I do.

Miriam (*kneeling at Annabel's feet, softly*) That's why I'm your sister. That's why I'm here, Annie.

She kisses Annabel's hands.

I love you.

Annabel (*uneasily*) Miriam, let's go in, now.

Miriam Sure.

Quite suddenly the lamp nearest them, Annabel's, flickers and dies. Only the one in the summerhouse now remains alight.

Annabel Oh, no!

Miriam (*springing up*) It's OK. It's out of oil. Hang on! Wait there!

Annabel Where are you going?

Miriam To fetch a torch. Back in a second.

Annabel We've still got the other lamp, why can't we take that one?

Miriam Because that'll run out in a minute. Bound to. Won't be a sec.

Annabel But we can both use the . . .

But Miriam has disappeared into the darkness, back towards the house.

Oh, for heaven's sake!

She hesitates.

Well, I'm not sitting out here on my own, I can tell you that.

She moves to unfasten the other lamp from the screw eye in the summerhouse wall. She fiddles irritably with it for a second but can't figure how to release it.

Dammit. Wretched thing!

She stands back and stares at the lantern in frustration. As she does this, it also flickers and goes out. Annabel is now alone in virtual darkness.

Oh, for God's sake!! Miriam! Miriam! Oh, no . . .

She gropes in the darkness in what she hopes is the direction of the house. She can evidently see nothing. She trips over one of the chairs and cries out. She is breathing heavily again.

Oh, bugger! Miriam! (*Yelling*) Miriam! (*To herself*) I can't even find my bag. (*Getting on to her hands and knees*) Where's my bloody bag?

She gropes about on the grass but fails to find it.

(*Starting to panic*) Oh, this is hopeless. (*Taking deep breaths*) Keep calm. Keep calm. She'll be back in a minute.

She waits, kneeling on the ground.

(*To herself*) Come on! Come on, Miriam! Where are you,
woman?

*Suddenly, in the darkness, something clangs against the
tennis-court fence. It's another tennis ball.*

What's that? Who's there?

She listens.

Who is that? Miriam? Who's in there?

*From the other end of the court, a man's voice is
heard, calling softly.*

Man (*off, in all but a whisper*) Annabel . . . Annabel . . .

Annabel (*rising to her feet*) What?

Man (*off*) Annabel . . .

Annabel (*incredulously*) Father? *Father?*

Man (*off*) Annabel . . .

Annabel Listen, who is this? Come out of there, do you
hear me? You come out this minute! You're not
frightening me. Come on.

*She moves tentatively towards the tennis court. Her
fingers make contact with the mesh.*

You come out, do you hear? Or I'm coming in. I say, I'm
not frightened of you. Come on! Come out at once!

Annabel pushes the gate slowly open.

I'm coming in, do you hear?

She cautiously enters the tennis court.
Just the sound of her breathing, quite laboured now.
She stands inside the court listening intently.

Where are you? I know you're in here.

The gate behind her slams shut violently. She turns with a cry and tries to open it but she has difficulty in the darkness locating the handle.

All at once a brilliant light shines from the other end of the court. Annabel, turning to look, is blinded by it. Simultaneously, the man's voice is heard, very much louder now.

Man (*loudly, off*) Annabel! . . . Annabel! . . . Annabel! . . . Annabel! . . . Annabel! . . . Annabel!

Tennis balls come hurtling down the court in rapid succession, some hitting the fencing, the occasional one hitting Annabel.

Annabel whimpers in terror and fumbles for the catch on the gate.

At last she finds it and manages to escape from the court. As she does so, abruptly the voice and the tennis balls stop and the light goes out.

Annabel stands moaning to herself in the darkness.

Annabel Help me, please! Dear God, somebody help me! Please!

From the summerhouse the sound of someone scrabbling at the trap door.

Annabel stands frozen in horror.

The trap lid is raised slowly. First a hand then the face and head and shoulders of Alice as she emerges filthy, bedraggled and bloody.

Annabel, transfixed by this apparition, begins to retreat. Her breathing has now become a series of wheezing rasps. As she backs away, she finally makes contact again with the tennis court fence. She slithers slowly down till she is sitting upright, propped against it. Her body gives a final couple of convulsions, goes rigid and she is suddenly very still, her eyes closed.

Alice climbs out of the trap door and walks over to

Annabel. She spends a moment checking her pulse for signs of life. Soon Miriam emerges from the far end of the court. She carries a ghetto-blaster.

Alice (*still busy with Annabel*) I thought you said she had a weak heart?

Miriam She had.

Alice She was as strong as a bloody ox.

Miriam But she's –

Alice Oh, yes. Don't worry, she's dead now.

She moves back to the trap and makes to close it.

Miriam (*staring at Annabel*) Should we put her in a chair or something?

Alice No! Don't move her. Leave everything as it is. Just make sure the tennis court is clear.

Miriam Yes, I will.

Alice, remembering something, steps back into the hole. It is now revealed as not being very deep at all. She retrieves a half-empty plastic bottle of water.

Alice It's a bloody good job we had this filled in. The way you dropped me this afternoon, I could have broken my neck.

She steps out of the hole and closes the trap.

Miriam It needed to look convincing.

Alice Alright, are you?

Miriam Yes, I just – keep thinking there's – something . . . nearly seeing things.

Alice You've frightened yourself, that's all.

Miriam Probably. (*She giggles a little nervously*)

Alice grabs Miriam's wrists and pulls her to her.

Alice (*gently*) Well done, little Mir, you did well, girl.

Alice kisses Miriam gently on the lips.

Miriam (*smiling*) Well done yourself, Lewis.

Alice (*mock aggressively*) Lewis! I'll give you Lewis . . . (*Releasing her*) What's the time, anyway?

Miriam produces a small pocket torch and shines it on her wristwatch.

Miriam Just gone twenty past two.

Alice Twenty past *two*? This was supposed to be over by midnight, wasn't it?

Miriam It took longer than I thought.

Alice You any idea how long I've been down that bloody hole? Three hours.

Miriam I'm sorry . . .

Alice Sort you out later, won't I?

Miriam giggles.

I need to get washed up. Get all this muck off.

Miriam I'll tidy up here.

Alice Don't touch her, will you? Leave her there exactly as she is till the morning. You get up at your normal time, see her bed's not been slept in, so when you find she's not in the house, you come down here looking for her, alright? Then you make the phone call.

Miriam Yes. I know . . .

Alice (*standing over Miriam*) She must have gone for a walk in the middle of the night. Had an attack. How sad.

Miriam Very sad.

Alice See you in a minute, then.

Miriam (*handing Alice the torch*) Here. Back-door key's in the usual place.

Alice (*as she moves off*) Ta! It's all ours now, isn't it? All ours, eh?

Miriam Yes. (*In a murmur*) All mine. (*Calling*) Alice!

Alice Yes?

Miriam When you get in, could you put the lights on again? So I can see what I'm doing. You know where it all switches on, don't you? In the basement.

Alice Sure.

Miriam Watch your step, though. There's a lot of water on the floor down there, for some reason. I think we must have had a leak.

Alice Bloody house. Sooner we sell it the better. (*Laughing as she goes*) Lewis! Where the hell'd you get Lewis, then?

> *Alice goes off. Miriam starts to tidy up. She replaces the chairs in the summerhouse and picks up Annabel's bag and puts it closer to her body, as if she had dropped it when she collapsed. She kisses Annabel on the forehead.*

Miriam Goodbye, dear sister . . .

> *Momentarily, both the mains lights in the summer house and the lights in the tennis court come on. It is briefly very bright. Just as suddenly all the lights flicker a couple of times and then go out again.*

(*Looking towards the house*) Whoops. Bye-bye, Lewis.

> *She continues with her tasks, placing the ghetto-blaster and the wine bottle ready to take back to the house.*

She takes another swallow from the wine bottle as she does this.

She now turns her attention to the tennis court. She pauses for a moment to remove her coat which she tosses on to the bench. Underneath she is wearing a silver party dress. It is quite old – designed for a young teenager rather than for a woman of Miriam's age. It is consequently rather tight-fitting and looks somewhat incongruous.

Miriam now goes into the tennis court where she starts to gather up the balls that have accumulated along the fence, rolling them back to the other end of the court.

The lantern in the summerhouse suddenly flickers into life.

Miriam turns, startled, and stares.

The wind chime again tinkles briefly.

She moves cautiously to the doorway of the court.

Slowly the rocking chair starts to move gently to and fro as if someone was sitting there.

Miriam stands transfixed. Whoever it is in the chair, she alone can see them.

The man's voice is again heard, softly from the summerhouse.

Man (*softly*) Miriam . . . Miriam . . .

Miriam is now motionless.

(*In horror, softly at first*) Father? . . . Father? . . . (*With a scream of sheer terror*) FATHER, NO!!

Still slumped against the fencing where she fell, Annabel's eyes open in a final deathly stare.
The lights fade to:

Blackout.

IF I WERE YOU

If I Were You was first performed at the Stephen Joseph Theatre, Scarborough, on 17 October 2006. The cast was as follows:

Jill Rodale Liza Goddard
Mal Rodale John Branwell
Chrissie Snaith Saskia Butler
Dean Snaith Andrew Brookes
Sam Rodale David Hartley

Director Alan Ayckbourn
Designed by Roger Glossop
Lighting by Mick Hughes
Costumes by Jennie Boyer

This production toured in 2007, opening at the Yvonne Arnaud Theatre, Guildford, on 17 January, with Richard Stacey playing Dean and Dominic Hecht playing Sam.

Characters

Mal Rodale
a sales manager, forties

Jill Rodale
his wife, early forties

Chrissie Snaith
their daughter, mid-twenties

Sam Rodale
their son, fifteen

Dean Snaith
their son-in-law, late twenties

Setting

Parts of the Rodales' home, including
their kitchen, sitting room and bedroom.

This also serves as an equivalent view of
a local showroom of the BFRS Retail
Furniture Warehouse.

Act One

Three of the rooms in the Rodales' comfortable,
conventional home.

First, a view of part of the upstairs (carpeted) master
bedroom, including a double bed, accessible from either
side, and a dressing table with stool. One door leading
to the en-suite bathroom and, ideally, another door to
the rest of the house.

Second, a view of the downstairs (carpeted) sitting
room including a sofa, coffee table and an armchair. All
angled to face the (unseen) TV screen. A single doorway
to the rest of the house.

Third, a view of part of the (lino-tiled) eating area
of the kitchen, including a table, a section of the fitted
units, a sink and a dishwasher, but neither the stove
nor the fridge, which are out of sight. This room has
one door leading to the rest of the house and, ideally,
another: the back door.

Overall the house has a tidy, almost unlived-in
appearance. Such furniture as we see is well maintained
and could indeed be new.

There's a feeling that we could be looking at one of
those furniture showrooms with their separate room
layouts. Which, later on, is what all this occasionally
becomes.

But at the start it is just before seven a.m. in the
Rodale home. The bedroom and the sitting room are in
virtual darkness. In the kitchen, the morning sun is just
beginning to glow through the blinds.

In the bed is Mal Rodale, a man in his forties. Mal is
currently fast asleep. Beside him, his wife Jill, a few years

younger, is already awake, silently counting the seconds till the alarm goes off.

In a moment, it does. Jill cancels it.

A beat. Then with a quiet groan she swings her legs out of bed, sitting for a moment in her nightdress, orientating herself. She heaves herself to her feet and walks blearily to the door.

Jill (*as she goes, softly, routinely*) Mal . . . Mal . . . wake up, now. Time to wake up.

A grumpy muttering sound from Mal, still half asleep under the covers.

He does not move. Jill goes off, sighing.

A silence.

Then a muttered oath from the bathroom.

(*Off, with a cry*) Oh, for God's sake! Mal!

A clatter as the lavatory seat goes down.

(*Off*) Is it so much to ask? I mean . . .

The lavatory flushes.

A moment later Jill returns, pulling on her dressing gown.

(*Sliding her feet into her slippers, to herself*) Is it so much to ask? Every single morning . . . (*Addressing the still inert Mal without looking at him*) Mal! Wake up, Mal.

More indecipherable, disgruntled muttering from Mal, under the bedclothes. Jill appears to understand him.

Yes, well, I keep telling you, you shouldn't drink so much, should you?

Jill draws back the curtains. The room brightens considerably as the morning light floods in.

Mal (*shocked by this*) Aaah!

Jill (*unmoved*) Time to get up.

Mal (*massaging his head*) Ooooh! Aaaaah!

Jill pads out of the room.

Jill (*as she goes, calling*) Sam! Wake up, now! Time to get up!

> *After a second, Mal sits up in bed and groans. He seems in some discomfort but this is the way Mal feels every morning first thing and he's used to it. He swings his legs out of bed and groans again, sitting in his T-shirt and shorts. Meanwhile, Jill enters the sitting room and, crossing to the windows, draws the curtains here as well. The room brightens.*

(*As the light hits her eyes*) Ooooh!

> *She studies the view for a second.*
> *From upstairs in the bedroom Mal begins his noisy early morning throat-clearing ritual.*
> *Jill hears this through the ceiling. She's used to hearing it but nonetheless she looks up, sighs and moves back to the door.*

(*As she goes, calling*) Sam! Sam! Time to get up!

> *As Jill goes out, Mal stands and moves to the bathroom, still continuing his loud throat-clearing. He goes off.*
> *Simultaneously, Jill enters the kitchen.*

(*As she enters, calling back though the door*) Sam! Come on! Wake up! Time to get up!

> *Jill picks up the electric kettle and empties it into the sink.*
> *Upstairs in the bathroom the sound of the lavatory seat slamming up again. More throat clearing from Mal, off.*

95

Jill starts to fill the kettle from the tap. Simultaneously offstage from the bathroom Mal noisily relieves himself.

Jill replaces the filled kettle on its stand. She locates two mugs and gets a couple of tea bags from a container in the cupboard. She places these ready in the mugs by the kettle. She seems to run out of energy at this point and stands totally motionless, staring at the kettle for several seconds waiting for it to boil.

In a moment, Sam, their son of fifteen enters the kitchen. He is half into his school clothes, still barefoot, carrying a bundle of his remaining clothes and his school bag,

(*Coming out of her trance, seeing him*) Oh, good. There you are.

Sam makes a loud snorting noise in his nose (apparently a subconscious version of his father's own ritual), dumps his stuff on the table and repeats the noise as he goes off again, presumably to the other part of the kitchen.

(*As he goes*) Don't do that, Sam. You sound like your father.

Upstairs, Mal now has on his white work shirt and boxer shorts. He clears his throat again. He is searching for his socks which he finds on the floor, his side of the bed. He sniffs them cursorily and, finding them satisfactory, sits on the bed and pulls them on, clearing his throat once more as he does so. Sam reappears in the kitchen with a soft drink from a newly opened can. He puts the can down and sits, snorting again.

Sam!

Sam (*unrepentant*) Sorry. (*He belches as a result of his drink*)

Jill sighs. It is a losing battle.

Sam finishes dressing, taking alternate swigs of his drink.

In the bedroom, on his bedside table, Mal's mobile rings. Mal, still with one sock on, glances at it and answers it.

Mal (*into phone*) What is it, Sandra? . . . (*He listens and frowns*) How ill? . . . Yes, but how ill is ill, Sandra? . . . (*Clears his throat*) Listen, Sandra, this happens every time there's a . . . oh, yes, it does, my love . . . yes, it does . . . it does . . .

As he talks, Mal goes off, clearing his throat again.

In the kitchen, Jill starts laying out a single breakfast place, cereal bowl, etc.

Jill Aren't you going to eat anything?

Sam Mum, can you sign something for me? (*He searches his bag*)

Jill You need more than a fizzy drink . . .

Sam locates a crumpled school parental permission form in his bag.

Sam Here. You need to sign it.

Jill What is it?

Sam Just something to sign. (*He finishes putting on his shoes*)

Jill starts to study the permission form.

Mal returns to the bedroom. He has managed, despite continuing his phone call, to get dressed a bit more. He is now searching for something he can't seem to find.

Mal (*into phone, as he enters*) . . . yes, and you know perfectly well how much I require you there today, Sandra, you know that . . . I feel let down, my love . . . well, that's certainly – well, that's certainly – well, that's certainly the impression I . . . Sandra, every bloody time an audit's due from Head Office . . . no, I'm not . . . I'm very sympathetic . . . *very* . . . that's not what I'm saying, Sandra . . . no . . .

Mal goes out again.
Sam is all but dressed now.

Jill (*still reading the form*) Shakespeare?

Sam (*casually*) It's nothing.

Jill You're going to be in Shakespeare?

Sam Probably. Maybe. Can you sign it, please?

Jill Don't let your father see this, will you?

Sam No, you can sign it.

Jill (*reading*) 'A Midsummer Night's Dream'.

Sam (*still ultra casual*) It's nothing.

Jill What is it? More of this acting, you mean?

Sam (*rising*) Probably won't even get in it.

He pads off in his stockinged feet.

Jill (*doubtfully*) Well . . . I don't know. You know how your father feels about all this acting, Sam.

The kettle has boiled. Jill pours water on the tea bags and then goes to fetch the milk. Meanwhile, Mal returns to the bedroom still on the phone. He now has on his suit and one shoe. Locating the other one finally, under the bed, he sits, putting it on with one hand as he talks.

Mal (*into phone as he enters, slightly more irritably*) . . . yes, I am . . . yes, but only when it's genuine, Sandra . . .

well, I'm sorry I don't think it is, my love . . . I'm sorry . . . no, I'm sorry, I don't . . . Sandra, listen . . . I know all about what women go through, don't bloody give me that, Sandra, I'm married to one, aren't I? . . .

Jill returns with a half-full bottle of milk.

Jill (*calling through the doorway*) Mal! Tea's here!

Mal (*into phone*) . . . listen . . . there's no point in getting hysterical, is there . . .?

Jill (*calling again*) Mal! Tea!

Mal (*into phone*) . . . listen, I'm not arguing – (*Yelling irritably through the door*) Alright! I'm coming. (*Angrily into phone*) . . . look, just you get your arse into work, Sandra . . . or you can forget the job altogether, alright? You have been told, girl. Take that as an official warning, Sandra. (*Disconnecting*) Bloody woman.

Mal leaves the bedroom in a bad temper.
Jill has finished making the tea. She pours the rest of the milk into a jug and finishes laying out the breakfast place with cereals, sugar, etc.
Sam returns with his shoes.

Jill (*as she busies herself*) So what made you want to do this?

Sam (*sitting*) What?

Jill This Shakespeare? What made you want to do Shakespeare?

Sam (*putting on his shoes*) Just for a laugh. She asked me, that's all.

Jill Who did?

Sam Mrs Easterly. She said would I be in it, like, you know.

Jill Mrs Easterly. Which one's Mrs Easterly?

Sam English teacher.

Jill Oh, yes. Tall woman, red hair.

Sam Yeah.

Jill The young one. Quite attractive.

Sam (*shrugging, a bit too casually*) Wouldn't know.

Jill Are you doing it up at the school, then?

Sam No, in the Gardens. It says there.

Jill What Gardens?

Sam Up at the Manor. Hadforth Manor Gardens. It says it all there.

Jill (*impressed*) Oh, those Gardens. I didn't know they had a theatre there.

Sam Open Air. On the grass. Look, just sign it, Mum. I have to bring it back by tomorrow at the latest –

Jill (*seeing Mal through the door*) Oh, there you are.

Mal enters the kitchen. He is now fully dressed for work in his suit, shirt and tie, plus briefcase. Jill immediately picks up the permission form from the table.
Sam simultaneously rises as he sees his father and moves away.
Mal, still angry, sits at the table without a word and starts to serve himself with cornflakes. Neither man acknowledges the other. Sam moves to the door. He has left his drinks can on the table.

Don't leave that there, Sam. In the bin. How many more times?

Sam shrugs, takes the can and puts it in the bin. He hovers in the doorway behind his father, signalling to Jill about the form.

Time for toast this morning, have you, Mal?

Mal No.

Mal is suddenly aware of Sam behind him and then of the piece of paper in Jill's hand.

What's that, then?

Jill What?

Mal That in your hand?

Jill Nothing.

Mal What is it? Give it here. (*He holds out his hand*)

Jill hesitates. Sam shakes his head at her.
Torn, Jill finally hands the form to Mal.
Mal reads it.
Silence.

What's all this then?

Jill It's just . . .

Mal (*turning to look at Sam*) You want me to sign this?

Sam stares at him.

You must be joking.

Jill It's just for fun. For a laugh.

Mal A laugh? There might be time for a laugh when you get your school work right. Judging from your reports of late there doesn't appear that much to laugh about, does there? (*Ripping up the form*) No way.

Sam stares at him, then without another word walks out of the door leaving his school bag behind.

Silence.
Jill gathers up the scraps of paper.

Jill (*close to tears*) You don't make things any easier, do you, Mal?

Mal Shakespeare! Poncing about in tights like a fucking fairy . . .

Jill Mal, don't start! Now, don't start!

Mal (*shouting through the door*) We've got one daughter, we don't want another one, thank you!

Jill Mal, stop it! Calm down!

Sam storms into the sitting room and throws himself into the chair. We now see just how upset he is. He sits, trying to recover.

Both of you. Between you. I can't take much more.

Mal (*slightly calmer*) I've got problems at work . . .

Jill Yes. Well, stop taking them out on him!

Slight pause. Jill recovers herself.

What's the problem at work, then? Another one?

Mal Nothing.

Jill waits.

We got the Head Office visit at the end of this week. And bloody Sandra's phoned in sick. Again.

Jill (*supportively*) Oh, she's worse than useless, isn't she?

Mal I told her, if she's not careful she won't have a job. It's common knowledge, they're downsizing. Closing branches here, there and everywhere. Slightest excuse. We could be next. We're on the list. I know for a fact, we're on the list.

Jill You said.

Mal Now him and his Shakespeare! Last in his class, bottom of everything . . .

Jill Well, that doesn't always follow. So were you at school, weren't you?

Mal That's beside the point. That's no excuse for him.

Jill I was. I was bottom of everything.

Mal That's the reason you have kids. So they can do better than you did. That's the only reason we have them, isn't it?

Jill (a *bit confused by the logic of this*) Well . . .

Pause.

Mal Well, there's always Chrissie.

Jill (*grimly*) We've got two children. Like it or not.

Mal We never had a problem with her, did we? I mean, once we got over the disappointment of her being a girl, never had a problem.

Mal eats for a second. Jill sits silent.

Never argued with us. Always did as she was told.

He eats.

Worked hard at school, didn't she? Top of her class, she was. Could have done anything. If she'd wanted to.

He eats.

Met Dean. Fell in love. Perfect couple. Got pregnant. Happily married.

He eats.

What she always wanted. Husband. Baby of her own.

Grandchild for you. What you always wanted. Happy ever after. Fairy-tale ending.

Jill is silent.

Isn't it?

Jill Don't be late now, will you?

Mal We got it right with her, didn't we? So why can't we get it right with him, eh?

Jill He's alright.

Mal He's not alright. He's not right at all. Why isn't he kicking a ball around? Same as other lads? Chasing girls.

Jill You know he doesn't like balls, he never has done . . .

Mal Well, he should do. He's a boy, for God's sake . . .

Jill He takes after me. I don't like balls. I've never liked balls.

Mal Prancing around in a park in tights . . . What sort of thing's that for a lad to be doing?

Jill It might not be in tights, we don't know . . .

Mal It's Shakespeare, isn't it? They all wear bloody tights. Bunch of shirtlifters.

His mobile rings.

Anyway, he's not doing it and that's final! I'm not having a son of – (*Glancing at his screen*) Oh, I'd better take this. Just a moment.

Jill (*sourly, in an undertone*) Yes, you'd better take it . . .

He gets up and moves to the door.

Mal (*into phone*) Yes? . . . Yes . . . (*Mouthing to Jill*) Just a minute . . . work.

Jill Yes.

Mal goes out.
 Jill stands unhappily.

(*Sadly*) Oh, dear. (*She looks as if she might cry*) Oh, dear!
Oh, dear!

She takes up her own mug of tea and sits at the table.
 Sam is still slumped in the sitting room.
 Mal now enters this, talking on the phone.

Mal (*into phone*) . . . look, I've told you before, love, if
you're going to phone me, then don't ever –

Mal sees Sam and stops talking abruptly.
 Sam immediately rises and walks straight past Mal
 and out of the room.

Listen, Sam, I –

But Sam has gone. Mal lowers his voice.

(*Into phone*) It's alright, just someone – (*Listening*) Yes, I
said . . . I said, I would . . . I *said* . . . Why should I say it,
then? . . . I said it . . . I did, I said! . . . When? . . . When
did I ever do that? . . . I've never done – *never* . . . Come
on, don't get like that again . . . I've got enough problems,
love . . .

Mal, pacing, becomes increasingly agitated. He's
 having a hard time. His increased pacing causes him
 to leave the room again. As Mal goes out of one door,
 Sam enters the kitchen to collect his bag.

Jill Sam –

Sam picks up his bag and makes to leave.

Sam. Don't just leave without . . . Please.

Sam (*turning in the doorway*) I really hate him, you
know. I hate him so much.

Jill No, you don't, not really, you're just –

Sam I'm leaving, Mum. As soon as I can, I'm getting out . . .

Jill Now don't be silly, you can't, Sam, you've got exams coming up –

Sam I've got to get away from him. You want to come with me, you can.

Jill Sam, he's having trouble at work at the moment, he's –

Sam Too bad!

Jill He doesn't mean half of it, he –

Sam And I hate the way he's treating you.

Jill Me?

Sam You know.

Jill What?

Sam You know.

> *Pause.*
> *Mal enters the sitting room again. He throws his mobile angrily into the sofa. He mouths a silent curse.*

What you doing protecting him, Mum? Always protecting him.

Jill He's my husband, Sam.

Sam (*sarcastically*) Great!

> *At this point Dean, late twenties, also in his work suit and tie bounces in.*

Dean (*cheerfully*) Morning, all.

Jill Morning, Dean. He's in the other room on the phone.

Dean Right. I'll rout him out. Morning, Sammy boy.

He aims a series of shadow punches at Sam's head and body.

Pow! Pow! Boof! Pow! Pow!

Sam (*not reacting, deadpan*) 'llo.

Dean goes off again.

Jill Listen, bring another form home tonight. I'll sign it for you. He need never know. They'll let you have another one, won't they?

Sam I don't know.

Jill Come on, Sam. We'll rise above it. We have before, haven't we?

Sam He's not worth it, Mum. Not at all.

Sam leaves.
Jill stands.

Jill (*despairingly*) Oh, men! Bloody men!

Impulsively, she rushes out.
Dean arrives in the sitting room to find Mal.

Dean Morning!

Mal continues to stare at his phone.

You fit then?

Mal Right.

He picks up his phone from the sofa and starts to leave.

Dean (*sensing Mal's mood*) OK?

Mal Whatever you do for them, Dean, they're never satisfied, are they? Always wanting more. Whatever you do, it's never enough. You try your best, you work your bloody balls off for them, it's still not enough. You found that out yet, have you?

Dean Well . . .

Mal (*as he goes*) Give it time, son, give it time . . .

Mal leaves the sitting room. Dean follows.
Jill enters the bedroom. She has a glass of water.
She sits at the dressing table and finds a couple of headache tablets which she pops from their tinfoil into the glass. She watches them dissolve, in one of her trance-like states again.
Mal comes into the kitchen followed by Dean.

(*Picking up his briefcase*) Right. Just a tick.

Mal puts the briefcase on the table, opens it and starts rifling through some papers.

Dean (*surveying the half-eaten cornflakes*) This yours? You haven't finished your cornflakes.

Mal Not this morning.

Dean Oh, I couldn't do that. I always need something to start the day. You know, cooked, like.

Mal What? Egg and bacon?

Dean And the rest. Sausage. Mushrooms. Fried bread. Baked beans. Black pudding. Fried potatoes . . .

Mal Yes, alright, that's enough . . .

He concentrates on his task for a moment.

What, every morning?

Dean Couldn't start the day.

Mal You're lucky. You must burn it up.

Dean I do. (*Indicating cornflakes*) Can I finish these?

Mal If you want. (*Giving up his search*) No, I don't seem to have it . . .

Dean (*sitting and starting to eat*) What's that?

Mal Invoice from those carpet suppliers. Be somewhere around. I'll find it. (*Puzzled*) Funny, I'm sure I had it . . .

In the bedroom, Jill swallows her glass in one. Under the next, she makes the bed. Mal rechecks his briefcase once more.

Chrissie cooks all that for you, does she? Every single day?

Dean Except Sundays. Then I do it. My turn. Boiled eggs.

Mal Fair enough. She doesn't mind, then?

Dean No. Bit tough on her when she was morning sick, but normally . . .

Mal How is she, my little girl? How's my Chrystal, then?

Dean Great.

Mal Looking after her, I hope?

Dean You bet.

Mal Little Liam OK?

Dean Magic. He's magic.

Mal That's what I like to hear.

Jill, once she has finished the bed, sits to study herself in the dressing-table mirror, pulling at the skin on her face, not liking what she sees.
Mal, downstairs, is going through his briefcase contents once again.

Dean Big game Saturday, then. (*He finishes his cornflakes*)

Mal Oh, yes.

Dean All hanging in the balance, isn't it?

Mal I'll be there, don't worry.

Dean Wouldn't miss it, eh?

Mal (*giving up his search*) No, Sandra must have filed it. God knows where it is if she's filed it . . .

Dean Got a match myself on Sunday. For the Heroes. Last of the season. Hadforth Heroes! Hey! Hey! Hey!

Mal Still in the first fifteen, then?

Dean What? Come on! Could they do without me, could they heck?

Mal I don't know. After that last game . . .

Dean It was in touch. Fly half was a yard over the line.

Mal Yeah . . . yeah . . . yeah . . .

Dean (*squaring up to Mal, mock aggressively*) Yeah.

Mal (*doing the same*) Yeah? Take you on, any day, kid.

Dean Watch yourself, old feller. Best wait for your mates.

Mal Come on, then.

Mal takes up his briefcase, starts to leave and then stops again in the doorway. Under the next, Jill gets up and leaves the bedroom, taking the glass with her.

(*Patting his pockets*) Now – do I have the bloody car keys? – I am getting old, you're right. (*Locating them in a pocket*) Yes, I do. Oh, Dean, by the way . . . I may need you to – you know – cover for me again, this lunchtime. If you don't mind.

Dean No problem.

Mal I need to sort this out. I'm going to have to sort it out with her today.

Dean No problem.

Mal (*affectionately*) Thanks, mate. You're about the only one I can trust, you know that, Dean.

Dean I'm here for you.

Mal She's a lucky girl, our Chrissie. I hope she knows.

He pats Dean on the shoulder.

Got herself a diamond, hasn't she?

Dean That's me. Girl's best friend, me. (*As they leave*) You up for a pint after?

Mal I'll need several. Sandra's off sick again, as well . . .

Dean Sandra? Not again!

Mal Bloody women . . .

Mal and Dean leave the kitchen.
A pause.
The house is silent.
Then Jill enters the sitting room. She picks up the TV remote control and points it at the (non-visible) set. A very upbeat announcer's voice is heard.

TV Voice (*brightly*) And now, coming up shortly, it's time to catch up on the latest goings-on at –

Jill immediately mutes the sound on the TV. The screen continues to flicker. She straightens one or two cushions, inspects the floor critically and leaves the room. In a moment, she enters the kitchen.
Moving a little like a sleepwalker, she starts to clear away the empty cornflakes bowl, the cereal packets,

milk, sugar, mugs, etc. She stacks the dirties in the dishwasher under one of the units. She wipes the table, gives a final look round and goes out again.

The lights change. We are now in the BFRS furniture showroom. The same layout although the items and areas are lit more dramatically with spotlights. The TV stops flickering. There is a background drone of showroom muzak. Mal and Dean enter, in full customer-service mode. They both wear earpieces and lapel mics clipped to their suits plus name badges, Dean's with simply his name, Mal's with 'Store Manager' under it.

Mal (*as they enter, already under pressure*) . . . OK, the best short-term solution, Dean, is as follows. You stand in for Charlie, here in Beds and Bedding, and I'll keep an eye on Kitchens and Fittings *and* man the office. We'll just have to pray there's not a run on white goods, cos if there is, we're in deep shit, mate. I'll pull Mary out of Lighting and put her on to Loose Fittings. That'll leave Bald Ron to cope on his own but beggars can't be choosers. Then we've got Big Debbie, God help us, covering Tiles, Rugs and Floor Coverings and she barely knows what day of the week it is anyway, the dozy bitch, but that's the best we can do in the circumstances. Alright, got that?

Dean (*a little confused*) I'll stay here, then, shall I?

Mal Don't move. Bloody Charlie. Why did his wife choose today?

Dean I suppose she couldn't help going into labour, could she? I mean –

Mal Why couldn't she hold the thing in for another three days, till after the audit? I'll give you a call on the radio. Good luck, mate.

*Mal steps through what was, until now, the invisible
'wall' between the bathroom and the kitchen areas.*

(*As he goes, into his lapel mic*) Hallo, George. Yes? Well,
you've got me, I'm afraid, George . . . Sandra's not here
this morning . . . she called in sick. What's your problem,
George, and I hope it's life-threatening, mate, because I
don't have time to waste, not this morning . . .

Mal goes out through the kitchen door.
    *Dean stands for a moment, in charge of the bedding
department. He straightens the cover on the bed
proprietorially.*

Dean (*spotting a customer*) Yes, madam? Can I be of
some assistance?

Dean goes out, adopting his dazzling sales smile.

*The lights change back to normal. The TV flickers
again as Jill enters with the vacuum cleaner.*
    *She plugs it into the wall and listlessly starts to
vacuum the already spotless carpet. She continues this
for some time, giving the impression that she could
probably have continued the task for a lot longer,
having little else to do.*
    *At this moment though, Chrissie, her daughter,
mid-twenties, enters and stands in the doorway. Jill,
concentrating on her task, is unaware of her for a
moment.*

Chrissie (*above the noise of the vacuum*) Mum? (*Trying
again a little louder*) Mum! (*A third try, even louder*)
Mum!

Jill finally sees Chrissie.

Jill Oh, hallo, love.

*Under the next, Jill switches off the vacuum cleaner
and starts to pack it away.*

Chrissie Am I early?

Jill Sorry?

Chrissie I'm not too early, am I?

Jill No, I don't think so. Why?

Chrissie I said I'd be round. Yesterday. We arranged – Girls' outing. Remember?

Jill Oh, yes. Sorry.

Chrissie Only you're not dressed. I thought I might be . . . a bit early. We said we'd go down the shops, remember.

Jill Oh, yes.

Chrissie You alright, Mum? You look terrible.

Jill Well, I haven't – you know – done my . . . I'll make us some coffee. Then I'll get dressed.

Chrissie I'll do that. I left Liam out there. You wouldn't believe it, the minute I get him out of the house, put him in the car, he falls asleep. I think that's what I should do at nights. Drive him round and round the block. (*Taking the vacuum*) Here, I'll take that.

Jill (*releasing the vacuum*) I can manage. You still wouldn't get any sleep though, would you? Not if you're driving . . .

Chrissie Joking, Mum, I was only joking.

Jill (*as they go*) Well, I never know when you're serious, Chrissie, and when you're not, these days.

They go out, Chrissie carrying the vacuum.

As they do so, the scene changes back to the showroom. The lighting changes and the muzak kicks in again.

Mal enters the bedroom while simultaneously Dean enters the kitchen. There is an even greater sense of impending emergency.

Mal Dean, what the hell are you doing in Kitchens, man? I told you to stay in Bedding!

Dean Sorry, Mal, Enid from Fitted Units, she was looking for you –

Mal You've left Bedding completely unmanned, Dean –

Dean – there's a phone call –

Mal – someone could just have strolled in and made off with a King Size.

Dean – for you, she said. Urgent.

Mal I couldn't even get you on the radio. What's happened to your radio, Dean? Don't say it's gone down again?

Dean No, I was in Kitchens, looking for you. You know the radios are rubbish in Kitchens . . . it's the aluminium. Look, Mal, Enid from FU, she says there's a phone call for you. A Mr Perkins from Eversley – she said he sounded quite agitated . . .

Mal (*moving back through the bedroom*) God, who'd be the manager . . . ?

Dean He said he's hanging on till he gets satisfaction. He'll only talk to you.

Mal What's his name again?

Dean Mr Perkins from Eversley.

Mal Oh, it's that bastard again, is it? I'll soon sort him out, don't worry . . .

Dean Now, Mal, don't lose it, mate. It never pays to lose it, Mal . . . Not with a customer.

Mal Some of them need thumping. (*As he goes*) And I've had this one up to here.

Dean makes to follow.

Dean (*calling*) Someone'll be with you in just one minute, sir . . .

Dean hurries off after Mal.

The scene changes back again.
Jill enters the kitchen with a mug of coffee. She sits. In a moment, Chrissie comes in and joins her.

Chrissie No, I say . . . I was up every ten minutes last night with him.

Pause.
Chrissie stares at her mother. Aware she is in a state.

They say you should leave them to cry, don't they? I've tried that. You just lie there listening to them crying all night. Either way, you never get any sleep.

Pause.

Still, they say boys are worst, don't they? Sam was the same, wasn't he? I remember he was.

Pause.

Yes, boys are worst. Till they get older, then you can scarcely wake them up at all, can you? Dean, he'll sleep through anything, Dean will. Sleeps straight through Liam. All he ever says is 'Oh God' and just turns over, you know. Men!

Pause.

Mind you, Dad used to get up sometimes, didn't he? For us? Even for me, he did. I mean, I know he used to for Sam early on but . . . that was different. Sam was always a bit special. But I remember Dad quite clearly. I couldn't have been more than . . . but I still remember him. If I'd had a bad dream or something. Standing by the bed. Always made me feel so safe. Knowing he was there. 'It's alright, Chrystal, any monster gets in, he'll have to deal with me first.' (*Reflecting*) He's always called me Chrystal. Why'd he start calling me Chrystal, do you know?

Jill (*softly*) He never cared for Christine.

Chrissie Well, no, I don't care for Christine either. But I'm not sure Chrystal's much better, are you? (*She laughs*)

Jill suddenly gets up and hurries from the room.

Mum?

Chrissie stands at a bit of a loss. This is evidently an ongoing situation.

Now, where did I put my coffee? (*Spying it on an offstage unit*) Oh, yes.

Chrissie picks up Jill's own mug and goes in search of her mother.

(*Going out*) Mum?

As she goes, the lights cross-fade to the showroom. Muzak once more.
  Mal comes into the sitting-room area.

Mal (*as he enters, into his lapel mic, irritably*) What is it now, George? . . . Listen, mate, it's your problem, you bloody deal with it, George!

Dean hurries on into the bedroom.

Dean How did you get on, then? With Mr Perkins?

Mal Oh, I sorted him out. He won't ring again in a hurry.

Dean You got rid of him, then. How'd you manage that?

Mal I told him to eff off. He says he's going to complain to Head Office.

Dean Head Office? That's in Düsseldorf.

Mal I don't care any more, Dean. His original order's gone missing as well. I don't know where the hell it is. His word against mine, as things stand. I've been through Sandra's filing but there's no record of a hard copy . . .

Dean Be on her computer probably.

Mal If you fancy trawling through her spreadsheets you're a better man than I am. I tried ringing her but she's not answering. I've half a mind to go round there and throw a brick through her window . . .

Dean Er – Mal . . .

Mal What?

Dean Are you still – you know – going off for – your lunch? Only it's five past.

Mal Oh, God, I'll have to phone her. No way I can leave here now, is there? (*He stabs a button on his phone*) And, Dean, there's an old bugger asleep on that Cherry Wood Queen Size in the main window. He's been there half the morning. This isn't a bloody dosshouse.

Dean Right. I'll kick him off.

Dean goes. Mal connects.

Mal (*into phone*) Hallo, love . . . listen, I'm sorry, I'm not going to be able to make it after all, love, not this lunchtime . . . (*A little taken aback by the reaction*) . . . no . . . well, so am I, love . . . so am – so am I . . . Yes,

well, no more than I am, love . . . I see . . . yes, I see . . .
oh, no . . . no, we can't have that, can we? . . . We don't
want that, no . . . not my little Trixie, no . . . (*Under
pressure*) . . . listen, I'll – I'll be there in ten minutes,
then . . . yes, I promise . . . ten minutes. Yes . . . bye-bye,
Trix . . . yes, I will . . . love you, darling . . . . yes, I love
you . . . and I love you . . . 'bye. (*Closing the phone*) Oh,
shit! (*Calling*) Dean! Dean, mate! I have to go out, after
all . . .

> As Mal goes off through the kitchen, the lights change
> back to the house and the muzak fades. Jill comes into
> the bedroom and sits in front of her dressing-table
> mirror. She has been crying and now tries to repair the
> signs with a little basic make-up.
> Chrissie appears in the doorway, having followed
> her up the stairs. She still holds their two coffee mugs.
> She puts Jill's mug down on the dressing table. Jill
> instinctively moves something under it to protect the
> surface. Chrissie sits on the bed and watches Jill for a
> second.

Chrissie (*at length*) We need to talk about this, don't we?

> *Silence. Jill does not react.*

(*Gently*) We do, Mum. I'm sorry, I know you don't like
to, but we do.

Jill Nothing to talk about, really.

Chrissie It's affecting us all.

> *Jill shrugs hopelessly.*
> *Chrissie almost subconsciously rubs her shoulder.*

What about Sam? Don't you care what it's doing to Sam?

Jill (*softly*) Do you think I'd still be here if it wasn't for
Sam?

Chrissie There must be something we can do . . . You're my mother. I hate to see you like this. You look terrible.

Jill Chrissie, saying that doesn't really help, love.

Chrissie Sorry.

Jill He's having an affair, Chrissie. That's all. It's what a lot of men do when they get – to a certain age. They feel – they need – you know – to re-establish themselves.

Chrissie Re-establish themselves? What does that mean?

Jill Ones like your father, anyway. Ones who can't bear to think of it gradually slipping away . . .

Chrissie Well, Dad's still attractive. Fairly. He's not lost it. Much.

Jill No. And he's out there now, isn't he, proving to himself he hasn't? All the same, he's not the man he was.

Chrissie How do you mean?

Jill He was . . .

A pause.

(*Smiling a little*) Then I'm not the woman I was, either. Look at me now.

Chrissie You still look –

Jill No, I don't. You said. I look terrible.

Chrissie You know I didn't mean –

Jill And you're quite right, Chrissie. It's six of one, my love. Not all him.

Pause.

Chrissie Who is she, do you know?

Jill Oh, some tottie from the make-up counter at Debenhams, I don't know. I don't care, really.

Chrissie Well, you should care. I'd care. If Dean went off and started doing that, I'd . . . (*She rubs her shoulder again*)

Jill Chrissie, you still love Dean. There's a difference.

Chrissie (*a beat*) And you don't love Dad?

Jill I don't know. Not much. Not really. Not just because of this. That's just a symptom. We've – gone our different ways, you know. As you do.

Chrissie (*unhappily*) I can't bear to think you don't love each other. You're my parents.

Jill shrugs hopelessly.
Chrissie sits miserably on the bed.

Jill It happens, darling. Nothing special.

Chrissie (*unhappily*) We are though. We're special. I think we are. We were. We used to be.

Jill We'll still be here for you, darling. Even if we separate. You know that. For you and Sam. Your dad would kill for you. You know he would. If you asked him to.

Chrissie I know. (*Rubbing her shoulder again*) I don't think that would be a lot of use just at present.

Jill has been observing Chrissie's gesture.

Jill What's wrong?

Chrissie What?

Jill You alright? You keep rubbing your shoulder. Is it worrying you?

Chrissie No, not really. Didn't even know I was doing that . . .

Jill What happened? You strained it?

Chrissie (*dismissively*) No, it's just a bruise. Nothing.

Jill Is it hurting then? You keep rubbing it.

Chrissie No, I just – my shoulder – I banged it on something – nothing.

Jill Let me see.

Chrissie No, it's nothing.

Jill Want some arnica?

Chrissie No, honestly. It's nothing.

Jill I've got some arnica. Sure?

Chrissie It's fine.

Jill You had that bruise the other week, didn't you? On your other arm.

Chrissie I'm a mother. When you're a mother you're always banging into things, aren't you? Comes with the job.

Jill (*unconvinced*) Does it?

She stares at Chrissie for a second.

I see. I'll get dressed then.

Jill goes out. Chrissie sits for a second.
She rubs her shoulder again abstractedly.

Chrissie (*half to herself*) Better check on Liam . . .

Chrissie collects up the two coffee mugs and goes off.

As she does so, the lights cross-fade to the showroom.
Muzak once more.
Mal comes from the kitchen.
Dean comes from the sitting-room area.

Mal (*as he enters*) Where have you been now?

Dean I got called away. There was a little bit of a crisis.

Mal Crisis, where?

Dean In Garden Furniture. George – he had a bit of a breakdown. Mrs Armitage sent him home.

Mal Sent him home? She's no authority to do that. There's another hour yet.

Dean Well. To be fair, Mal, I don't think she had a choice. He was sitting under one of the umbrellas, just crying, you know. Didn't look so good for the customers. No option really.

Mal Should have dressed him as a bloody gnome, no one would've noticed the difference. (*He starts to move off*)

Dean By the way – it's a girl, apparently.

Mal What is?

Dean Charlie. His wife had a girl.

Mal (*sourly*) Lucky him. God! Roll on closing time.

Mal marches off through the sitting room.

Dean Seven pounds, three ounces . . . apparently. Right.

Dean goes off through the bedroom door.

The lights change back to the house and the muzak fades. Chrissie comes into the kitchen still with the two coffee mugs. She now starts to rinse and dry these.
In a second, Sam enters, still in his school clothes.

Sam Oh . . .

Chrissie Hallo.

Sam You, is it?

Chrissie This'll be me.

Sam Where's Mum?

Chrissie Getting dressed.

Sam Oh. (*Glancing briefly at his watch*) Right.

He dumps down his bag and goes off to the fridge.

Chrissie You right, then?

Sam (*off*) OK.

Chrissie How's school?

Sam (*off*) OK.

Chrissie (*continuing with her task*) Good.

Sam returns with a can of soft drink.
He sits and watches her.

Sam That your baby out there, is it?

Chrissie That's the one.

Sam It's turning blue and choking, did you know?

Chrissie (*unmoved*) Oh, dear. Yes, he does that round about this time of day.

Sam Thought you'd like to know.

Chrissie And his name's Liam. For the hundredth time.

Sam Liam. (*He considers*) That's mail backwards. Did you know that?

Chrissie Yes.

Sam You should write on him 'please forward'.

Chrissie (*mirthlessly*) Oh, ha-ha-ha.

Sam If his surname was Layor. L–A–Y–O–R – Liam Layor. Then he'd be Royal Mail backwards.

Chrissie So he would. Only his name's Snaith.

Sam H-tians. Liam H-tians. Not as good, is it? Sounds Dutch. Maybe you should consider changing your name. For the sake of the child.

Chrissie Maybe you should consider changing your jokes. For the sake of my nerves.

Sam (*getting up*) See you, then.

Chrissie See you.

Sam moves to the door, leaving the can on the table. He runs into Jill, now dressed, who enters.

Sam Hi, Mum.

Jill Hallo, Sam . . . Had a good day?

Sam Great.

He goes out. Jill sees the can on the table.

Jill (*calling him back*) Sam! Back!

Sam reappears.

In the bin. Please.

Sam Sorry.

Jill How many times do I have to say it?

Sam returns and puts the can in the bin.

I think he's just waking up, Chrissie.

Chrissie Yes, it's nearly time for his feed . . . I'll give him something.

Sam A food parcel.

Chrissie You'll get a clip round the ear in a minute.

Jill He's been very good. Not a squeak all day.

Chrissie He's saving it for later.

Chrissie goes out.

Jill Did you bring another form?

Sam Form?

Jill You know the permission form? For the Shakespeare?

Sam Oh, yes. Hang on. (*He puts down his bag and rummages through it*) No point though. He'll never let me do it, will he?

Jill He need never know.

Sam He'll find out. Good news is – we had the auditions today with Mrs Easterly and – ta-ra – I got the part I wanted . . .

Jill Did you? Oh, good.

Sam She said I was right for it and I was. I was brilliant. Here.

Sam hands her the form.

Hide it from him this time.

Jill I'll sign it now. Got a pen?

Sam Somewhere. (*He produces a pen*) Just sign there and the date.

Jill (*doing so*) Right. If you'd – like me to help you with your words or anything . . .

Sam (*surprised*) Oh, well, thanks.

Jill Just take you through them, you know. If you want.

Sam May take you up on that, Mum. Maybe tomorrow. See you later . . .

He makes to leave.

Jill Sam . . .

Sam Yeah?

Jill Do you know yet if you'll be wearing tights?

Sam What?

Jill Only I think it would be easier for your dad if you weren't having to wear tights . . .

Sam No, I won't be wearing tights.

Jill You won't?

Sam It's not that sort of part.

Sam goes.

(*Off*) Goodness me, sister! Are you going to put that huge thing into his little tiny mouth?

Chrissie (*off*) Look, Sam, just sod off, will you!

Jill (*hurrying out*) Now, now, now. Stop that, you two. Sam! Stop teasing your sister!

Jill goes off.

As she does so, the lights cross-fade to the showroom. Mal enters through the sitting room.

Mal (*as he enters*) Right, that's it. Closing time. We're off.

Dean comes on through the bedroom.

Dean Pub time, then?

Mal Queen's Head, here we come. And I tell you, if Sandra's not here tomorrow . . . I left her a message on her machine. Be here or die. Come on, then. Are you fit? First one's on me.

Mal goes out through the bedroom.

Dean (*following him*) You're on. (*Fumbling for his mobile*) I'd better phone Chrissie, tell her to hold my dinner.

Dean goes out after Mal.

The lights cross-fade back to the house.
Jill enters the sitting room where the TV is still silently flickering away. Jill is drawn to something happening on the screen. She stops to watch.

Jill (*as she watches, to herself*) Oh. There now. Oh.

Chrissie enters in a moment.

Chrissie What you watching?

Jill Oh, you know . . .

Chrissie (*recognising the programme*) Oh, yes.

They both stand watching.

Jill Ha! I guessed that, didn't you?

Chrissie Yes.

Jill Him and her.

Chrissie Yes.

Jill Bound to happen.

Chrissie Sooner or later. He sleeps with anything that moves. He does.

Jill (*frowning*) Yes.

Chrissie Sorry.

They watch some more. In the kitchen, Sam enters with a self-made sandwich in one hand and his copy of A Midsummer Night's Dream *in the other. He is absorbed in the text in between mouthfuls. He sits at the table.*

The two women continue to watch the screen during the next.

Chrissie Why do you always watch it with the sound down, Mum?

Jill I think it's more interesting.

Chrissie You can't hear what they're saying, though.

Jill Most of the time you can tell.

Chrissie I suppose.

Jill Leaves you free to get on with other things, then, doesn't it?

Chrissie I suppose so. Dean just phoned. They're in the pub. Surprise! He'll meet me here on his way home.

Jill Hope he doesn't intend to drive.

Chrissie No, it's usually me. (*At the screen*) Oh, God, look, she's going to catch them at it this time, isn't she? She'll chop 'em both up with a meat axe if she catches them, won't she? About time she did. It's been going on long enough. These two. I can't believe she doesn't know by now.

Jill She knows. She's known for ages.

Chrissie You reckon?

Jill You always do. You know it, the minute they start.

Chrissie Oh, look at that. They always cut away to something else, don't they? Just when things are getting interesting.

Jill Well, it's early evening.

Chrissie Yes.

Jill Mind you, later on, they don't cut away soon enough, in my opinion. You want to sit down?

Chrissie Might as well.

Jill (*as they sit*) Get Sam his tea in a minute.

Chrissie Get his own, can't he? His age?

Jill Him? If I don't get him something, I doubt he'd eat at all.

Chrissie You ought to get a job, Mum. You really ought to. Hanging around here all day on your own. No wonder you get depressed. I know I keep saying it, but you ought to get out.

Jill Yes, you're probably right. I think I've lost my nerve, you know. You realise it's been fifteen years since I did a proper job? I mean, I don't count the part-time ones, I mean a *proper* job. You know, proper.

Chrissie Well . . .

Jill I was good, you know. Had a good future. They told me. The youngest Personnel Officer they'd ever appointed. Not even called that now, is it? Human Resources, or something. It was all your fault.

Chrissie Me?

Jill If you hadn't come along . . .

Chrissie Don't blame me. I'm going back. Soon as he's in nursery school. I'm back to work. I'm not hanging around.

Jill Unless you decide on a second.

Chrissie We'll see.

Jill looks at her for a moment.

Jill Listen, if there's anything you want to talk over, Chrissie. You know . . .

Chrissie Yes, OK.

Jill I'm here.

Chrissie OK.

Silence.

(*At the screen*) Oh. Look at that. They're at it again.

Jill I'm amazed she has the energy.

They watch for a second.

Chrissie It's nothing I can't cope with, don't worry, Mum.

Jill There's always something you can't cope with, love.

They continue to watch the TV.
   In a moment, Dean enters the kitchen through the back door. Sam is still reading at the table, mouthing the words silently. Dean is slightly drunk.

Dean (*cheerfully*) Evening. Evening, Sammy boy! (*Aiming a series of shadow punches at Sam's head*) Pow! Pow! Boof! Pow! Pow!

Sam (*continuing to read, without looking up*) She's in the other room.

Dean What you doing? Homework?

Sam Just reading.

Dean What's this, then? Dirty book, is it?

Sam Pretty dirty. Shakespeare.

Dean Shakespeare! Bloody hellfire! (*As he goes*) Shakespeare! Who does he play for, then?

Dean goes out again.
   Sam continues to read.

Jill (*at the screen*) I always like this one. He makes me laugh.

Chrissie He's even funnier when you can hear what he's saying.

Jill You can tell from his face, though, can't you?

Dean appears in the sitting-room doorway.

Dean Right. I'm here.

Chrissie (*without turning*) Hallo.

Jill Hallo, Dean. Mal with you?

Dean Putting the car in the garage. What are you watching, then? (*Staring at the screen*) Oh, this rubbish. You coming?

Chrissie In a minute. It's nearly over, this.

Dean You've got the sound down. Why've you got the sound down?

Chrissie Mum prefers it with the sound down.

Dean You can't hear it with the sound down, can you?

Dean takes up the remote and points it at the TV.

Chrissie Dean! What are you doing?

Dean Teletext. Want to see the scores, do you mind?

Chrissie Mum's watching this.

Jill (*muted*) Doesn't matter.

Chrissie (*angrily*) No, come on. Give it here. Dean!

Dean evades her grab for the remote.

Dean Oh, look at that! Three – nil.

Chrissie Sorry, Mum.

Dean (*switching the TV back*) There you are! Back to normal.

He tosses the remote on to the sofa beside Jill.

Chrissie (*giving up*) Come on, then. I'll drive.

Dean I'll drive.

Chrissie Not with Liam in the car, you're not.

Dean Give us the keys . . .

Chrissie I'm driving. Look at you, practically falling over . . .

Dean I am not. Listen, don't make out I'm drunk.

Chrissie (*kissing Jill*) Night, night, Mum.

Dean Don't tell me I'm drunk, girl, when I'm not.

Chrissie (*moving to the door*) Come on then . . .

Dean No, that really pisses me off, that. When you talk like that.

Chrissie (*embarrassed by his behaviour*) Dean! Come on, please!

Dean No, do you know that? It really pisses me off.

Jill Don't talk to her like that, Dean.

Dean What?

Jill She's your wife. Don't talk to her like that. Show her a bit of respect.

Dean You just keep out of it, mother-in-law. Please? This is just between us, if you don't mind most awfully.

Jill is silent. Despite the jokey nature of the previous exchange, there is an atmosphere in the room.

Thank you. So much. (*To Chrissie*) Come on, then, wife of mine. Let's collect his lordship, shall we?

Dean goes out. Chrissie stands awkwardly.

Chrissie (*still embarrassed*) It's just talk. He doesn't mean it.

She fumbles through her bag for her car keys.

Jill I hope he doesn't.

Jill rises and moves to Chrissie.
She hugs her, nearly catching her daughter off-balance.

Chrissie (*wincing*) Ow!

Jill Sorry. Forgot.

Dean (*off*) Come on, then! If you're coming. We want our dinner.

Chrissie See you tomorrow, eh?

Jill See you tomorrow. And we will do the shops. Promise.

Chrissie goes out.
Jill moves back into the room. She sits, deep in one of her trance-like states.
In a moment, Mal enters the kitchen. He has his briefcase and a takeaway.
Sam is still sitting at the table reading, totally absorbed.

Mal Hey, Sam. Listen –

Sam rises at once and makes for the door.

Listen, son, I'm sorry about this morning, I was probably –

But Sam has gone.

(*Angrily*) Don't fucking walk away from me when I'm talking to you!

He slams the takeaway on the table.

Jesus!

In the sitting room Jill, hearing this, runs to the door.

Jill (*calling*) Sam! Sam!

Sam (*off, as he passes the sitting-room door, yelling*) Forget it!

Jill (*going off after him*) Sam!

Dean appears in the kitchen doorway.

Dean Alright, Mal?

Mal stands, gripping the table, breathing deeply, trying to calm down.

Problem, is there? Mal?

Chrissie appears in the kitchen doorway long enough to take in the tableau.

Chrissie We'll be in the car. Don't be long.

She goes out again.

Mal She has poisoned that boy against me. Do you know that?

Dean Jill?

Mal He was a good boy. Gutsy. You know. Real fighter. Took on anyone. When he was five. Now look at him. Halfway to – It's her. It's all her doing, that. All of it.

Dean Well . . .

Mal starts to unpack his takeaway during the next and put it to reheat in the offstage oven.

Mal It's all her doing, you know. Kept giving him books for Christmas. Story books. Dolls.

Dean Dolls?

Mal You know. Toy people. He's a lad. He doesn't want all that. Then it was a doll's house. He had a bloody doll's house when he was five. Had his head stuck in it, jabbering away to himself for hours. Till I took it away, chucked it on the tip. Now it's theatre.

Dean Theatre. Well.

Mal Theatre. When he was born, you know, I had this dream, the way you do, you know, as a bloke does with his son, it's only natural – something a woman, she'd never understand – but you'll know what I'm talking about, Dean, I know you will, what with having Liam and that – I was determined Sam'd grow up and do things I never could. Never had the opportunity to do. Good job, not like mine, you know, better than that – professional – maybe shine at some sport or other, you know. I wasn't even bothered which. Football preferably, obviously, but if not . . . Just so's I could point at him and say, that's my lad, there. Now, what's he doing . . . ?

Dean Shakespeare.

Mal What?

Dean He was reading it just now. Shakespeare.

Mal Enough to break your heart, isn't it?

A car horn sounds outside.

Dean I'd better be going.

Mal (*clasping Dean's shoulder*) Thank God for you, Dean. You and Chrissie and little Liam. My hope for the future, mate. You three. Don't let me down. Or I'll come looking for you.

Dean (*squaring up to him*) Oh yeah?

Mal (*doing likewise*) Yeah!

Dean Yeah!

Mal Yeah!

Mal thumps Dean's shoulder. They smile.

Dean See you tomorrow.

Mal Tomorrow, mate.

Dean starts to leave.

Mal And Dean . . . (*Pointing at him*) I'm holding you to that.

Dean points a finger back at Mal in a final gesture of male solidarity and finally goes.

Jill appears in the bedroom. She has changed back into her night things. She turns down the bed.

Mal, meantime, goes off. In a moment, he re-enters the sitting room. He carries with him his now opened takeaway (a curry), a spoon and fork and an open can of lager. He sits on the sofa. He stares at the silent TV screen and scowls with distaste.

He plays with the remote until he finds something he fancies.

Jill leaves the bedroom again.

Jill (*off, calling*) Sam! Sam!

Mal hears her but ignores it. Instead he eats, drinks and watches TV.

Mal (*to the screen*) Go on, girl, go for it! Yes! Whooaarr!

In a moment, Jill enters the kitchen. She glances round and, seeing it empty, she straightens a chair or so and goes, taking Mal's briefcase with her.

The lights snap off in the kitchen.

Mal continues to eat, drink and watch TV.

Jill appears in the sitting-room doorway. She looks at the TV and looks away in distaste.

Mal is probably aware of her but doesn't acknowledge her.

Jill I'd have cooked you something, you know. I had something in. I could have made you something. You only needed to ask.

Mal (*still watching the TV*) I'm fine.

Jill Well, I expect you had lunch, did you? I expect you had a good lunch?

Mal I had a sandwich.

Jill Oh, dear, mustn't miss out on your lunch, must you?

Mal I won't.

Pause.

Jill (*suddenly, angrily, snatching at the remote control*) And would you mind not watching things like that when I'm in the room, please? Would you mind?

Jill darkens the TV screen with the remote which she throws back on the sofa.

Mal Hey! What you doing? What's wrong with that?

Jill (*as she goes*) And Sam's locked himself in his room again. I don't know what you said to him this time.

Jill goes out.

Mal takes up the TV remote and brings back the TV picture with the sound up loud.

A burst of cheesy music. Mal watches for a second but the magic, such as it was, has gone out of his viewing. He switches the TV off again.

He goes back to his dinner but after one more mouthful gives up.

Mal (*re-tasting the food*) That's bloody revolting, that is.

Jill re-enters the bedroom. She has removed her dressing gown. She sits on the bed in her nightdress. She starts to cry quietly.

Mal swills the rest of the lager, slams down the can and goes off swiftly, abandoning his half-eaten meal on the coffee table. The lights snap off in the sitting room.

Jill hears Mal coming up the stairs.

She swiftly moves to the dressing table and starts to remove what little make-up she has on.

Mal enters the bedroom. During the next there is a long, long silence. Not a look, not a word exchanged between them. Mal comes and goes, as he gets undressed.

Jill continues with her face. From the bathroom the sounds of the lavatory seat slamming up and of Mal relieving himself, cleaning his teeth, etc.

Finally Jill gets into bed. She turns off her light and lies back, staring at the ceiling. Mal returns in his T-shirt and shorts. He gets into bed beside her and switches off his own light.

Pause.

Jill (*at length, from the darkness*) We have to talk, Mal.

Silence.

Mal, we have to. We do.

Slight pause.

Mal There's nothing to talk about, is there?

Mal turns over, his back to her.

Jill (*softly*) Oh, God help us.

A silence. Dawn starts to creep up, as before, through the downstairs kitchen blinds.

The bedroom and sitting room grow lighter, too.
Sometime in the night, though, Jill and Mal have switched personas.
Externally, they still look identical but, beneath the skin, as it were, Jill now inhabits Mal's body while Mal inhabits Jill's. It takes a moment for them both (and us) to realise this. As well it might.
For simplicity's sake, both characters despite their changes of persona, will be referred to by their original names, since they are played by the same actor.
The alarm rings. In a moment, Mal (now Jill) cancels it.
A beat, then with a quiet groan he swings his legs out of bed, sitting for a brief moment, orientating himself.
He heaves himself to his feet and walks blearily to the door.

Mal (*as he goes, softly, routinely*) Mal . . . Mal . . . wake up, now. Time to wake up.

A grumpy muttering sound from Jill, still half asleep under the covers. She does not move. Mal goes off, sighing. A silence. From offstage, a scream from Mal.
A moment later he returns in near panic.
He clutches Jill's dressing gown in his hand.
He stares at himself in the mirror.

(*Touching his face, in horror*) What's happened? What's happened to me? Mal! Mal! Wake up! Wake up!

More indecipherable, disgruntled muttering from Jill, under the bedclothes.

(*Shaking Jill awake*) Mal, please. Wake up. Help me! Mal! You have to help me . . .

Jill sits up in bed.

Jill (*grumpily*) What's going on? What do you think you're doing, woman – (*Breaking off and staring at Mal, aggressively*) Who are you, then? What the bloody hell are you doing in here, mate?

Mal Mal . . . it's me. It's Jill.

Jill Jill?

Mal *Jill.* (*Slight pause*) Mal, it is!

He starts to giggle. He stops.
  The truth slowly dawning on them both.

Jill *Jill?* (*Staring at Mal*) Oh, my God.

She lifts the sheet slightly and stares down at herself.

(*Looking at him, horrified*) Then who the hell am I, then?

Blackout.
  End of Act One.

Act Two

The same.

A few moments later.

Mal is still Jill.

Jill is still Mal.

Mal sits on the stool at the dressing table.
Jill sits on the bed.
A silence. The first shock is over.
Panic is beginning to set in.
Particularly for him.

Jill I don't know what we're going to do. I don't.

Pause.

I can't go to work like this. How can I go out looking like this?

Mal I don't see why not. I went out looking like that.

Jill Ah, but then you were you. Weren't you? Now you're me. And I'm you. Look at me.

Mal Put some make-up on. You'll feel a bit better.

Jill *Make-up?*

Pause.

I mean, look at me.

Mal Don't keep saying that. It doesn't help.

Jill I mean – all this . . . (*Indicating her breasts*) What am I going to do with these?

Mal I don't know. You were happy enough to stare at them before. You can sit in front of the mirror, now, can't you? Jiggle them up and down to your heart's content. You'll find the novelty soon wears off.

Jill I wish you'd stop making jokes, woman. What the hell is there to laugh at?

Mal Nothing. Absolutely nothing, Mal. I'm sorry, I'm just trying to keep calm. One of us has to. Otherwise I think I'm going to have a panic attack. And that is not going to help either of us, is it?

Jill (*getting up, agitated*) What are we going to do? What the hell are we going to do?

Mal (*also rising*) Mal! Sit down, for God's sake. You're a grown man, now pull yourself together. (*Indicating the stool*) Sit! Sit!

Jill sits.

Now listen, I would like you to know that I'm not exactly over the moon at being lumbered with all this, either. All these – extra bits. I nearly died of fright in there, did you know that? And you left the seat up again.

Jill Sorry.

Mal Well, you won't be doing that any more anyway . . .

Jill Look, will you just shut up, woman! What are the lads going to say? How can I face them like this?

Mal Well, you can't is the short answer. You'll have to stay here and I'll have to go to work.

Jill You can't do that. You can't do my job.

Mal I'm going to have to try, aren't I? I doubt you can do mine but you're going to have to try your best, as well.

143

Jill Oh, dear God!

Mal It's the only way, Mal. Think of the kids. Sam. You said it yourself, he's having identity problems. How's he going to react if he discovers his mother's his father and his father's his mother? We have to keep things as normal as possible.

Mal *Normal?*

Jill Look, with any luck it won't last. It may only be temporary. Just a temporary – personality exchange.

Jill Really? I've never heard of that.

Mal No, nor have I but it will have to do for now, won't it? And unless you want to lose your job, I'd better get ready for work. Dean'll be here soon.

Jill Oh, God. How can I face him?

Mal You're not going to have to, are you? I'm going to have to face him.

Jill What am I going to do?

Mal You're going to go downstairs and make sure Sam has something to eat before he goes to school. Then once you've seen him off, you come up here and get dressed. Make yourself presentable.

Jill (*head in hands*) This is a nightmare. I can't do this.

Mal I'll leave you a list of things to do. It's not difficult.

Jill I can't do it.

Mal (*sharply*) Mal! For God's sake, pull yourself together! (*More calmly*) Listen, Chrissie will be round later with Liam. I promised her we'd look round the shops together, you'll enjoy that.

Jill What, you mean dress shops?

Mal What other sort of shops do you look round? By the way, if you want to try anything on you're a size twelve, European thirty-eight.

Jill I'm not doing it, Jill. I cannot do it. I'm sorry. I'll be a laughing stock. No way!

Mal stares at her.
  Sam comes into the kitchen, half dressed as usual.
He dumps his stuff on the table.

Sam Mum? Mum? (*To himself*) Where is everyone? (*He snorts*)

Sam goes out again, in search of life.

Mal Alright. If you prefer it then, I'll stay here and you can go to work. Put your suit on, suck your chest in, try and make your voice a bit deeper and maybe no one'll notice. Dean or Sandra – or all the lads you have a drink with afterwards in the pub. Or – the people you have lunch with.

Jill stares at him.

But, then again, even if they do notice – well, you'll have given them all a *really* good laugh, won't you? So look on the bright side, Mal, I would.

Jill considers this.
  Sam sticks his head into the sitting room.

Sam Mum? (*To himself*) Abducted! They've all been ab-d-u-u-u-c-ted!

He snorts again and goes out.

Jill (*reluctantly*) Just for today, then.

Mal One day at a time, anyway.

Jill It's not going to work, Jill. Not in a million years.

Mal Why not? Why should anyone ever suspect? Eh? Unless you keep calling me 'Jill', that is.

Jill What am I supposed to call you, then?

Mal Mal, Jill. You call me Mal. And I'll call you Jill, Jill. Or dear. Or dearest. Or if you're really good, clever girl. Now, go on, off you go downstairs. (*Handing her the dressing gown*) And I should put this on or you'll give the postman a heart attack.

Mal goes off.

Jill (*appalled*) Bloody hell.

She pulls on her dressing gown and awkwardly slips her feet into her slippers, bending to do so.

Oh, heck . . . (*Straightening, hitching up her bust*) These bloody things weigh a ton, and all.

Jill goes off making the equivalent of Mal's earlier throat-clearing noises.
Sam comes back into the kitchen.
He has the usual soft-drink can in his hand.
He snorts. He takes out his Shakespeare text again and sits studying it.
In the bedroom, Mal comes back dressed in shirt and boxer shorts.

Mal (*sniffing his shirt*) Ugggh! Hasn't he a single thing to wear that's *clean*? He's only got to put them in the basket there, for God's sake. All he has to do!

Mal finds his last-night's socks again just by the bed.
He picks them up, sniffs them cautiously and recoils.

Uggh! I don't believe this. Men! They're animals!

Mal goes off again in search of cleaner socks.

Jill meanwhile enters the kitchen.
Still clearing her throat.
Sam jumps slightly and hides his book.

Sam Oh!

Jill Morning.

Sam Thought you were Dad.

Jill You did?

Sam Yes.

Jill Well, I'm not.

Sam No. I know you're not.

Jill I'm your mum.

Sam I know.

Jill Right.

She takes the kettle and starts to fill it at the sink.
The sound of Mal relieving himself in the bathroom upstairs.

Mal (*off, horrified*) Aaaaaah, nightmare!

Jill puts the kettle on.

Jill Right. Breakfast. What you want? Cornflakes?

Sam No, thanks, Mum. Don't want anything.

Jill Got to have something! Come on! (*Opening the cupboard*) Cornflakes? All Bran? Special K? Muesli? Take your pick. Going, going, gone! Cornflakes, there you are!

Jill bangs the cornflake packet in front of Sam.

Sam (*a little bemused by her brusqueness*) It's OK. I'll just have the drink. I never eat breakfast, you know that, Mum.

Jill produces a bowl and spoon.

Jill Bollocks! Most important meal of the day.

She slams the bowl and spoon down on the table in front of Sam.

Bowl! Spoon! There you go! Now, eat!

Sam (*startled*) You feeling alright?

Jill What?

Sam You're sounding like Dad.

Jill Am I? Well, I'm not.

Sam (*muttering*) Do without two of you.

Jill (*sharply*) What? What did you say?

Sam Nothing.

Jill Eat!

Sam Right.

Sam serves himself some cornflakes, very puzzled by his mother's behaviour.
In the bedroom, from his bedside table, Mal's mobile phone rings.
Mal enters, now with clean socks on, glances at his screen and answers it.

Mal (*into phone*) Hallo . . . oh, hallo, Sandra . . . (*He listens and frowns*) Oh, dear . . . oh, dear . . . you're not? . . . No better? . . . Oh, I'm sorry to hear that, Sandra . . . what's the problem exactly? . . . Yes . . . no, I'm feeling fine, no . . . what's the problem with you? Tell me. (*Listening sympathetically*) . . . oh . . . oh, I see . . . oh, dear, Sandra . . . oh, that's horrid for you . . .

As he talks, Mal goes off.
In the kitchen, Jill waits for the kettle to boil.

Sam (*still seated*) Any milk is there, Mum?

Jill In the fridge. You know where the milk is.

Sam (*staring at her, rising*) Yes, right.

Sam moves off to the fridge. As he goes he belches as a result of his drink.

Sorry.

Jill Better out than in, son.

Jill starts to make two mugs of tea.
Sam, during the next, returns with the bottle and sits and pours milk on to his cornflakes.
Mal returns to the bedroom. He has managed, despite his phone call, to get his trousers on. He is carrying his shoes. He now sits on the bed during the next and puts them on one-handed.
Jill takes the milk from Sam and pours it into the cups on top of the tea bags.

Mal (*into phone, as he enters, still very sympathetic*) . . . no, well, as I say . . . that can't be normal, Sandra, it really can't be . . . not as regularly as that, love . . . no . . . no . . . no, that can't be right . . . no, you need to see someone, you really do, Sandra . . . no, it's probably nothing at all, love, but you need to be sure, Sandra, don't you . . . in your own mind . . . (*He listens*)

Sam Any sugar is there, Mum?

Jill Haven't a bloody clue.

Sam Right.

Mal (*into phone*) . . . yes . . . mmm . . . mmm . . .

Jill Better have a look. She'll have some somewhere.

Sam Who will?

Jill I will.

Mal (*into phone*) . . . yes . . . mmm . . . mmm . . .

Sam Right.

Jill and Sam both search the kitchen in both the onstage and offstage cupboards and drawers.

Mal (*into phone*) . . . yes, it's a worry otherwise, isn't it . . . yes . . . you never know the next . . . no . . . you never know the next . . . no . . . you never . . . no, you never . . . yes . . . no, well you can't carry on like this, can you? . . . no . . .

Mal goes out again.
Jill and Sam are still on their search for sugar.

Jill (*producing a box*) Eureka! How about this, then?

Sam That's no good.

Jill Why not?

Sam They're sugar lumps.

Jill It's sugar, isn't it?

Sam You can't put sugar lumps on cornflakes, Mum.

Jill Why not?

Sam Because you can't. It's stupid. You can't put sugar lumps on cornflakes.

Jill (*excitedly*) Alright! Alright! I'm doing my best!

Sam (*alarmed*) OK. OK. Sorry.

Meanwhile, Mal returns to the bedroom still on the phone. He now has his jacket on.

Mal (*into phone as he enters*) . . . yes, alright, Sandra . . . yes, you phone me the minute you've got an appointment

. . . yes . . . no, that's alright, my love . . . the most important thing is to get you right, isn't it . . . ?

Jill Perhaps your – dad will know.

Sam What?

Jill Where we keep the sugar.

Sam Dad? He won't know. He doesn't know anything.

Jill (*calling through the doorway*) Tea's here!

Mal (*into phone*) Yes, alright then . . . I'll wait to hear from you . . . 'bye, Sandra . . . not at all . . . no, you're too valuable to lose, Sandra . . . 'bye-bye, love.

Mal rings off.

Jill (*calling again*) Tea! (*As an afterthought*) Mal!

Mal (*calling through the door*) Coming! (*To herself*) This suit smells like a brewery.

He stands in front of the dressing-table mirror for a second. He reaches into a drawer and takes out a perfume atomiser and for a moment is tempted to spray himself with it.
He decides to resist the urge and leaves the bedroom.

Jill (*frustratedly, giving up her search*) Well, I don't know where it is. How the hell should I know where it is?

Sam Don't worry, Mum. I'll eat them without sugar.

Jill Good lad.

Sam You're sure you're OK?

Jill (*snapping*) Of course I'm OK.

Pause.

Sam You seem a bit – angry.

Jill Do I?

Sam Tense, you know.

Jill Well, I am tense.

Sam Right.

Mal looks into the sitting room, still darkened, shakes his head and goes and draws back the curtains, sniffing the air distastefully. He sees the half-eaten takeaway and the lager can still on the table.

Mal (*picking them up*) He only has to put them in the bin, all he has to do.

Mal leaves the sitting room.

Sam Is it like – you know – like your hormones?

Jill My what?

Sam You know – your hormones?

Jill No, it's not my bloody hormones.

Sam Sorry.

He eats his cornflakes, rather meekly.
Mal enters the kitchen briskly, still carrying the discarded takeaway and the empty lager can.

Mal (*dumping these in the rubbish bin*) All you have to do – put them in the bin – That whole room reeks of stale curry. Morning, Sam.

Sam (*bemused*) Morning . . .

Mal Don't you want some sugar on those? Here.

Mal produces the sugar container and puts it on the table beside Sam. He then grabs a can of air-freshener from under the sink and a cloth.

(*Waving the can at them both*) Air-freshener. Under the sink for further notice. Alright?

Mal goes out.

Jill (*after him, rather lamely*) Don't forget your tea, love . . .

Sam and Jill exchange a look.
Jill smiles and shrugs. Sam barely manages to smile back. He is growing rather concerned.

Sam What's he doing, clearing up?

Jill Well, he . . . he must have felt like it.

Sam Have you had a word?

Jill What?

Sam A word? With him? You're always saying you're going to have a word with him. You know – about you clearing up after him.

Jill Yes. I've had a word.

Sam Well done, Mum. Brilliant.

He eats some cornflakes.
Jill sips her tea.
Mal comes into the sitting room. He wipes over the table with the cloth, briefly sprays the air with a few squirts of air-freshener and leaves again.

(*During this*) By the way – did you mean what you said . . . after school . . . before he gets back, you know . . . ?

Jill Sorry?

Sam My lines. Going through my lines. In the play. Shakespeare.

Jill Shakespeare. Right.

Sam If you're still on for that?

Jill Yes, I'm – still on.

Sam Hey, I must go. I need to be early this morning. (*Rising*) Thanks for signing the form.

Jill Form? What form?

Sam I should have a lie-down, Mum. When we've all gone. You look terrible. See you later.

Mal enters the kitchen.

Mal (*as he enters*) Now, Sam, have you had enough . . .?

Sam (*abruptly*) Bye, Mum . . .

Sam sweeps past Mal and out of the door.

Mal Well, don't just – (*Indicating the table*) Just look at that! Every morning!

Jill (*a little belatedly, after Sam*) Hey, don't just walk away and leave things for your . . . father.

Mal instinctively starts tidying away Sam's breakfast debris. Jill, equally by instinct, stands watching him.

Don't forget your tea.

Mal You're going to have to look out for him, you know. I mean you just can't ignore him any more, Mal. He needs you. Like it or not, you're his mother now and he needs you.

Jill What am I supposed to do? I gave him breakfast.

Mal (*holding up the box*) What? Sugar lumps. Well done.

Jill (*frustratedly*) Oh, I can't cope with this. How can I cope with this?

Mal You're just going to have to. Till we get it sorted out. Look, before I go I'll make you a list. Just the basics. Nothing difficult. I did a big shop at the beginning of the week, we should be alright for food.

Mal takes a kitchen pad and pencil and, sitting at the table, starts to make a list. Jill watches him miserably.

Jill (*unhappily*) I don't know how I'm supposed to cope with Sam. He wants me to hear his lines when he gets back. Shakespeare.

Mal (*writing*) You'll have to do it then, won't you? I promised him. You can't let him down. I'll try and keep your end up. You'll have to try and do the same for me.

Jill How are you going to manage at work? Never mind about me. How are you going to manage? It's a complicated job, mine.

Mal Can't be that complicated.

Jill Dealing with people all day. Staff. Managing, motivating them. I had to go on a course. They sent me on a course, you know. Five days.

Mal (*still writing*) I know. I know. You got legless in Prestatyn for a week.

Jill We've got staff off sick. Maternity . . .

Mal Maternity? Someone had a baby, did they?

Jill Charlie Dilling – in Beds and Bedding. His wife had one yesterday.

Mal Oh, lovely. Boy or girl?

Jill Haven't a clue. Anyway. He's off sick. Well, at least Sandra's back at work. That's one thing.

Mal No, she's not . . .

Jill After the message I left on her phone last – what did you say?

Mal She phoned your mobile. I've just spoken to her. Told her she was to take time off, see a doctor and get herself sorted out.

Jill You did what?

Mal She's a silly girl. Stuffing herself with painkillers every month . . . Where's the sense in that?

Jill Oh, my God! Now what are we going to do . . . ?

Mal *We* are going to manage without her. (*Holding up the list*) Can you read that?

Jill What, all this?

Mal Come on, it's perfectly simple. (*Reading*) 'One. Make bed.' You can do that, surely. 'Two. Vacuum sitting room and hall . . .'

Jill What's this one then?

Mal Plumber. Look out for the plumber. He's supposed to come and look at that cold tap in the kids' bathroom. It's been dripping for weeks. He keeps promising to come but he never does. Three-minute job. Alright? Cope with that?

Jill I don't know . . .

Mal Well, do your best. Just don't turn your back on him, he likes to touch your bum. And don't forget Chrissie's round this morning, too.

Jill Shopping.

Mal You'll enjoy that.

Jill Oh, yes.

Mal Seeing Liam.

Jill I suppose.

Mal Of course you will.

Jill Never going to play football with him now, am I?

Mal I don't see why not.

Jill It's not the same. You don't play football with your grandmother, not if you're a lad. Oh God! There's the match on Saturday.

Mal You can still go.

Jill What, with the lads? Me and the lads? You're bloody joking.

Mal Well, you can go with some of the girls, then.

Jill Girls?

Mal Yes. I'll find you a few. One or two I know are quite keen on football.

Jill (*sitting, sinking her head in her hands*) Oh, no!

Mal Well, suit yourself. Just don't ask me to go with you, that's all. Once was quite enough . . . Where's Dean got to? He should be here, shouldn't he? Listen, go upstairs and put some clothes on. Go on. It'll be alright, Mal. Don't worry. It'll all be fine.

He kisses Jill on the top of her head.

(*Gently*) Off you go. That's it.

Jill gets up and goes slowly to the door.

Jill (*hesitating in the doorway*) Jill?

Mal What is it? What's the problem now?

Jill What am I going to wear?

Mal Whatever you like, love, there's plenty in my wardrobe to choose from. Not too casual, not if you're going out later.

Jill A dress?

Mal No. Trousers if you prefer. Try and look a little bit smart, that's all. Don't want to let Chrissie down, do you?

Jill No.

Mal And, Mal, just a little bit of make-up, love. You look terrible.

Jill Right. (*As she goes*) Everyone keeps telling me I look terrible . . .

Jill goes out.

Mal Dear, oh dear. Men!

From his pocket, his mobile rings.

(*Retrieving the phone and studying the screen*) Oh. Now, who can this be, I wonder? (*Answering*) Hallo . . . Oh . . . yes . . . hallo, dear . . . yes . . . yes . . . oh, how nice . . . no, she's not in the room, just me . . . oh . . . oh, you must look lovely in that . . . I wish I could, too . . . I'm glad I bought it for you . . . yes, it was sweet of me, wasn't it? . . . Yes . . . well, we all need spoiling occasionally, don't we? . . . You more than most . . .

Dean enters, dressed for work as before.

Dean (*cheerfully*) Morning, all. Sorry I'm late . . . (*Seeing Mal on the phone*) Oh, beg your pardon, mate . . .

He steps back respectfully.
Jill comes into the bedroom, still clutching her list.
She stands for a second. She puts the list down on the dressing table and goes out again.

Mal (*still on the phone*) . . . yes . . . yes . . . listen, I'm sorry, dear, I can't talk now. I'm just on my way to work. Yes, I'll talk to you later. 'Bye, now, 'bye. (*He rings off*) Sorry about that. Good morning, Dean.

Dean Doesn't give up, does she?

Mal What?

Dean (*indicating the phone*) Don't you give in to her, mate.

Mal I certainly won't.

Dean Treat 'em mean, keep 'em keen, eh? That's my philosophy.

Mal Oh, you find that works for you, do you, Dean?

Dean Sorry?

Mal I'm amazed.

Dean (*laughing, uncertain*) Hey! Watch it? Eh? Yeah? Yeah?

Dean goes through the ritual on his own.

Yeah? Yeah! Yeah! (*Running out of steam, rather*) Anyway.

Jill returns to the bedroom.
    She carries a top and trousers which she now holds up against herself in front of the mirror. They clash horribly. Even she can see this.

Jill (*irritably*) Oh, I don't know, do I? How am I supposed to know?

Jill goes out again.
    Mal finishes tidying the kitchen.
    Dean sits at the table and watches him.

Dean Any road, sorry I'm late. Chrissie and me, last night, we had this slight altercation.

Mal Did you?

Dean Nothing serious. Blow over. You're dead right about women, though, Mal. Seriously.

Mal Am I?

Dean Oh, yes.

Mal Really? I never thought I understood them, at all.

Dean You? You read them like a bloody book, mate, I tell you. (*Sitting*) Like you were saying yesterday, whatever you do for them, they're never bloody satisfied, are they?

Mal finds a dishcloth, wets it under the tap and starts wiping the work surfaces.

Whatever you do – whatever you . . . (*Noticing Mal*) What you doing?

Mal Just wiping these over.

Mal sets about the work surfaces while Dean warms to his theme. Mal shoots Dean the odd venomous look but is evidently trying his best to retain self-control. Jill comes back with a second clothes combination which she rapidly rejects as well. She goes out again.

Dean (*puzzled*) Oh. No, whatever you do for them . . . it's never quite enough, is it? I mean, as you said, you try your best, you work your balls off for them, it's still not enough, is it? You were spot-on there, mate. I mean, take what you're doing now, that bit of cleaning, if she was in here, if Jill was here – don't get me wrong – she'd be saying, oooh, don't forget that bit in the corner, wouldn't she? Or, ooh, look you missed that bit! Wouldn't she? Eh?

Dean laughs. Mal continues, grimly.

No, it's all one-way, mostly. When you think about it? All about them being appreciated, isn't it? I mean, take last night with me and Chrissie – I mean, don't get me wrong, Mal, I think the world of her – but I mean the entire conversation was about what *she'd* done for *me*. What about all the things I've done for her, eh? I said to her, bloody hell what about all the things I've done for you then, eh? So we finished up having this – this altercation, you know. And this morning, she's still sulking. Refusing to get up. Well, except to feed the baby, of course . . . So I had to get the breakfast. Do it myself. Boiling eggs . . . all that.

Mal Nice change for her, anyway. Breakfast in bed.

Dean You're joking. She didn't have breakfast. Wasn't my turn, was it? Fair's fair.

Under the next, Mal finishes wiping the surfaces and, as he passes behind Dean, squeezes the wet cloth over his head.

I mean, let's face it, women, they'll turn anything to their own advantage, won't they? To suit themselves? I mean, take the other – (*Jumping up in alarm*) Hey! What are you doing?

Mal Sorry.

Mal wrings out the rest of the water in the sink, and puts the cloth neatly out to dry.

Dean Careful.

Mal Ready for off, then?

Dean Sure. Waiting for you. Do you – er – want me to cover for you again, this lunchtime? For your – lunch appointment?

Mal Sorry?

Dean You know. While you – you know – you have your lunch?

Mal Oh, my lunch. No, not today.

Dean No?

Mal Probably – disagree with me.

Dean Right. Sorry. I thought you were . . . sorry. None of my business.

Mal Come on. We're going to be late.

Dean moves to the door ahead of him and goes out momentarily.

(*Checking*) Car keys? Yes. Right. Here I go, then. (*Softly*) Brace yourself, girl.

Dean returns with Mal's briefcase.

Dean Don't forget this.

Mal Oh, thanks.

Dean (*as they go*) How's Jill? Is she any better today, is she?

Mal How do you mean?

Dean Well, she seemed in a bit of a mood, yesterday.

Mal She's in a worse one today, I can tell you . . .

Mal and Dean leave.
    From the bedroom, frustrated sounds from Jill.

Jill Oh, dammit. Sod you! Do up, you bastard. (*With another effortful grunt*) Hah! At last.

A pause. Then Jill comes on, rather red in the face from her struggle, wearing trousers and putting on a top over her bra.

They're easy enough to get off but they're buggers to put on.

She stares at herself for a second.

Well, that's going to have to bloody do. (*She sits on the stool*) I'm knackered already. (*Catching sight of herself in the mirror*) God, I do, I look terrible.

She opens a drawer, then another until she locates some make-up. She stares at it somewhat bemused.

I don't know. There's tons of the stuff. Decorate a bathroom with all this.

A sequence as Jill experiments with a little make-up. The results while a bit haphazard are not as horrendous as they might have been.

(*At length, surveying the results of her handiwork*) There you go. Gorgeous. Pull anyone now. Now, where's my list? (*Locating it*) Make bed. Right.

She gets up and pulls the bed over somewhat cursorily. The results would hardly meet with her spouse's approval.

That's that, then. Piece of piss. Next.

She goes out consulting the list. In a moment, she enters the sitting room.

Vacuum. Where's she keep that?

She picks up the TV remote control and points it at the (non-visible) set. She rattles through about thirty channels at lightning speed, never giving a single programme a chance to settle.

No. Nothing. Too early for sport. Not late enough for sex. Vacuum cleaner . . .

Jill goes out again for a moment and then returns with the vacuum. She plugs it in, as before, and starts going over the floor. After a second, Jill stops and examines the carpet.

Not sucking up properly, is it? Not picking up. I don't know, why can't she keep things maintained? She only has to tell me.

She turns the cleaner over and examines it.

Alright, we'll soon sort you out.

Jill gets up and goes to the door.

Leave it to a bloke, love. Leave it to a bloke . . .

As Jill goes out of the sitting room, leaving the up-ended vacuum cleaner, the lights cross-fade to the showroom and background muzak once more.
    Mal and Dean enter, as before, from the bedroom. They have earpieces and lapel mics clipped to their suits plus their name badges.

Dean (*as they enter*) . . . well, I think the best thing, Mal, if I might suggest, since you're asking me, is to do the same as we did yesterday. I'll stand in for Charlie, here in Beds and Bedding and you keep an eye on the office as well as Kitchens and Fittings. I mean, if push comes to shove we could always pull Mary out of China again . . . but that didn't work so well yesterday, did it? I mean –

Mal What about flowers?

Dean Flowers? We don't have a flower department.

Mal For Charlie's wife? Has anyone organised flowers? I think it would be nice if we sent her flowers, don't you?

Dean (*dubious*) We've never done it before . . .

Mal Well, I think we should have done, don't you, Dean?

Why don't you go round the departments now, make a collection. Have a whip-round? I'll phone the florist's . . .

Dean It's not usual. What about Beds and Bedding? Who's going to –

Mal I'll look after that as well, off you go. (*Touching her earpiece*) I don't know how long I can wear this thing. People keep jabbering in my ear.

Dean You'll need to keep that on, Mal, or you'll be out of contact. You need to remain accessible.

Mal I'll be accessible. Don't worry about that. Off you go.

Dean Right.

> *Dean starts to go off through the bedroom doorway, shaking his head in amazement.*
> *Mal goes out through the kitchen door.*

Flowers? He's going off his head . . .

> *As Dean goes off through the bedroom, the lights change back and the muzak fades.*
> *Jill returns to the sitting room with a large metal toolbox.*

Jill (*putting down the toolbox*) This thing's got heavier. Now then, let's have a look at you, you little bugger.

> *She switches off the vacuum at the wall socket and then squats down on the floor and begins to dismantle the machine with a screwdriver.*

> *The lights cross-fade to the showroom. Muzak again. Mal enters from the bedroom. As he does so, he gets a call via his headset.*

Mal (*into his headset*) Hallo . . . . who's this, please? Oh, good morning, George . . . yes . . . Dean said you might call me . . . I see . . . well, I think it's best if you dealt with that yourself, don't you, George? . . . Well, she's your customer . . . no, I'm not expecting you to . . . you can't do better than your best, can you, George? . . . That's what my mother always told me . . .

Dean enters through the bedroom behind Mal.

Dean (*urgently*) Mal . . . Mal . . .

Mal Yes, Dean? (*Into headset*) . . . Excuse me one minute, George . . . (*To Dean*) What's the problem?

Dean (*grimly*) Mr Perkins. From Eversley. He's back again.

Mal Really? Is that bad?

Dean He's not taking a no. Not this time.

Mal No?

Dean No. He's demanding a yes.

Mal Well, I suppose I'd better talk to him.

Dean I think you'll have to, Mal. He says he's prepared to overlook what you called him yesterday – you know, the language – seeing it was in the heat of the moment, like – but he's demanding satisfaction, this time . . .

Mal Right. (*Starting to move off*) Mr Perkins?

Dean From Eversley.

Mal What did I call him, yesterday, can you remember?

Dean No, but try not to call him anything else, Mal. He's a retired minister and he's not at all happy. Try not to lose it again, won't you?

As Mal and Dean go off through the bedroom, the lights change back. Muzak fades, In the sitting room,

Jill now has the vacuum cleaner in several pieces.
Chrissie enters the kitchen. She wears dark glasses.
She puts away her car keys and dumps her bag down
and goes out again.

Jill (*growling, as she struggles with the vacuum*) Come on
. . . come on, you bastard . . . yes . . . you little bastard . . .

Chrissie, during this, enters the sitting room, stops
and watches Jill with some surprise.
    She removes her sunglasses.
    She has evidently been crying.

Chrissie Mum?

Jill Oh, hallo.

Chrissie What are you doing?

Jill Trying to get this thing off. I think there must be a
blockage, you see. It's not sucking up properly. I've
managed to strip down most of it but – Oh, it's a bugger,
this last bit. Whoever designed this . . .

Chrissie Mum, ought you to be doing that?

Jill It needs fixing.

Chrissie Yes, but do you know what you're doing?

Jill Course I know what I'm doing . . .

Chrissie Don't you think you ought to get a man to look
at it?

Jill (*affronted*) What do you mean, 'a man'?

Chrissie Someone who knows. Take it in and have it
looked at if it's not working.

Jill No way. Soon fix this. Don't worry.

Chrissie You sure? You're getting filthy.

Jill Come on, bit of dirt . . .

Chrissie It was working yesterday, wasn't it?

Jill Was it?

Chrissie Well, you were using it. Would you like me to help you?

Jill It's no problem. Leave it to me. I'll just get this last bit free and then we'll get down to the nitty—

Chrissie Have you checked it's not full?

Jill What?

Chrissie That it doesn't need emptying?

Jill Emptying?

Chrissie It possibly just needs emptying, Mum.

A long pause. Jill surveys the remains of the vacuum, the various sections she's removed and finally back to the vacuum again.

Jill (*at last*) That'll probably do it, yes. (*Deflated*) I'll put it back together, then.

Chrissie No, Mum, don't bother. We'll put it away in the cupboard and leave it for Dad. Dad can do it.

Jill You'll be lucky.

Chrissie Dad understands these things. I mean, he's useless at most things but with things like this, he's brilliant, isn't he? Leave it to Dad, Mum.

Jill (*reluctantly*) Right.

Chrissie Come on, we'll clear it all away and then have a cup of coffee, shall we?

Jill OK.

They start to collect up the bits.

Chrissie Mum, did you mean to wear that today? Do you mind me saying?

Jill How do you mean?

Chrissie That top with those trousers? Was that deliberate?

Jill Yes.

Chrissie Well, it looks a right mess.

Jill Does it?

Chrissie If you don't mind me saying. Terrible. (*She picks up the toolbox*)

Jill No, I'll take that, it's heavy, love.

Chrissie (*taking the vacuum with her other hand*) I can manage, Mum. You just bring the bits.

Jill No, Chrystal, you can't carry all that, love, you'll –

Chrissie (*as she goes*) I can manage . . . (*As she goes*) Be quiet out here. Liam's just got off.

Chrissie goes off, leaving Jill to bring the loose bits.

Jill (*as she follows, muttering*) I wish people would stop telling me I look terrible.

Chrissie and Jill leave the sitting room.

As they do so, the lights cross-fade to the showroom. Muzak once more. Mal enters from the bedroom, answering his phone as he enters.

Mal (*into phone*) . . . no, I said, I don't think I can come round, not today, I'm sorry . . . well, we can't always get what we want in this world, can we, Trixie? Particularly when it doesn't even belong to us in the first place . . .

now, don't get like that . . . Trixie, if you could only hear yourself, love . . . shouting and screaming like a school-girl in a tantrum . . . quietly, dear, quietly now . . . you'll make yourself ill . . . Trixie . . . Trixie . . . I'm ringing off now . . . I'm not talking to you while you're like this . . . I'll talk later when you've calmed down . . . goodbye . . . (*Firmly*) No, I said goodbye, Trixie. (*He rings off*) Dear, oh dear! I thought I was bad enough sometimes.

Dean appears in the kitchen area.

Alright, Dean?

Dean How d'you get on? With Mr Perkins?

Mal Oh, I sweet-talked him. Don't worry about him.

Dean Sweet-talked?

Mal He was just looking for an argument, that's all. I wasn't prepared to give him one. I know the sort, I've met them before.

Dean Really?

Mal Oh, yes. Promise them nothing but agree with everything. It's usually the way to deal with men like that.

Dean Is that a fact?

Mal I'll be in the office if you want me. Looks as if it needs a proper tidy. Poor Sandra, I'm sure she's a wizard on computers but her paperwork's a disgrace. (*As he goes through the bedroom*) Customer over here needing attention, Dean.

Dean (*following Mal off, bemused*) Oh, yes. *Sweet*-talk?

Dean follows Mal off through the bedroom.

The lights cross-fade back again to the house.

Chrissie enters the kitchen with a mug of coffee. In a moment, Jill, also carrying a mug, comes in and joins her at the table.

Jill Sleeping like a log.

Chrissie Told you. Always the same, minute he's in the car. You should have been round at our place last night. Yelling and screaming.

Jill Real tantrum, was it?

Chrissie I'll say. And that was just us two.

Jill What?

Chrissie Nothing.

Pause. Jill stares at her.

Nothing. I've said, nothing you can do. We'll sort it out between us. We have to.

Jill continues to stare.

Nothing. I've said.

Another silence.

No, I was thinking about what we were saying yesterday, Mum. I think the problem for Dad, he's like most men, he lives in a sort of fantasy land, doesn't he? Well, they all do really, don't they? In their different ways. Most of them, most of the time. Dean, Sam, Dad. Liam probably eventually. But then we don't help, do we, because quite often we sort of protect them, don't we? Keep the truth from them. Frightened of hurting them, I suppose, little blossoms. I mean. I say things to you, Mum, I'd never dream of saying to Dad. Not in a million years. It's the same with you, isn't it? I mean, this affair of his. You've been playing along with it, but in the end, face it, the only one who's really getting hurt is you. What you should have probably done is said to Dad, 'Listen, I know you're having an affair with this woman, so for goodness' sake stop pretending you're not, making all these secret phone calls, pathetically sneaking out in your lunchbreaks as if nobody knew, just go ahead, fuck her senseless and then come back home and let's get on with our marriage, for God's sake.' Only you can't really say that to him, can you?

Silence. Jill sits somewhat stunned.

You alright, Mum?

Jill I don't know.

Chrissie Sorry. Shouldn't I have said that? I haven't upset you again, have I?

Jill I just feel I've just been run over by a large truck.

Jill suddenly gets up and hurries from the room.

Chrissie Mum?

Chrissie stands at a bit of a loss.

Oh, God. I can't say a thing right, can I?

Chrissie picks up Jill's own mug as well as her own and goes off in search of her mother.

(*Despairingly calling, as she goes*) Mum? Mum, I'm sorry . . .

As she goes, the lights cross-fade to the showroom.
    Muzak once more. Dean comes on from the sitting room. He sees something off through the bedroom entrance and hurries over.

Dean (*calling*) Hey, you, off! Off there! I warned you yesterday!

Mal enters from the bedroom entrance.

Mal What's the problem?

Dean Look at him. That old bugger. He's back again in the main window, kipping on the Cherry Wood Queen Size . . . Hey, you!

Mal No, leave him, Dean. He's an old man, he's not doing any harm. Besides, he's fast asleep. It's a good advert for the bed, isn't it?

Dean Not if he pisses on it in the window, it won't be.

Mal Good point. In that case, go and get him a cup of tea from the machine and wake him up nice and gently, how about that?

Dean Tea? What, in the main window?

Mal Off you go. Good advert.

Dean goes, further bemused.

(*Into his headset*) Hallo, George . . . back again, are we? Now, tell me, how did you get on, George? . . . Good, good . . . six sun-loungers, well done . . . you see, you can do it . . . a little bit of confidence, all you need . . .

As Mal goes off through the kitchen, the lights change and the muzak fades. Jill comes into the bedroom and sits in front of her dressing-table mirror.

She is still stunned from her previous conversation with Chrissie.

Chrissie appears in the doorway, having followed her up the stairs. She still holds their two coffee mugs. She puts Jill's mug down on the dressing table and sits on the bed.

Jill (*at length*) So let's get this straight – she –? (*Pause*) He –? (*Pause*) I – knew all along?

Chrissie That's what you told me.

Jill Yes. Well, I probably did then.

Chrissie You said you did. From day one.

Jill Then why didn't I say something? Do you suppose? To me – to him?

Chrissie I don't know. Sometimes, you know, you both start off talking about it and it finishes up with him thinking that because you've both talked about it, he now has your full permission to carry on with it. You know men. Twist anything to suit themselves, sometimes.

Jill (*a bit mystified*) Oh.

Chrissie You'd lose him altogether, then.

Jill Right.

Chrissie Dad's still a good looking man. Miss Tottie from the make-up counter, she gets wind you've relinquished your claim, she'll be in there like a dose of salts.

Jill You reckon?

Chrissie Younger woman, older man. Have him jumping through hoops in no time, poor bugger.

Jill Probably.

Slight pause.

Chrissie Mum . . . you didn't mean that yesterday, did you? Please say you didn't really mean it. That you don't love Dad any more? You didn't mean that, did you? Look, he's a silly, stupid, pig-headed bloody man and he's treated you so badly he deserves to have it cut off, but please don't walk away. Give it another go. Think of Sam, Mum. Both of us.

Jill sits silent.

(*Softly*) It would break my heart, if that happened, it really would.

174

Jill rises and, crossing, holds Chrissie.

Jill It'll be alright, love. I won't let anything happen to hurt you, Chrystal. I promise.

Still clinging to Jill, Chrissie laughs.

What's that?

Chrissie You called me Chrystal. Only Dad calls me Chrystal.

Jill laughs and, growling, gives Chrissie another squeeze.

(*Wincing slightly*) Ah!

Jill What is it?

Chrissie Sorry.

Jill Alright?

Chrissie Yes, just . . .

Jill What?

Chrissie (*rubbing her shoulder*) It's just that bruise. Still got it.

Jill What bruise?

Chrissie On my shoulder here. I told you.

Jill (*drawing away from Chrissie*) How did you get it?

Chrissie I said – I banged it on something – Nothing.

Jill Banged it on what?

Chrissie It's nothing. Don't keep going on about it, Mum. I've said. It's nothing. You sort out your own problems. (*Rising*) I'd better go and check on Liam.

Jill (*growing angrier*) Banged into what? Now tell me.

Chrissie I'll be downstairs. (*She turns to leave*)

Jill (*shouting*) Don't fucking walk away from me when I'm talking to you!

Chrissie stops, startled.

Sorry.

Chrissie (*after a second*) It's only if he gets a drink or two inside him, that's all. He – he expects things, you know, and I can't – always satisfy him, you know, the way he wants it – just at the moment. I know some women, they get over it just like that. Practically having it away before they're out of the maternity ward, but . . . it's probably partly my fault.

Jill (*shocked*) You control yourself, don't you? If you love your wife and respect her, then you learn to control yourself, surely?

Chrissie I suppose. Nice to think it always happened like that, wouldn't it?

Chrissie goes out. Jill stands frustrated.
In a moment, she kicks the bed and leaves the bedroom as well.

As she does so, the lights cross-fade to the showroom.
Muzak once more. Dean comes on from the kitchen as Mal comes on from the sitting room. He has some kitchen gloves and some cleaner.

Mal I sent off the flowers, Dean. Pass it round the staff, will you? Got a lovely bunch of mixed blooms. Carnations. Roses. Mostly pink, you know. Seeing it's a girl.

Dean (*guardedly*) Lovely, Mal. (*Seeing what Mal is holding*) What you doing, now, then?

Mal Oh, that office is filthy. Filthy. How can anyone bear to work in there . . . ?

Dean Right. You on for a pint later, then?

Mal A what?

Dean A pint? You know, Queen's Head? With the lads?

Mal (*uncertain*) I'm not sure . . . I'm not sure about that. I'll see.

Mal goes off through the bedroom.

Dean (*feebly*) It's my shout . . . (*As he goes, to himself*) He's lost it. He's completely lost it . . .

Dean goes off through the sitting room.

The lights change back and the muzak fades as Chrissie comes into the kitchen with the two coffee mugs. She now starts to rinse and dry them. In a second, Sam enters, still in his school clothes.

Sam Oh.

Chrissie Hallo.

Sam Here again?

Chrissie Yep.

Sam Where's Mum?

Chrissie Upstairs, I think.

Sam Oh. Getting dressed, is she?

Chrissie No, she's dressed today. Sort of dressed, anyway.

Sam Ah.

He dumps down his bag and goes off to the fridge.

Chrissie OK, are you?

Sam (*off*) OK.

Chrissie School OK?

Sam (*off*) OK.

Chrissie (*continuing with her task*) That's good.

Sam returns with a can of soft drink. He sits and watches her.

Sam Hey, this'll interest you. Did you know that Liam Snaith . . .?

Chrissie Oh, God, here we go again . . .

Sam Liam Snaith is an anagram for Animal Shit, did you know?

Chrissie Do you have nothing better to do at school than sit and make up daft jokes about my child?

Sam I'm interested in his welfare. I'm his uncle, aren't I?

Chrissie God help him. Haven't you any homework to do or something?

Sam I'm going to do this. In a minute.

He produces a book from his school bag.

Chrissie What's that?

Sam Shakespeare.

Chrissie Shakespeare. Didn't know you were into that.

Sam I'm in the play. Got a part. Da-da!

Chrissie Does Dad know?

Sam Yeah. Ripped the form up, didn't he? Typical.

Chrissie You're still doing it, though?

Sam Mum signed another one for me. She's going to hear my lines for me.

Chrissie I wouldn't bother her, not today, Sam.

Sam She promised. I'm going to be word perfect before we start. I'm going to amaze them. Mrs Easterly and that.

Chrissie Mum's a bit – a bit out of sorts today, Sam. I wouldn't bother her.

Sam She's always out of sorts. So's Dad. He was this morning. Really, really, *really* odd. Started trying to make me breakfast.

Chrissie Dad did?

Sam Weird. I was so surprised, I almost spoke to him.

Chrissie Something's strange. Can't put my finger on it.

Sam You think maybe they're both – you know – maybe getting senile?

Chrissie Not yet.

Sam It can happen at any age. I was reading. It can happen at your age.

Chrissie No, it can't.

Sam There's senile people of thirty. There was apparently this young woman, she was having a baby and when she woke up from having it, she'd aged seventy-five years –

Chrissie Oh, bugger off . . .

Sam (*rising*) True.

Sam moves to the door, leaving the can on the table. He runs into Jill, who is about to enter.

Hi, Mum.

Sam goes out.

Jill Hallo, Sam . . . I think Liam's just waking up out there, Chrystal. Chrissie.

Chrissie Yes . . . I'd better feed him.

Sam reappears.

Sam (*smiling sheepishly at Jill*) Sorry, Mum.

Jill What?

Sam (*picking up the can from the table*) Forgot. Sorry.

Jill (*who hadn't noticed*) Oh, well done.

Sam puts the can in the bin.

Sam Mum, are you feeling OK to go through my lines, are you?

Jill Lines?

Sam For the play, you know. Like you said.

Jill still looks blank. Chrissie shakes her head at Sam.

The Shakespeare. You said you would.

Jill Oh, right. Right. I thought . . . I thought your dad said you couldn't do it?

Sam Yes, he did. Still.

Jill Well . . .

Sam Never stopped us before, did it? I mean if we only did things he let us do, things he wanted us to do, we'd never do anything at all, would we?

Jill No.

Chrissie Sam, don't push Mum. You'd don't have to do it now, Mum, do it another day . . .

Jill No. If I said I'd do it, then I'll do it. If – if I promised.

Sam Great. Thanks.

Chrissie (*softly to Sam*) Go gently with her.

Chrissie goes out.

Sam Shall we go in the other room, then? In case he comes back? Don't want him interfering, do we?

Jill No.

Sam Just you look . . .

Jill Terrible. I know.

Sam After you, Mum.

Jill and Sam go off.

As they do so, the lights cross-fade to the showroom. Mal enters the sitting room.

Mal (*as he enters, calling*) Oh, Dean . . .

Dean comes on through the bedroom.

Dean That's it then, is it? Home time?

Mal I had a thought, Dean. The staff have worked very hard today. Especially George in Garden Furniture. He really tried his best. I was very proud of him.

Dean George? He's a plonker . . .

Mal Now, Dean, don't pre-judge people. For all you know, someone's maybe saying that about you somewhere and you wouldn't like that now, would you? Listen . . . I thought it'd be nice if we bought them all a drink, don't you? Well, on the firm. Buy them all a drink on the firm.

Dean On the firm? You mean everyone?

Mal Be a nice gesture, wouldn't it? I've so enjoyed today, I can't tell you.

Dean There's dozens of them.

Mal Well, push the boat out for once. They won't all come anyway, some of them'll want to get home, I expect, but it's the gesture . . . (*Into lapel mic*) Hallo . . . all departmental heads can I have your attention, please. Would you inform all staff that, as soon as they've finished, Mr Snaith and I will be in the bar of the – (*To Dean*) – where was it –?

Dean Queen's Head –

Mal – the Queen's Head and we'll be happy to buy you all a drink. Just the one, mind you. (*He laughs. To Dean*) Come on, then. What are you waiting for?

Mal goes out through the bedroom.

Dean (*following him*) Right. (*Fumbling for his mobile*) I'd better phone Chrissie, tell her to hold my dinner.

Dean goes out after Mal.

The lights change back.
Jill enters the sitting room followed by Sam.
Jill sits in the armchair.

Jill So. What is it you want me to do?

Sam (*handing her the script*) If you just read the first bit from here – see, scene two, here – then I'll say my bit and you just stop me if I get anything wrong.

Jill Right.

Sam I'll stand up. He'll probably be standing up. I mean, we haven't started yet but I think he'll be standing up.

Sam stands a bit away from Jill, his back to the door.

Sam Right. Here we go then. Bit nervous in front of you.

Jill Right. (*Reading*) *Quin:* 'Francis Flute –'

Sam Quince.

Jill What?

Sam Quin. That's the character's name. It's short for Quince. His name's Quince. Peter Quince, he's a carpenter –

Jill That's not a bad trade, you know. Carpenter.

Sam Really?

Jill You could do worse than that. What's he do? The one you're playing, then?

Sam Francis Flute? He's a bellows mender.

Jill Not a lot of future in that these days, is there? (*Going to read again, then hesitating*) Listen, son, you're really set on this acting thing, are you?

Sam Don't know. Maybe.

Jill You enjoy it?

Sam Yes.

Jill Do your – do you have friends who act as well? With you? You know.

Sam Yes. One or two. Why?

Jill (*casually*) I was just – wondering. Boys are they?

Sam Yes. Some of them.

Jill Girls?

Sam Some girls, yes. You know, to play the girls' parts, like. You know.

Jill I just wondered if you'd got – you know – other reasons for – you know – for wanting to be in the play. Like a – you know – a special friend.

Sam How do you mean? Special friend?

Jill You know like a – like a – girl or something?

Sam No. I don't have many friends that are girls.

Jill You don't?

Sam I find most of them a bit stupid, you know. Talking about their boyfriends. Texting and giggling and that.

Jill But you do have – then – special friends among the boys, do you?

Sam No, no one special. Mum, what's this all about? Why are you asking this?

Jill I was just interested, you know. Interested in you, that's all. I was wondering if you had a special reason for wanting to do something like this, that's all.

Sam I said, I enjoy it. And, you know, because she asked me.

Jill Who asked you?

Sam I told you. Mrs Easterly.

Jill Mrs Easterly?

Sam My English teacher. She asked me and I said OK, I'd give it a go.

Jill Nice, is she?

Sam (*casually*) Yes, she's pretty nice, yes.

Jill Elderly, is she?

Sam About thirty-something. I thought you said you remembered her, Mum?

Jill You tell me about her.

Sam Well, she's tall – pretty tall. Quite thin, you know. (*Describing her with his hands*) Not thin – you know – but in places she's thin . . . And then she's got quite long red hair and – very green eyes . . . and – she laughs a lot –

great smile . . . when she smiles at you. You know. (*He stops, rather embarrassed*)

Jill Sounds like you fancy her.

Sam (*smiling*) Wouldn't mind giving her one. (*Immediately penitent*) Sorry, Mum.

Jill rises and moving to Sam, claps him on the shoulder.

Jill (*moved*) That's my boy.

Sam (*confused*) I was only joking, Mum, she's a teacher, for God's sake! And she's married.

Jill Well, what's that about, eh? When did that ever – (*Checking herself*) Quite right, lad, quite right. Married woman. Always respect that.

Sam I will. Mr Easterly's the PE teacher. He's huge.

Jill (*sitting down again*) Right. Let's do this Shakespeare.

Sam We'd better. Dad'll be home in a minute.

Jill (*finding her place in the text again*) 'Quin:' – no, Quince, isn't it? – '*Quince:* Francis Flute, the bellows mender.'

Sam Here, Peter Quince.

Jill (*reading*) '*Quince*: You must take Thisbe on you.'

Sam 'What is Thisbe? A wandering knight?'

Jill '*Quince*: It is the lady that Pyramus must love.'

(*Under her breath*) Bloody hell, here we go.

Sam What?

Jill Nothing. Carry on.

Sam 'Nay, faith, let me not play a woman; I have a beard coming.' (*Slight pause*) That's it then, thanks, Mum.

Jill That it? That all you say?

Sam In that scene, yes, that's all he says. Except later on there's an *All*. When we all say, 'That would hang us, every mother's son.'

Jill Not much of a part, is it? This Flute? Doesn't get to say much, does he? Hey, what about this one later on? This *Tita*? He goes on a bit.

Sam No, that's Titania, Mum. Queen of the Fairies.

Jill (*hastily*) Oh, well, you don't want to get into that.

Sam No, he says a lot more, Francis Flute, later on when he's doing Thisbe –

Jill The woman's part?

Sam Look, I'll show you. Thisbe has this death speech. I nearly know that. Thisbe's just found her lover, Pyramus, dead, like in *Romeo and Juliet*, you know, and she's so upset she goes and kills herself then. Listen. I think I know it. I think I do.

> *He positions again and starts to perform for Jill. What Sam lacks in technique and sophistication, he makes up for in sincerity and simplicity. Jill, despite herself, slowly gets drawn in.*

Sam So. Thisbe comes in. And she sees him, you know, lying there and then she says:

> Asleep, my love?
> What, dead, my dove?
> O Pyramus, arise!
> Speak, speak! Quite dumb?
> Dead, dead! A tomb
> Must cover thy sweet eyes.

> *At this stage, Chrissie enters quietly and lingers in the doorway, listening to Sam.*

186

These lily lips,
This cherry nose,
These yellow cowslip cheeks
Are gone, are gone:
Lovers, make moan!
His eyes were green as leeks . . .

Er . . . hang on . . .

Sam hesitates losing his words, momentarily.
  Simultaneously, Dean looks in at the kitchen
doorway. He is, as yesterday, slightly drunk.

Dean Evenin' all. We're back. (*Seeing no one*) Oh.

Dean goes out of the kitchen again.

Jill Go on, Sam . . .

Sam Oh, yes. I remember –

O, sisters three,
Come, come to me,
With hands as pale as milk;
Lay them in gore,
Since you have shore
With shears his thread of silk.
Tongue, not a word;
Come, trusty sword.
Come, blade, my breast imbrue –

Mimes stabbing himself and falls to his knees.

And farewell, friends;
Thus Thisbe ends;
Adieu, adieu, adieu.

Sam lies down on the floor feigning death.
  Jill and Chrissie watch enthralled.
  Dean chooses this moment to enter noisily.

Dean (*as he enters, loudly*) Excuse me! Just want to catch the half-time score, ladies, do you mind . . .

Chrissie Dean, don't! Sam's doing his –

Dean Oh, hallo, Sam. What you doing down there, mate? Having a kip?

Chrissie (*holding Dean back by an arm*) Dean, don't –!

Dean (*shrugging free from her grasp, brusquely*) Don't do that, come on!

Dean moves to the coffee table, stepping over Sam, and picks up the TV remote control.

Jill (*rising, furiously*) Don't you interrupt my son in the middle of his Shakespeare, you pillock!

Chrissie (*startled*) Mum!

Sam (*incredulous*) Mum!

Dean Eh?

Jill grabs the remote and tries to wrestle it from Dean.

Jill (*angrily*) Give me that, give it to me!

Dean (*winning the tussle*) Come on, let's see the screen. Just for a minute, that's all!

Dean pushes Jill reasonably gently to one side. This is, in retrospect, the wrong thing to do.

Jill Don't you push me, you bastard!

Jill throws a punch which catches Dean, totally unprepared, on the jaw. Dean goes down with a crash. Almost immediately, Jill hops about nursing her hand which probably received more damage than Dean's jaw.

Chrissie (*alarmed*) Dean!

Sam Mum!

Sam goes to see to his mother.
Chrissie goes to kneel beside the poleaxed Dean.

Chrissie Dean! Are you alright? Dean?

Sam Mum!

Jill (*nursing her hand*) Bloody hell!

Chrissie Is it broken?

Jill Feels like it.

Sam I don't think so. You can still move your fingers. That was fucking amazing, Mum!

Jill Don't swear in front of your mother . . .

Chrissie Put something cold on it, Sam, prevent the swelling.

Sam Come on, then, Mum . . . (*To Chrissie*) Is he still alive?

Chrissie Yes, he'll be alright.

Sam Pity.

Sam and Jill go out.
Chrissie tends to Dean.

Dean (*sitting up, groggily*) What happened there?

Chrissie She punched you.

Dean Who did?

Chrissie My mother.

Dean Your *mother*?

Chrissie Yes.

Dean My God!

Chrissie Come on, Dean, up you get. We'll go home. I'll fix you something to eat.

Chrissie helping Dean to his feet, assists him to the door.

Dean (*as they go, incredulously*) Your mother punched me? Your *mother*?

As Chrissie and Dean leave the sitting room, Sam helps Jill into the kitchen.

Sam Sit down there, Mum. I'll get you something. Frozen peas are best. Have we got any peas?

Jill (*sitting*) I haven't the faintest idea.

Sam Wait there.

Sam goes off momentarily.

Jill He's got a head like a rock, that lad. Always suspected he had.

Sam returns with a packet of frozen peas.

Sam Here!

He dumps the packet on to Jill's hand, resting on the table. Jill reacts with a cry.

Sorry.

Jill That's worse than the bloody bruising.

Sam Sorry. (*Looking at Jill through new eyes*) I think you're amazing, Mum.

Mal enters the kitchen and takes in the scene. Sam continues to minister to Jill's hand.

Mal (*only slightly drunk*) Evening. Had a good day then, dearest?

Jill Wonderful.

Mal Just been out for a quick drink. Sorry I'm late.

Chrissie comes into the kitchen, supporting Dean.
Dean stops short in the doorway as he sees Jill.
Chrissie collects her handbag.

Chrissie Evening, Dad.

Mal (*mystified*) Hallo, Chrissie. Hallo, Dean.

Dean, still in shock, stares at Mal.

Dean alright, is he?

Chrissie (*propelling Dean out ahead of her*) Once he's had his dinner. See you tomorrow, Mum. Night all.

Sam Night.

Jill Night.

Mal (*still mystified*) Night.

Chrissie (*returning briefly, to Sam and Jill*) Oh, don't spread it around what happened to him, will you? He'd never live it down at the rugby club. Just a secret between us, alright? If it comes to it, I'll be the one to spread it around, don't worry.

Chrissie goes out.

Mal What on earth's been going on?

Jill Nothing to worry about. I think that's enough of that now, Sam, thanks all the same. I'm beginning to get frostbite. I'll go upstairs in a minute. Run it under the tap. (*Aware that Sam is in the room with them, to Mal*) So you had a good day then, you say? Dear.

Mal Yes, dearest, I think it was – a good day, yes –

He takes the peas from a slightly startled Sam.

I'll put those away, shall I, Sam – (*Going off to the fridge*) We, all of us, we've just been out for a quick drink . . .

Jill All of us? Who's all of us?

Mal Anyone who wanted to come. About twenty or thirty of us, in the end –

Jill Twenty or thirty? Who paid for that?

Mal (*returning*) The firm did.

Jill My God!

Mal Just the first round. Oh, by the way, sorry, I'm afraid I scraped the car getting into the garage just now.

Jill Oh, for –

Mal Sorry, love. I keep telling you we don't need a car that size, we really don't. And I certainly shouldn't have been driving it after two glasses of white wine, I tell you that.

Jill (*appalled*) You've been drinking white wine?

Mal Yes. It isn't bad at all in there, the Queen's Head.

Jill White wine? In front of the entire staff?

Mal Not bad at all.

Jill (*shaking her head*) I'll be upstairs.

Sam who has been staring at them both, bemused, now makes to follow Jill.

No, Sam, you stay here. Have a chat with your – father.

Jill goes out.

Mal (*after a slight pause*) Have you had your supper, Sam?

Sam (*awkwardly*) – Er . . . no.

Mal I'll cook you something, shall I?

Sam (*alarmed*) – Er, no, thanks, Dad. No way.

Mal I think I've got a couple of instant ones in the freezer. Would you like one of those? There's a chicken or there's a fish one, I think. You know, the salmon in that sauce. You liked it last time you had it, remember? Well, I heard you – liked it the last time you had it. Your mother said you liked it the last time you had it, anyway.

Sam No, thanks.

Mal Omelette? I'll make you an omelette. Cheesy omelette. One of my fluffies – one of your mother's special – fluffy ones.

Sam What's going on here? You've taken up cooking, Mum's punching the daylights out of people –

Mal At least have a sandwich. I'll make you a sandwich. (*Concerned*) Sam, you must eat something. Please. Please.

Sam stares at him, knowing something is wrong but unable to tell what.

Sam (*reluctantly*) OK.

Under the next, Mal locates the ingredients and swiftly and adroitly makes Sam up a sandwich. Sam watches fascinated by his father's newly acquired culinary dexterity.

Mal (*as he does this*) What happened with Dean, then?

Sam Mum punched him.

Mal (*unsurprised*) Yes, I thought she might. To do with Chrissie, I take it?

Sam No, I was – Dean interrupted my Shakespeare and she decked him.

Mal Good for her. Cheese OK for you?

Sam Yeah.

Mal Shouldn't really. Give you nightmares. You know, tomorrow, as soon as I get home, I'm going to cook us all a proper meal. All of us, sitting down together for once. You, me and – and your mother. (*Completing the sandwich*) There. That'll have to do you for now. Just pop the plate in the dishwasher when you've finished, will you, Sam?

Mal presents Sam with the sandwich.

What do you say, then?

Sam Thanks, Mum. Dad. Sorry. Ta.

Sam heads for the door.

Mal Sam – you'll do your Shakespeare for me sometime, won't you?

Sam Sure. If you want.

Mal I'd love it. I'll probably go up early tonight. It's been a long day.

Mal instinctively moves to kiss Sam on the cheek but checks himself, in time.

'Night – son. (*Unconvincingly*) Yeah! Yeah! Yeah!

Mal claps Sam rather awkwardly on the shoulder in a gesture of male solidarity.

Sam Night, Dad . . .

Sam goes out, still rather dazed.
Mal busies himself in the kitchen, tidying up.
Jill enters the bedroom, wearing Mal's T-shirt and shorts.

Jill (*catching sight of herself in the mirror*) No. Wrong.

Jill goes out of the bedroom again.
Sam comes into the sitting room and sits eating his sandwich and reading his script.
In the kitchen, Mal finishes tidying up and now calls up on his mobile. He takes a deep breath.

Mal (*getting the answering service*) Hallo, Trixie . . . it's me . . . I've just got home . . . Trixie, I don't know where you are at the moment, why you're not picking up . . . but I had to call to warn you . . . Trixie, she knows . . . she knows all about us . . . and, Trixie, she's dangerous, love . . . please God, she never finds out your address. I'd hate for anything to happen to you . . . she's like a woman possessed . . . punching people – threatening to kill them, I . . . Trixie, I can't talk now she's coming back in the – oh my God! What's she got in her hand? Trixie – (*She rings off, abruptly. Muttering*) Sleep well, dear.

In the bedroom, Jill comes back in dressed in her nightdress. She gives herself one more look in the mirror and gets into bed and lies there absently massaging her hand.
In the kitchen, Mal gives a final look round and goes out.
In the sitting room, Sam finishes his sandwich, gets up and also leaves the room.

Mal (*offstage*) Goodnight, Sam.

Sam (*offstage*) Goodnight, Dad.

In a moment, Sam comes into the kitchen with his plate. He puts it into the dishwasher.
Mal meanwhile looks into the sitting room for a look round.

Mal Everything off? Good.

Mal goes out again. The lights in the sitting room go off.

Sam (*looking round the kitchen, to himself*) It is. It's aliens. It has to be.

Sam leaves the kitchen. The lights in the kitchen go off. In a moment, Mal enters the bedroom, taking off his jacket. He sees Jill in bed.

Mal You've still got your make-up on.

Jill (*dourly*) I know. I'm expecting the plumber.

Mal It's alright for you. You don't have to get the sheets washed, do you?

Jill I think I do now.

Mal Well, suit yourself then.

Mal goes out.

Jill (*calling to Mal*) I plugged my razor in to recharge. You'll need it in the morning.

Mal (*off*) Thank you. What have you done to my vacuum? It's all in bits.

Jill I was – emptying it.

Mal (*off*) Oh, there's an easier way, you know. You coped alright, then?

Jill Alright. (*Reflecting*) Good to talk to Sam again, anyway. Even if he was talking to you.

Mal (*off*) I hear he did his Shakespeare for you?

Jill Yes.

Mal (*off*) Was it good?

Jill Yes – he – was quite good, you know. For a lad, you know. (*Pause*) I can't do this for long, Jill. Staying home all the time. I'll need to get out. Get a job.

Mal (*off*) I'm not stopping you.

Jill Amazing you didn't go crazy all these months.

Mal (*off*) Yes, wasn't it?

The main lights in the bedroom now go off so that it is lit solely by the two bedside lights. Mal re-enters, dressed for bed in his T shirt and shorts.

(*Sitting at the dressing table*) Look, I didn't like to say it earlier but – I wouldn't wear that top with those trousers again, will you, love? I loathe that top, I never wear it.

Jill Then why have you still got it?

Mal (*taking a jar of face cream from a drawer*) Oh, I've dozens of things I hate and I still keep. Never get round to throwing them away. (*Seeing he has face cream on his hand*) No, I don't need this, do I? Well, no harm, is there? What the hell.

Mal rubs cream into his face.

(*As he does*) Listen, Mal, I have to tell you – whatever happens, I'm going to carry on working, love. Today, I got a taste for it. I mean I was rusty but it all started coming back to me. I felt – ten years younger. I mean, I think I was technically five years older but . . . you understand?

Jill Fair enough.

Mal (*getting into bed*) Maybe we could work together.

Jill How do you mean?

Mal I could do with someone in that office. It's chaos in there.

Jill Ah, well, Sandra's off, isn't she?

Mal Hooray! The Queen of Filing . . . .

Jill Well, I'm not working for you . . .

Mal I wouldn't employ you . . . Want the light out?

Jill Yes.

Mal I won't sleep, mind you. I never do.

Jill Nor will I.

Mal Oh, ho-ho. That'll be the night.

Together they switch their bedside lights off. The room is in near darkness.

(*As they do this*) No, I think honestly, Mal, once I'd got over the initial shock . . . Chrissie was quite right. I should have gone back to work, ages ago. Retrained. But, you know, you lose confidence, don't you? After all these years. And if things aren't . . . I was amazed the way I slipped back into it . . . some differences, yes. Computers and card machines . . . but people haven't changed, though . . . they're still the same, aren't they? . . . Mal?

Gentle snoring from Jill.

Mal? Straight off. How does he do it? (*With a sigh*) Alright. Here we go. One sheep . . . two sheep . . . three sheep . . . why do they always have to be sheep? Why not cows for a change? . . . Or Trixies? One Trixie . . . two Trixies . . . three Trixies . . . four Trixies . . . five Trixies . . . six Trixies . . .

In the darkness, her voice slowly fades out as it first merges with and is then replaced by Jill's voice.

Jill . . . six Trixies . . . seven Trixies . . . eight Trixies . . . nine Trixies . . . ten Trix— (*She stops*) Mal? Mal?

Mal is now the one snoring gently beside her.

Jill switches on her light again.

Mal! Wake up! Mal!

Mal (*sleepily*) What is it? What is it now, woman? I only just got off to . . . Off to . . . Off to . . . Hang about.

Silence.

Jill We've changed back.

Mal switches on his light. He looks at Jill.

Mal We have, haven't we?

Jill We have.

They take this in for a second.

Mal Thank God for that.

Jill Thank God.

Mal Back to normal.

Jill (*rather sadly*) Yes. Back to normal. What do you think could've –?

Mal Don't know. Could have been a dream. Could just have been a dream.

Jill What? Both of us? At the same time?

Mal No, well, maybe not.

Jill Anyway, my hand still hurts like hell, thank you very much.

Mal Sorry, love.

Jill No, you did right. He deserved it.

Mal Well. That's that then, isn't it?

Mal switches off his light again.
Slight pause.

Jill Mal, we can't pretend it didn't happen. I mean, that would be such a waste, wouldn't it. Everything's changed now for both of us. We can't simply ignore it, can we? Can we, Mal?

Mal No, we need to talk it through, you're quite right, love. We definitely need to talk things through, don't we?

Pause.

Don't you think? Jill?

Slight pause.

Jill (*snuggling up to him*) In the morning, love. Let's talk in the morning, shall we?

Mal (*holding her to him*) Yes, we'll talk in the morning, love.

As they both lie there contentedly in each other's arms, Jill reaches out and switches off her own light and there is a:

Blackout.

LIFE AND BETH

Life and Beth was first performed at the Stephen Joseph Theatre, Scarborough, on 22 July 2008. The cast was as follows:

Beth Liza Goddard
Gordon Adrian McLoughlin
Martin Richard Stacey
Ella Ruth Gibson
Connie Susie Blake
David Ian Hogg

Director Alan Ayckbourn
Designed by Pip Leckenby
Lighting by Kath Geraghty
Music by John Pattison

This production toured in 2009, opening at the Yvonne Arnaud Theatre, Guildford, on 21 January, with the part of Connie being played by Eileen Battye and that of David by Terence Booth.

Characters

Beth Timms
fifties, recently widowed

Gordon Timms
sixties, her late husband,
formerly a maintenance engineer

Martin Timms
thirties, their son, a car salesman

Ella Packer
late twenties, his girlfriend

Connie Bunting
fifties, Beth's sister-in-law, also a widow

David Grinseed
fifties, widower, a clergyman

Man Police Officer
(voice only)

Woman Police Officer
(voice only)

Place

Beth and Gordon's living room
in a suburban semi-detached house

Time

Christmas Eve and Christmas morning,
only last year

Act One

A modest sitting/dining room in a fairly modern semi-detached suburban house. Dining table, easy chairs, coffee table, TV etc. In one corner a cat's empty bed-basket.

A single door to the hall and the rest of the house. In one wall, a service hatch with twin doors connecting to the kitchen. A fireplace with a 'coal-effect' electric fire. Next to it, a set of superfluous fire tongs.

Beth, a pleasant woman in her fifties, is sitting on the sofa. Across from her in the armchair sits Connie, about the same age, fidgeting awkwardly.

Between them, on the coffee table, the remains of tea things for two, biscuits etc.

The TV, on low, is playing a carol service from somewhere or other. We deduce it must be Christmas time. There is little evidence of this otherwise. One or two cards dotted about, nothing more.

The women appear to have run out of conversation. While Beth is quite happy with this, it's evidently not a situation that suits Connie.

Connie (*after a long pause*) Well . . .

Beth (*vaguely, agreeing with her*) Mmmmm . . .

Connie As I say . . .

Another pause.

He was remarkable, wasn't he . . . ?

Beth (*vaguely*) Oh, yes . . .

Connie Treasure. Absolute treasure. They broke the mould . . . when they . . . didn't they? Everyone adored him, didn't they? I mean you, you simply worshipped him, didn't you? The ground he stood on?

Beth Yes, I was very fond of him.

Connie Oh, come on, you adored him. We could all see that. No, I mean, face it, Beth, you couldn't have done better, could you? Better than Gordon? As husbands go, I mean . . . as husbands go . . .

Beth Yes. Well, he's gone now, hasn't he?

Connie God rest his soul.

Beth Yes.

Pause.

Connie He was a wonderful brother to me, too. My big brother, I called him. I mean, I know I was a little bit older than him but only by a year or so. But I always thought of him as my big brother. I couldn't have asked for better. Always looked out for me, always took care of me. I only had to lift the phone –

Beth . . . yes . . .

Connie – he was always at the other end, Gordon. Sorting me out.

Beth Yes, you were often on the phone to him . . .

Connie Well, he was my brother. I was his sister. All on my own, wasn't I?

Beth I know.

Connie . . . All on my little own . . . No. Gordon was always the special one. I know my parents felt he was. I mean, from the minute he was born almost. I don't think it was just because he was the boy. It would have been the same even if he'd been a . . . He was always remarkable . . . reading early . . . writing . . . multiplying in his head, you know . . . Me? I couldn't keep up with him. Didn't even try. You know when I was about eight or nine, it must have been, Dad took me to one side and he said, don't get me wrong, Connie. Me and your mum, we still love you, we both still think the world of you, but even though you're the eldest, we're going to need you to step aside, love, make room for young Gordon. You're going to have to let him past. Like in a race. He's lapping you, you see, Connie. He's been round three times to your one and he's still passing you . . .

Beth He shouldn't have said that to you.

Connie No, it was true, Dad was being honest, he was only being honest with me . . . all the time I was growing up. I could always feel Gordon, breathing down my neck. No, he was like that, my dad. He always came straight to the point, I admire that in a man . . .

Beth Still, it was only his opinion, wasn't it? You never know, you might have come on later –

Connie Later?

Beth You might have been a late developer, if they'd given you a year or two.

Connie I never developed at all, did I?

Beth Not surprised after that.

Connie Well, we'll never know now, will we? Nearly forty years ago. I could have been a scientist, couldn't I? Or a surgeon?

Beth (*slightly dubious*) Possibly.

Connie Now look at me. Stocktaking at Porters.

Beth You've done well.

Connie But I could have done better. I know I could. If

I hadn't stepped aside for Gordon. He had the best of everything. He had the biggest bedroom. Best education. We all made sacrifices for Gordon.

Beth Well, maybe you shouldn't have done, Connie.

Connie Well, I had no say in it, did I?

Beth I mean, Gordon never became a scientist or a surgeon either, did he?

Connie No. But we all thought he might have been . . .

Beth Health and Safety Officer at Twistletons. That's a far cry from brain surgeon . . .

Connie They spent every penny they had on him. I never got my doll's house. Dad couldn't afford it. Nor a pony. I always wanted a pony. All I got was his hand-me-down tricycle. The day he got his new fairy cycle . . .

A pause. Connie reflects back gloomily on her life.

Beth (*trying to lighten the mood*) Oh well, under the bridge now, isn't it?

Connie That's where I feel my life's gone, Beth. Under the bridge and into the drain . . .

Beth (*reflecting, smiling*) Fairy cycle! Think I had a fairy cycle . . .

Connie . . . into the sewer . . .

Beth (*indicating the TV*) Oh, this is a lovely carol, isn't it? It's one of my favourites . . . Do you mind if I turn it up a bit?

Beth operates the remote. The volume on the TV increases. Beth hums along with the carol.
Connie starts to cry. Beth is aware of this and attempts initially to ignore it. Connie gets louder, eventually competing with the TV.

(*Turning off the TV, slightly irritably*) Connie, do try and cheer up, love. Come on now, it's Christmas.

Connie (*tearfully*) It's alright for you, Beth.

Beth What do you mean, it's alright for me? I've just lost my husband, for heaven's sake . . .

Connie Yes, and I've just lost a brother . . .

Beth You weren't even that fond of him, were you?

Connie I was, I adored him.

Beth You just said he ruined your life . . .

Connie What a terrible thing to say. That's a terrible thing to say, Beth, about my brother. About your late husband . . .

    Beth makes to respond. Then checks herself.

Beth (*after a deep breath*) Maybe you'd like to unpack your things? I've put you up in the spare room. I hope that's alright?

Connie Oh, that'll do me. I won't sleep much anyway.

Beth . . . I gave it a good airing . . .

Connie . . . never sleep these days . . .

Beth . . . I put Martin and his friend Ella in our room . . . in my room . . .

Connie Your room? Where are you sleeping, then?

Beth I'll have the couch here . . .

Connie The couch?

Beth This sofa bed, it pulls out . . .

Connie That's not very fair on you, is it . . . ?

Beth It makes quite a nice little bed, this sofa. We used it a lot in the old days. Whenever we had a full house . . .

Connie . . . Turning you out of your bed . . .

Beth . . . it's no problem. I'll be up first, it's not a problem . . .

Connie . . . this is meant to be a break for you . . .

Beth . . . I'm not sleeping that much lately, either . . .

Connie . . . we agreed, Martin and I, you're not to lift a finger. It's a Christmas for you to put your feet up. What sort of rest would it be, if you're going to be down here sleeping rough?

Beth It's really rather comfy. Gordon even used to . . . at the end, you know, when he couldn't . . . cope with the stairs . . . before he was . . . (*She tails away*)

Connie (*sympathetically*) Yes . . .

    A silence.

Still, it could get a bit chilly down here in the night, couldn't it? Once the heating goes off.

Beth I can always put the fire on.

Connie Be careful you don't gas yourself with the fumes. I was reading, you know, about this entire family –

Beth It's electric.

Connie Oh. (*Pause*) Still got his basket, I see.

Beth What?

Connie (*indicating the cat basket*) Wagstaff's basket. Still got it, have you?

Beth Yes.

Connie Just in case he . . . ?

Beth Comes back.

Connie No sign of him?

Beth No. Day of the funeral he just went out through the cat flap in the kitchen there, never came back. Never came back for his tea.

Connie Oh, well. They say they can sense it, can't they? Animals? They say they hate change almost as much as we do. He probably missed Gordon. He sensed Gordon had gone for ever and it upset him so much he ran off . . .

Beth He didn't even like Gordon.

Connie Beg your pardon?

Beth Wagstaff couldn't stand him.

Connie Oh, he must have liked Gordon, surely . . . ?

Beth He used to hiss at him whenever he came near.

Connie Everybody adored Gordon.

Beth Wagstaff didn't.

Silence.

You going to church later on? For the midnight service tonight?

Connie Yes . . . I'll go along . . . Support David, you know . . .

Beth Support who?

Connie David Grinseed. The Reverend Grinseed.

Beth Oh, yes . . .

Connie I always call him David. He prefers it if his close friends call him David. I know him as David, anyway.

Beth Yes, of course, he did the funeral, didn't he? I'd forgotten his name was David.

Connie Well, it's not everyone he . . . you have to get to know him for a little while first.

Beth He was very pleasant.

Connie Oh, yes.

Beth It was a nice funeral.

Connie Oh, he always does a good funeral, David. Quiet manner. Sympathetic.

Beth Yes. Have you been to many of them, then?

Connie Beg your pardon?

Beth Funerals? You sound as if you've been to several.

Connie Well . . . as I say, I try to support him, you know.

Beth I see.

Connie It's not only funerals. I mean, I go to his weddings as well.

Beth Christenings?

Connie One or two. If I'm not working. I don't join in, you know. I'm just there for support. David's not married. He lost his wife a few years ago. (*Mouthing*) Cancer.

Beth Oh, sad.

Connie So he's just a bit lonely. Currently. Yes, David's a lovely man once you get to know him.

> *Pause.*
> *Connie is a little flustered. Beth stares at her.*

(*Turning her attention to the tea things*) I'd better clear all this, hadn't I?

Beth No, no, Connie, I can easily . . .

Connie Beth, I've told you, you're doing nothing. You're not lifting a finger till New Year's Eve . . .

Beth I can easily rinse them through –

Connie (*fiercely*) Sit down! You're to sit down, now!

Beth (*feebly*) You don't even know where anything goes –

Connie Then you can show me . . .

Beth What's the point of that? It's just as easy for –

Connie Sit!

Beth (*sitting again, muttering*) It's my house . . .

Connie Not for the next few days, it's not. You're to treat this place just like a luxury hotel, do you hear?

Connie starts for the door with the tray.

Beth Probably should have done that, really . . .

Connie Done what?

Beth . . . if we'd thought of it. Gone to a hotel.

Connie (*dubious*) Oh, I don't think so. I wouldn't fancy that. Not at Christmas time. Not in a strange hotel.

Beth Might have been rather nice. A bit of an adventure, really . . .

Connie We don't want adventures at our time of life, do we? Certainly not at Christmas.

The doorbell rings.

Beth (*rising*) Oh, that'll be them!

Connie (*putting down the tray*) Don't worry, I'll let them in.

Beth They're early. Traffic must have been good.

Connie Wait there, wait there. Luxury hotel, remember?

Beth (*unconvinced*) Yes . . .

Connie (*as she goes*) Here goes the chambermaid . . .

Beth sits for a moment, then rises and stares round the room. Her gaze finally alights on the empty cat bed.

Beth Where have you got to then, you little bugger? (*Sighing*) Oh, well.

She turns towards the tea tray where Connie left it. Beth seems intent on taking it out to the kitchen but, before she can move to it, the tray jumps slightly, as if shaken, causing the crockery to rattle.

(*Startled*) Oh! (*She stares at the tray, puzzled*) That's odd.

Beth moves to examine it but, before she can, Connie, flushed with excitement, enters. She leads in David, a clergyman in his late fifties, at present in official mode, i.e. visiting a recently bereaved parishioner whom he doesn't know terribly well.

Connie (*in a hushed tone*) Beth. It's David. Come to see you.

Beth Oh.

David Hallo, Mrs Timms. I'm sorry to burst in on you on Christmas Eve. I just wanted see how you're doing. I hope this isn't entirely the wrong moment . . .

Beth (*bit flustered*) No. Do come in. We were just . . . having tea. Would you care for some?

David No, no, thank you.

Connie You sure, David? It's no trouble . . .

David No, please, I know traditionally vicars are always up for free teas . . . but not just at present, thank you. If truth be told, the day I've just been having, I could probably do with something stronger . . .

Beth Well, there's some beer, I think. I got some beer in for my son . . .

Connie (*with her*) There's some beer, David . . .

David No, that's awfully kind but no thank you. I'm here for a briefest second. I just wanted a quick word with Mrs Timms. I promised her I'd look in weeks ago . . . make sure she was coping OK.

Beth Do sit down, won't you?

David Thank you.

> *He continues to stand.*
> *Slight pause.*
> *David looks at Beth, smiling.*
> *Beth smiles at David, rather shyly.*
> *Beth looks at Connie.*
> *David looks at Connie.*

Connie (*a little put out*) Well, I'll . . . I'd better wash these up, then. (*Picking up the tray*) You just shout if you need anything, David.

David Thank you, Connie.

Connie That's me. Connie cook and chief bottle-washer . . .

> *David laughs politely.*

I'll just be in the kitchen.

> *She goes out with the tea tray.*

Beth Please, do sit down Mr – er – Reverend –

David (*doing so*) David, please. David.

Beth David.

David Everyone calls me David. It's Beth, isn't it? You don't mind if I call you Beth?

Beth Everyone else does . . .

David Listen, Beth . . . I know we met, of course, at the service –

Beth Oh, yes. Briefly.

David Funerals are always such awkward, emotional occasions. Sometimes I find it's better to leave things a week or two. Just to let the – (*gesturing vaguely*) the – things to settle a bit.

Beth Yes.

David But I enjoyed our talk together afterwards.

Beth (*frowning*) Did you?

David You don't remember?

Beth I remember a few words, I – (*She shakes her head*)

David Well, it was more than a few words, we did have quite a chat. You obviously don't remember?

Beth I'm sorry. It was – one of those days, you know. Sorry.

David No, no, why should you? So, Beth. Tell me, how's it been without – er – without – Graham?

Beth Gordon.

David Gordon, I'm sorry. How's life without Gordon? Bit tough still, is it? I imagine it must still be tough. People I spoke to said you were both very close.

Beth Well, it's strange, really. I mean, I miss him, of course. I couldn't not miss him. Gordon. He was always there, you see. Till he went.

David Yes, yes. It was a very special marriage, I imagine. And he went quite suddenly, your sister tells me?

Beth Sister-in-law . . .

David Sorry.

Beth Connie's Gordon's sister. She's not my sister . . .

David Sorry. Bit guilty of not quite doing my homework, I'm afraid. So it all happened suddenly? That must have been the most terrible shock.

Beth Yes, it was quite sudden, really. He had the fall at work, of course . . .

David Oh, dear. Now remind me, where did he work?

Beth Twistletons Engineering. He fell off a ladder. He should never have been up there in the first place, especially not with him being in charge of Health and Safety, but he insisted . . . Never listened to anyone.

David What was he doing up this ladder?

Beth Trying to rescue this lad. Who should never have been up there either. Not with the lad having vertigo. Gordon clearly told him to come down the ladder at once as he was contravening mandatory Health and Safety procedures. Only he panicked.

David Gordon panicked?

Beth No, the lad panicked. Gordon didn't panic, Gordon never panicked. He climbed up the ladder to rescue the lad. Only this lad was so terrified, his hands were gripped tight to the ladder. And when Gordon tried to lever them open, he fell off.

David The lad fell off?

Beth No, Gordon fell off trying to lever the lad off the ladder. The lad's fingers stayed gripped tight.

David Heavens!

Beth They had to cut the whole ladder down with the lad still clinging to it. Took him and the ladder off to A&E. Eventually they had to operate.

David On the ladder?

Beth No, on the lad. The ladder was cast iron. They had to put the lad under and ease open his fingers from the ladder. He'd gone into spasm, you see.

David Poor lad, poor lad.

Beth Yes, he recovered quickly enough, though.

David Oh, good.

Beth More than Gordon did. He broke his back.

David Oh, that's terrible. How terrible!

Beth That was the start of it. When they finally let him home, practically the first thing he did was to fall off a chair.

David Oh, heavens! Just quietly sitting, was he?

Beth No, he was standing on it. In the kitchen, out there. Trying to fix something, as usual.

David Not the sort of thing he should have been doing with a recently broken back, surely?

Beth He was always fixing things, Gordon. Very keen on DIY.

David Well, you know what they say. Ninety per cent of accidents occur in the home, don't they?

Beth Something like that. Most of them were Gordon's.

David (*looking to change the subject*) Well, anyway . . .

Beth Have-a-go hero, that's what they called him in the paper.

David Yes, yes . . .

Beth That's not what I called him. Bloody stupid idiot, I called him. (*Slight pause*) Sorry.

David Well, you know, Beth, most of us do tend to feel angry occasionally with those we love most, don't we? Sometimes it's almost irrational. Possibly because we care so much about them that we grow angry if they injure themselves, we tend to feel their hurt almost as if it were our own. When they finally leave us alone in the world – particularly a relationship as close as yours – it's practically a sense of betrayal, isn't it? I know, in my own case, my late wife . . . she . . . (*he hesitates*) . . . I mean, it was months, years before I finally . . . But I prayed for guidance . . . and eventually, Beth, the realisation came to me, I saw that, no, this isn't the way I should be remembering her, not with anger or with bitterness, not with resentment . . . that wasn't the way. I must let all that go, mustn't I? Rather I should remember her with love. And, finally, after all those endless months of anguish, I found peace and contentment. It's not a matter of forgetting, Beth. Heaven forbid that we should ever forget. It's rather a case of *how* we remember, do you see?

Beth Yes.

David I sense, Beth, that you loved your husband, you loved Gordon more than you loved your own life . . .

Beth Yes, well, I . . .

David And that love was a beautiful and special thing, Beth. The love between a husband and wife can be the most precious there is. Our Lord intended it that way and – aside from our love for Him, of course – the love that exists between a husband and wife is the strongest. But when the day finally comes to say au revoir – well, it's rather like that lad with the ladder, isn't it? We need to learn to let go. Release the fingers, relinquish that grip, you see?

Beth Right . . . right.

David Because rage, anger, disappointment, frustrated unrequited love, sense of betrayal, they're all negatives, aren't they? There's an old song, you know. I don't expect you know it, Beth, probably before your time. I can't remember who wrote the words – possibly Johnny Mercer? Sammy Kahn? It goes something like this: 'You've got to accentuate the positive . . . eliminate the negative . . . cling right on to the affirmative . . . and don't mess with Mr In-Between.' You see?

Beth No, I can't say I know that one.

> *David is standing quite close to her now, their eyes on each other. Silence.*
> *A scratching sound from the kitchen hatch.*
> *They become aware of this. David looks puzzled.*

(*Frowning*) Excuse me, please.

> *She moves swiftly to the hatch and pulls it open to reveal a startled Connie clutching the milk jug.*

Connie (*startled*) Oh, sorry!

Beth Sorry, Connie, did you want something?

Connie No, I was just . . . wondering . . . wondering where this . . .

Beth (*brusquely*) In the cupboard over the sink.

Beth closes the hatch abruptly and moves back to David.

I beg your pardon, David, you were saying?

David (*vaguely, a little bemused by this last*) Was I –? Yes, I . . .

Beth Don't mess with Mr . . .

David In-Between. Yes.

Beth Yes.

David I hope that's been of help, Beth.

Beth Yes, it's been most helpful, thank you.

David Life is for living. I really believe that.

Beth Oh, yes. I mean that's the reason we're all here, isn't it?

David You're still young – for a woman. You're attractive.

Beth Thank you.

David Life is ahead of you. Seize it with both hands. Make new friends, explore new places. Turn a new page, Gerald is a past chapter . . .

Beth Gordon.

David Go on! Push the boat out! Take that dog of yours for a long walk, why don't you?

Beth Dog?

David He's out of his basket, anyway. He's eager to find a way forward. Come on, I bet he hasn't had a walk for days, has he? He's probably even now scratching at the back door, dying for a walk.

Beth He's a cat.

David Well, then . . . do whatever you do with cats. Pick it up and cuddle it. Get used to sharing your love again, Beth . . .

Beth Wagstaff's gone.

David Who?

Beth The cat. He walked out, he just wandered off.

David Oh dear. How long's it been gone?

Beth About six weeks ago. He left the day of the funeral.

David Ah, well. They say animals often sense things, don't they? They have an instinctive sense of when things aren't all they should be.

Beth I wish he'd told me . . .

David Ah. Would that they could speak sometimes.

Beth . . . I'd probably have left with him.

David Yes?

Beth But then . . . I couldn't do that, could I? Not the day of the funeral . . .

David No, we're not like cats, are we?

Beth I can now, though, can't I?

David How do you mean?

Beth Walk away. My life's my own again, isn't it? Free as a bird.

David That's the spirit. (*He smiles at her*) Good on yer, Beth.

Beth (*smiling at him*) Thank you.

They stand for a moment looking at each other.

David (*awkwardly, shyly*) Beth, would you . . . would you mind if I – if I –?

Beth Would I mind what, David?

David Would you think it – terribly . . . if I –?

Beth If you what?

David If I said a prayer for you? Would you mind?

Beth Oh. No, not at all. Why not? I have a Buddhist friend who's chanting for me somewhere . . . the more the merrier.

David Thank you. These days, some people, they rather object – in principle, you know. Best to check first. (*He clasps his hands and closes his eyes*)

Beth What, now? You're going to say it *now*?

David Yes.

Beth With me here?

David Do you mind?

Beth Might make me feel a bit weird, you know. Hearing myself discussed.

David I promise I'll only say . . . Of course, if you'd rather I –

Beth No, you carry on, David. Don't mind me.

> *David prepares to resume his prayer.*
> *Beth waits rather self-consciously.*
> *The front doorbell rings again.*

Oh, that's probably them. My son, Martin and his friend. Would you excuse me a moment . . . (*She goes to the door*)

David Of course.

> *Beth, on her way out, nearly collides with Connie.*

Beth Oh, beg your pardon, Connie . . .

Connie (*going*) I'll go, Beth. I'll let them in, don't worry.

Beth Sorry to interrupt you, David. Do carry on.

David Well . . . maybe this is . . . not the time. I'll save it till I get to church.

Beth Perhaps that'd be best. Probably be stronger from there. (*She smiles at him*)

David (*smiling*) Possibly.

Voices are heard from the hall. In a moment, Connie comes back in.

Connie (*as she enters*) They're here . . . they've arrived . . .

Martin, in his thirties, enters behind her. Although he is rarely less than ebullient, he is especially so at present, in anticipation of this occasional, somewhat exceptional meeting with his mother. Unsure of how he'll find Beth's state, he has characteristically opted for seasonal bluster.

Martin Knock-knock! We're here! At last! Hallo, Mum! (*He embraces her*)

Beth (*reciprocating*) Martin!

David, rather affected by this family reunion, steps back smiling.
   Connie remains in the doorway where she is soon joined by Ella, a rather pale, currently red-eyed woman in her late twenties who also stops to witness the meeting of mother and son. Ella has the aura of a woman nursing a grievous insult.

Martin (*holding Beth at arm's length*) You're looking well, Mum. You're looking fantastic. Isn't she, Auntie Connie? Fantastic.

Connie Oh, yes, considering . . .

Martin You both are, you both are.

Connie . . . considering, yes.

Martin Sorry we're a bit late. Deviated from the sat nav. Took a detour, got a bit lost.

Beth You're not late.

Martin Someone, who shall remain nameless but certainly wasn't me, misread the map.

Beth I think you've put on weight, son.

Martin Possibly, possibly. (*Indicating Ella*) If I have, then you can totally blame that one. Mum, this is my friend Ella. Ella, say hallo to everyone.

Ella smiles, a rather subdued response.

Beth Hallo, Ella . . .

David (*shyly*) Hallo, there.

Ella gives another of her half-hearted smiles.

Martin No word of a lie, this is no exaggeration, Ella is one of the great cooks in the country –

Beth Well . . .

Martin – present company always excepted, Mum. Ella is known locally in Dorchester as the Cholesterol Queen . . . I'm joking, I'm joking, love . . .

Beth I hope you are.

Connie Honestly, Martin! You never know with him, do you?

Martin So, I'm warning you in advance – be prepared for a simply fabulously gastronomic Christmas. No calories spared. Now! Listen! We're here, we've arrived – no thanks to our map-reader here. We're now going to unload the four-by-four – we're jammed to the gunnels – Mum, you're to relax, put your feet up, take it easy. From this moment on, we're taking over . . . You're not to do a single thing from now on, do you hear? Have you told her that, Auntie Connie? Mum's to do nothing?

Connie I keep telling her . . .

Martin Do nothing. That's an order.

Connie . . . not that she listens to me . . .

Martin (*turning to leave*) Right. You fit, Ella? Let's get going. Let's make this place a bit more festive, shall we? (*Seeing David for the first time*) Oh, hallo, squire, where did you spring from?

David Hallo, there.

Beth Oh, Martin this is the Reverend – the vicar –

Connie Martin, this is David –

Martin Oh, how do you do?

David Hallo. David Grinseed . . .

Martin You stopping for Christmas as well, are you?

David No, no, no . . . I was just –

Beth He's visiting.

Connie David's just visiting –

David Passing through. Checking on – Beth here. Yes, I can see everything's under control – if you'll excuse me, I'll be . . .

Martin Not stopping for a beer?

David No, thank you . . .

Martin Something stronger, then? Whisky?

David No. Really, I –

Martin Little one? Single malt. We brought the single malt, didn't we, Ella? Didn't manage to drop that, did you? Whole carrier bag, full of stuff. Baileys, Apricot Brandy, Tia Maria . . . Right down the stone steps in the car park. Place smelt like a brewery . . .

Beth Oh, dear . . .

Connie I've done that in my time.

Martin I told her, you'll be popular with Mum now. She'll overlook the Baileys and the Apricot Brandy . . . but she'll never forgive you for the Tia Maria . . . that's Mum's special tipple, Tia Maria . . .

Beth Never mind, doesn't matter. Actually, I think I still have some left over from last year . . . Never got round to . . . what with . . . Anyway, it was never my . . . it was more . . . he liked a drop, occasionally. I sometimes – joined him, you know . . . keep him company . . . special occasions . . . like this.

A silence.

Martin Yes, yes.

Connie Yes.

David (*after a slight pause*) Look, I wonder, if you'd mind – before I go – might I suggest that we all of us share in a brief prayer for Beth – just a short one – together – to remember – (*He concentrates for the name*) her husband . . .

Beth (*softly*) Gordon . . .

David Yes. And of course your father, Marvin . . .

Martin Martin.

David I think that might be a nice idea. Fitting. Especially at this time of year. When we're – when we're all gathered.

Connie Lovely.

Martin Yes. Why not?

Connie makes to kneel down.

David (*anticipating her*) No, no, we don't need to kneel down – I don't think that's – If we could simply stand in a circle – a family circle, as it were . . .

They all shuffle, rather self-consciously, into a small tight circle in the middle of the room.

That's it . . . Dear Lord . . .

Martin Should we be joining hands?

David No. This isn't a séance . . . just a quick prayer . . .

Martin Right . . . right . . .

David Dear Lord – we ask You at this time to remember Beth, loving wife of – Gordon. We ask You to help her overcome her overwhelming loss of her beloved partner, her rock, her protector, the companion and mainstay of her life. And, although Gordon will remain for ever in her heart, nevertheless we ask You to guide Beth to seek out a new and fulfilling future, bringing her new horizons and fresh companions throughout the remaining years of her life. Keep her in health and grant her happiness and give her courage in the years ahead to overcome her loss. Amen.

Connie Amen.

Martin Hear! Hear!

Beth (*softly*) Thank you.

David Well, if you'll excuse me. I have to slip away . . . busy time for me . . .

Martin Must be.

David Hopefully see you later, Connie. At the carol service.

Connie I'll be there, David. As usual.

David If I can tempt anyone else . . . you'd all be welcome.

A slight pause. He looks expectantly at their faces.

No? Oh, well. Another year, perhaps? It's usually great fun. (*As he goes*) Happy Christmas, all.

Beth/Martin (*muttering rather guiltily*) Happy Christmas.

Connie (*following him off*) I'll see you out, David.

David (*off*) No need, Connie, no need . . .

Their voices continue out in the hall for a moment or so.

Beth Perhaps we should have said yes. I felt a bit guilty saying no.

Martin We didn't say no. We didn't say anything. Right, let's start unpacking, shall we? You sit down, Mum, leave it all to us. Can you open the back, Ella love?

Beth After I got a free prayer . . . (*Sitting*) We should have said we'd go, you know.

Martin Well, you can, Mum. (*Handing Ella the car keys*) There you go. We two'll carry on here. Get things organised, won't we, Ella?

Ella goes out without acknowledging him.

Beth I don't want to go on my own. Be no fun on my own.

Martin Auntie Connie's going. You can go with her.

Beth No. I don't . . . No, it doesn't matter.

Martin You sit there. Can I get you anything? A drink?

Beth Not at the moment, I've only just had tea.

Martin (*peeling off his jacket*) Right. Get going then. Give Ella a hand. I tell you we've brought mountains of stuff. Presents . . . booze . . . food to feed an army . . . Sit there, you're not to move!

> *Martin goes out.*
> *Beth gets up after a second and, rather restless, moves to the window and gazes out.*

Beth Oh, what's he driving now, a tank? (*Seeing something*) What's that out there? (*Calling through the window*) Wagstaff? Wagstaff!

> *Connie enters with a glass of wine in her hand.*

Connie I hope you don't mind, Beth, I helped myself to a little drink.

Beth (*still distracted*) Go ahead.

Connie Very quiet that girl, isn't she?

Beth Probably shy.

Connie Right little chatterbox. You want one?

Beth (*continuing to gaze out of the window*) No.

Connie What's the matter?

Beth I thought I saw something just now. Out there in the bushes. I thought it might have been Wagstaff – come home for Christmas.

Connie I think he's probably gone for good. Cheers!

Beth Cheers!

Connie Well, I have to say. You've made a big hit with David.

Beth Really? Have I?

Connie You know you have. He was all over you. Even had your own private prayer, didn't you? I mean, I think the least he could have done was to include Gordon's son, not to mention his own sister . . . We never got so much as a mention . . .

Beth Yes, that was a pity. I think he has trouble remembering names . . .

Connie He can remember mine. All about you, wasn't it?

Beth Well, don't blame me. I didn't ask him. I never told him what to say, did I?

Connie David's a very vulnerable person, Beth. You shouldn't toy with him if you don't mean it.

Beth I beg your pardon. Toy with him? What on earth are you talking about?

Connie You know what I mean. With his feelings. You can turn a man on a sixpence, you can. Always could do, all the years I've known you.

Beth I don't know what you mean.

Connie You know.

Beth I don't.

Connie You know. (*Significantly*) Mervyn Jacobs.

Pause.

Beth If you want my opinion, Connie, I think you've just been listening at too many doors.

Connie What on earth do you mean?

Beth You know.

Connie I have no idea what you're talking about.

Beth You know. (*After a pause, puzzled*) Mervyn Jacobs.

A dignified silence. Both women try to rise above it.
Ella enters, laden with bags and boxes. She stops short in the doorway.

Kitchen's straight along the hall, love. The door facing you.

Ella goes out again.

(*To herself, drily*) The house is small enough. No wonder she has trouble reading maps. Who the hell's Mervyn Jacobs when he's at home? Oh, yes, wasn't he the bloke you were keen on, once? What about him?

Connie It's Christmas time, isn't it? We'll say no more about it, shall we?

Beth Please, let's not.

Martin enters with an artificial Christmas tree.

Martin Knock-knock! Brought this in from the garage. I'll come and set it up in a minute.

Beth Oh, you shouldn't have dragged that in, Martin.

Martin Why not?

Beth We don't need it. It's just us.

Martin We always have this tree in here. Traditional, isn't it?

Connie Oh, yes, nice to have a tree.

Martin Ever since I was a kid, Dad would set it up. Every Christmas. Wouldn't be the same, would it? All the presents round the base there. Magic.

Beth Well, I've not bought anyone very much this year, I'm afraid . . .

Connie Nor have I . . .

Beth . . . what with one thing and . . .

Connie No.

Martin We have. You should see that SUV out there. Masses. Mountains.

Connie Oh, you shouldn't have . . .

Martin Most of them for you, Mum.

Connie Oh.

Beth Oh, Martin, you shouldn't waste your money, you know I –

Martin I want to, Mum. And I don't consider it wasted. You need a bit of spoiling, especially this Christmas. Listen, I'm going to shift the rest of the stuff into the kitchen, then I'll come back and do the tree. Then we're all having supper in here. Ella's in there now getting that under way . . .

Beth Is she?

Martin I told you, you're to leave everything to her, Mum. She's Cordon Bleu trained.

Beth She won't be able to find anything . . .

Martin Don't worry, once she sets foot in a kitchen Ella's like a fish in the water. Different woman. She's a bit – shy, you know at the moment . . .

Beth Well, if she needs any help, we're just through here – I'm just through here . . .

Martin No trouble tonight. Tonight's just a cold collation. She plans to start the big stuff tomorrow, wait and see. That's when she plans to really pull the stops out. She's got a chart, you should see it. Planned the entire week right down to the last detail.

Beth Well . . .

Connie Lovely. Let's leave it to her, then. You know me, I can hardly boil a tea cosy.

Martin Well, you can skivvy, Auntie. You don't mind a spot of skivvying, do you?

Connie (*unenthusiastically*) No.

Martin Then, straight after supper, I'm going to set those garden lights up. Need to do those before we go to bed.

Beth Lights?

Martin The whole place is in darkness out there. We can't have that, can we?

Beth No, Martin, we don't need all that, surely? It was only your father, he –

Martin Family tradition. What would Dad have to say? The place wouldn't be the same, would it, without the flashing reindeer? Need our flashing reindeer, don't we? Wouldn't be the same without Boris . . .

Martin goes.

Beth He doesn't need to do that.

Connie He wants to do it.

Beth I always hated all that. It was like Blackpool out there . . .

Connie It's for his father, Beth. For once, it's not for you. Martin's doing it in memory of his father. Surely you can appreciate that? Surely you can?

Beth remains silent.

Now, I'm going to help myself to another little drink, if I may. Then before we have supper, I'm going to have a quick bath.

Beth You do that.

Connie What time are we having it? Supper?

Beth As soon as she's ready, I suppose.

Connie Cold collation. Not sure I like the sound of that.

Beth Cold meat and salad, that's probably all it'll be.

Connie Well, if she's Cordon Bleu I think the least she could have done is heat something up.

From the kitchen behind the hatch an almighty crash and breaking glass. Simultaneously a cry from Ella as she bursts into tears.

Whatever's that? What's happened?

Connie rushes out of the room to investigate.

Martin (*off, from the kitchen*) Not on there, I said NOT ON THERE!

Beth Oh, dear God!

Beth hurriedly crosses to the hatch and opens it.

Martin (*off, in mid-flow*) I told you, didn't I, not to put it on there – I told you –

He breaks off as he presumably sees Beth.
Ella continues to sob softly in the background.

Beth (*surveying the damage through the hatch*) Oh, dear. Everything alright?

Martin (*off*) Yes, yes, fine, Mum. Small accident, we'll cope with it, don't worry.

Connie (*off, as she enters the kitchen, alarmed*) Oh, no! Whatever's happened?

Martin (*off*) It's alright, Auntie. We're dealing with it.

Connie (*off*) What a terrible mess!

Beth (*faintly*) There's a dustpan and brush under the . . . Oh, God.

> *Beth gives up and closes the hatch.*

(*Muttering*) I think I am going to need a drink at this rate.

> *She starts randomly to tidy the room, straightening a chair here, an ornament there.*

Oh, I feel like a spare sock on a one-legged sailor.

> *Another clatter from the kitchen.*

(*Reacting to this*) Oh, I can't stand it a minute longer, I –

> *Beth heads determinedly for the door. She nearly collides with Martin who is holding an opened can of beer from which he occasionally quaffs.*

Martin Whoops! Now, Mum, where do you think you're going? Sit down!

Beth I can't bear this, I feel I'm under house arrest. I need to be doing something, Martin.

Martin I told you there's nothing for you to do . . .

Beth It's Christmas! All this sitting down's not good for me, it feels unnatural.

Martin All in hand.

Beth Sounds like it.

Martin Slight accident, that's all. Nothing serious.

Beth Sounded as if she'd dropped the china cabinet . . .

Martin Nothing that can't be replaced. Now then – (*Turning his attention to the Christmas tree*) I'll just set this up. Plug it in. Away we go.

> *Under the next Martin erects the tree, standing it in the corner of the room. It is one of those floor-standing artificial trees with detachable feet, on which the branches hinge for packing purposes. The lights have been previously attached and wired to the branches. It all requires a certain amount of straightening and artistic branch 'grooming' which Martin does in due course.*
> *Beth watches him.*

You alright there, Mum? Can I get you anything?

Beth No, thanks, Martin. Not at the moment.

> *Pause. She watches Martin.*

I am going to be allowed to go to the toilet on my own, I hope?

Martin Only if you put your hand up.

Beth So long as I know.

Martin That's the trouble with you. Can't bear sitting still, can you? Not for a minute. Spent your life running after Dad and me. Time you sat down, isn't it?

Beth I'm not used to sitting down. I'm used to being on my feet. Doing things.

Martin There's nothing to do, I keep saying . . .

Beth There's masses to do, Martin. I mean, you three can't . . . I mean, how can you possibly . . .? I mean, it's Christmas Eve . . . this time of year I'm usually rushed off my feet. Wrapping and stuffing things . . . hanging the holly. (*Unhappily*) There's masses . . .

Connie looks in, holding a refilled wine glass.

Connie That's all cleaned up in there, anyway. Down on my hands and knees as usual. Just going up for a quick bath, get changed. (*Indicating her glass*) Oh, I helped myself, I hope you don't mind, Beth.

Beth Help yourself.

Connie Oh, that looks nice, Martin.

Martin It will do. Eventually.

Connie (*as she goes*) Lovely and Christmassy.

Connie goes out.

Beth I hope she's not going to get pissed again, like she did last year.

Martin I'll keep an eye on her, don't worry.

Beth Trying to ride the flashing reindeer. That really had your dad going.

Martin Bloody hell, yes. Burnt her legs, didn't she?

Beth That's not all she burnt. I got through that much Savlon . . .

Martin (*now absorbed*) How about you? Fancy a drink?

Beth No. I'll wait till supper.

From the kitchen, behind the hatch, the sound of a dropping saucepan lid.
They both register this but then choose not to comment.

You don't need to go to all this trouble, Martin, you really don't. Not just for me.

Martin (*intent on his task*) Yes, I do.

Beth Not just for me.

Martin For me as well. I need to do it for me. And for Dad. He'd expect it.

Beth I don't think he would. Why do you feel he'd expect it?

Martin He just would. I know he would.

Beth Why?

Martin I'm his son.

Beth And?

Martin He took care of you, didn't he? All your married life. All thirty – whatever years of it . . .

Beth Thirty-three.

Martin Devoted to you. Like you were to him. He looked after you, saw you right, gave us a home. Worked his socks off, didn't he? We never wanted for nothing, not really. He did everything a man should do.

Beth (*gently*) I looked after him, too. I did a little bit as well, Martin.

Martin No, but he was, like, the provider, wasn't he? Once you'd stopped work, when you had me – and then Karen – nursing her, till she . . . Dad was the sole provider, wasn't he? Now it's fallen to me. I know I could never be quite what he was for you – no way – I mean, you two were that close, weren't you? Friends of mine, they used to say you and Dad, you were the perfect couple . . .

Beth We had our moments . . .

Martin Let's face it, you never argued, did you? All the time I was growing up, I never once heard a cross word between you. Lads at school, they said their mums and dads used to go at it like hammer and tongs sometimes.

Beth No, we never argued. I sometimes didn't agree with him but I never argued with him . . .

Martin Never an angry word here . . .

Beth . . . there was no point, really . . .

Martin . . . I could never live up to that . . .

Beth . . . he never listened to me . . .

Martin . . . never. You heard me in there. Yelling at Ella. Yelling at her. Dad would never have done that, would he?

Beth No, your dad never yelled.

Martin I made her cry, didn't I, you heard me. That's terrible.

Beth Yes, well, she's over it now, isn't she?

Martin I yelled at her in the car coming here, as well . . . I don't know what comes over me . . .

Beth Well, sometimes, you know it's good to have a good yell . . .

Martin Not when it makes someone cry, it isn't.

Beth Well, occasionally women need a good cry, you know. They enjoy it, Martin. Some women. Your Auntie Connie does. She loves a good cry.

Martin You don't cry. I've never seen you cry, Mum.

Beth No. I don't cry very much. I didn't think I'd cry at the funeral, but I did. Surprised me. Oh, and I cried when

242

Karen finally went . . . but . . . All I'm saying is that some women, you know, they weep buckets. They're always bursting into tears. Your Auntie Connie cries at TV adverts. Maybe Ella's one of those. You never know.

Martin Most of the women I've gone out with start crying sooner or later.

Beth You've not had a lot of luck with your women, have you?

Pause. Another clatter from the kitchen which again they both register and then choose to ignore.

Martin (*finishing with the tree*) Right, that's it, that'll do. Plug it in, let's have a look at it.

Beth Oh, well done. That looks lovely, Martin.

Martin (*plugging the lights into a wall socket*) And – the moment of truth!

Martin switches on. Nothing happens.

Typical.

Beth Not working?

Martin No.

Beth Probably just a bulb.

Martin Typical.

He starts tightening each bulb separately, working his way round the tree.

Beth I don't know why they make them like that, do you? I can't see the point, can you? One bulb goes out, they all go out. Why do they make them like that, do you know? I mean, if they all go out, how's anyone supposed to know which one of them it is that's just gone out. Why do they make them like that, do you suppose?

Martin (*who hasn't the foggiest*) Well, they design it . . . in series – you know, in phase . . . because of electrical resistance, you know . . . safety . . . optimum loading and so on . . .

Beth I mean, if one bulb goes in here, they don't go out all over the house as well, do they? Your dad explained it to me once but I couldn't follow it. Not after the first ten minutes, anyway.

Another crash from the kitchen.

Martin No, I think it may be the plug. I'll just fetch the toolbox.

Beth Under the stairs, where it usually is.

Martin goes out.
More sounds from the kitchen. This time a series of thumps as of someone hitting a stove with their hand.
Beth cautiously moves to open the hatch. As she opens it, the thumps grow louder. Ella's effortful grunts are also heard.

You alright there, love?

The thumping continues.

If you're trying to get that oven door open . . . a little tip. You need just to lift it slightly first, love.

More thumping.

No, you just have to lift it first. It's a safety feature. Just lift it – that's it.

The thumping stops.

It's a stupid stove. My husband insisted we got one. Full of these safety features, it's hopeless. Drives you mad. Oh, look, warm bread, how lovely. I love warm bread. If you need a hand, just give a yell, won't you?

Beth closes the hatch. As she does so, Martin returns with a large toolbox.

Martin Knock-knock! Back again!

Beth I was just seeing she was alright.

Martin She's alright. I've seen her cook up a three-course dinner for ten. No hassle.

Beth Really?

Martin Didn't even break sweat.

During the next he sits by the tree and starts to unscrew the plug.

Beth She seemed to be having trouble getting the oven open . . . Still, that stove, it's got a mind of its own.

Martin Ella's more used to industrial stuff, you know.

Beth Yes?

Martin You know. Big industrial ranges.

Beth Well, I'd better lay the table. At least I can do that.

During the next Beth goes to the sideboard and locates cutlery, mats, cruet, etc. Including two new Christmas candles. She starts to lay the table for four.

(*As she does this*) What does Ella do exactly? You did tell me, didn't you?

Martin Chef. She ran her own restaurant for a bit.

Beth Really?

Martin That's how we first met, actually. Went there to eat a couple of times. Only unfortunately it closed. Nothing to do with her, mind you.

Beth No . . .

Martin Not her fault, at all. Dodgy partner. He ran off with the money.

Beth Oh, dear . . .

Martin So she's, like, between restaurants, you know. Freelancing. Mind you, she's no shortage of offers. There's demand for her. All around the Dorchester area, you know. She's a bit special, really. In the catering world. Special . . .

Beth You're fond of her then?

Martin Oh, yes. She's –

He concentrates on the plug for a second.

Come on, come on, you little . . .

Beth waits.

She's – Ella's – just amazing. (*He shakes his head at the memory*) Poetry. You've no idea. I couldn't begin to tell you, Mum. Not without making you blush. You know.

Beth I'm pleased for you, son. Are we having pudding, do you know? I don't know whether we need spoons and forks . . .

Martin (*studying the plug*) Oh, there we are! There we are. Cause of the trouble. Loose wire.

Beth Oh, well done.

Martin Pulled loose, that's all.

Beth Can you fix it?

Martin No problem.

As he reassembles the plug, the hatchway opens from the kitchen.

Beth Is it ready, then? Oh, wonderful . . .

*Two plates are pushed through. They contain a quite
pleasantly presented, modest sized salad concoction,
vertically arranged.*

I'll take them from here, love, I'll take them.

Martin Hey, I'm starving.

Beth Doesn't this look amazing. (*Calling to Ella*)
Incidentally, is there a pudding, love? Only I was
wondering to lay spoons and . . . (*Getting little apparent
response*) No, probably not.

Beth takes the first two plates to the table.

(*As she does so, quietly, to Martin*) By the way, I've put
you both in our room.

Martin Right.

Beth I thought you'd prefer it in the double.

Martin (*thumbs up*) Thanks, Mum.

*Connie enters. She is transformed. Clothes, hair,
makeup.*

Beth Well, look at you!

Martin Auntie's smelt the food!

Beth (*putting the plates on the table*) All dressed for
dinner?

Connie Well, I thought I'd make the effort, you know . . .
and with me going on later . . .

Beth Oh, yes. Look at this, Connie, doesn't it look
delicious?

*Ella passes two more plates through the hatch. Beth
takes them.*

Connie (*looking at the food rather dubiously*) Yes . . .

Beth Whoops, this one's rather toppled over. I'll have to have this one.

Martin (*completing his plug*) That's done it!

Beth Would you mind bringing the white wine from the fridge, Ella? If you wouldn't mind?

Ella closes the hatch.

Oh, now glasses, we need glasses. Connie, would you mind? In the cupboard there. We need four. We'd all like a drop of white wine with our dinner, wouldn't we?

Connie (*getting out the wine glasses*) I'll stick with the red.

Beth Suit yourself. (*Opening the hatch*) Ella, could you bring the red through as well, please – oh, she's gone.

Martin I'll get it.

Martin goes out with the toolbox. He hasn't yet switched on the Christmas tree lights.

Connie That bathwater was a bit tepid, you know, Beth.

Beth Oh, dear. Well, nobody's had one recently. It's the immersion probably, playing up again. I'll have to get the plumber. Don't ask me. Gordon was the only one who understood it. It's full of override features.

Ella enters, rather flushed from her labours, carrying the white wine and a covered basket of warm bread.

Beth Doesn't this all look lovely. Bravo!

She gives Ella a little round of applause which Ella hardly acknowledges.

Now, how are we all going to sit? I'll be here, as always. (*At one end of the table*) Ella, would you like to sit here, love? (*To Beth's right*) Connie, you go here and – Martin can go at the end. In his dad's place.

Connie Man of the house.

Beth Yes. Now you must tell me how you do this, Ella. I can never get it looking like this . . .

Connie It looks quite simple, really . . .

Beth I can never get mine to stand up. It's a great art, I imagine? Getting it to stand up? (*Pouring wine for herself and Ella*) It looks delicious, don't you think, Connie?

Silence.

(*Calling*) Come on Martin, where are you? We want to eat! We're all starving hungry in here!

Connie Well, I hope this keeps us going. It needs to last us through till breakfast, doesn't it?

Martin enters with a bottle of red wine.

Martin Sorry. Had to open a fresh bottle, that one was practically empty.

Connie Well, if we're still hungry after this, we'll just have to fill up on sweet. I presume there's a sweet?

Beth – er . . .

Connie Martin?

Martin . . . er . . . I'm not sure.

Beth Well, this looks very filling, anyway. We don't need too much, do we? Spoil our appetite for tomorrow, won't it? Now, do sit down, we're all dying to start.

Connie Try not to eat it all at once.

Martin Now, who's this red for? Just for you is it, Auntie Connie? May I –?

Connie Thank you.

Beth I've put you up that end, Martin, in your . . . where your dad used to sit . . .

Connie Man of the house.

Martin Right. Oh, we haven't got the Christmas tree, have we? Just a tick. (*He goes to the tree*) We must have the lights. And – let there be light.

Martin clicks the wall switch. There is a small bang and all the lights go out. They are now lit only with the residual street light glow from the window.

Beth ⎱ Oh, no!

Connie ⎰ What's happened?

Martin Whoops! Sorry about that, ladies! Technical fault.

Beth It's the fuse.

Martin Yes, it's probably the fuse. Don't panic, girls. I'll find the fuse box. Fix it in no time.

Beth Under the stairs. I'll go, if you like.

Martin No I'll go, I'll do it. No sweat. I'm a dab hand with fuses. If I can find my way.

Beth Martin, have your supper first. Tell you what, we can light the candles, can't we?

Martin Oh yes, why not? Dinner by candlelight. Very romantic.

Beth Anyone got a light?

Martin I've got one. I've got one here. If I can find my way.

Martin gropes his way back to the table.

Connie Oooh!

Martin Sorry, Auntie Connie. Now then. Here we go.

Martin lights one of the candles. It gives sufficient light to reveal at the other end of the table, in the seat reserved for him, the figure of Gordon.
   Beth, who appears to be the only one of them who can see her late husband, rises in alarm.

Beth Oh, my God! It's him!

Martin Mum! What is it, Mum?

Connie Beth, what's the matter with you?

Ella looks alarmed.
   Beth sways for a moment and swoons to the floor in a heap.
   Ella gives a small scream.

Martin } Mum!

Connie } Catch her!

As they gather round Beth in consternation, Gordon remains seated in his ghostly light until a:

Blackout.

End of Act One.

Act Two

SCENE ONE

The same. An hour or so later.

The table has been cleared, the settee bed has been made up and, although the Christmas tree remains unlit, the main lights have been restored. The room is now lit by a single table lamp standing on the sofa's side table, now serving as a temporary bedside light. Outside in the garden, behind the closed curtains and thus not too noticeable at present, a light pulses on and off, evidence that the illuminated reindeer is now functioning.

Beth, in her nightclothes, is sitting up in bed staring at the corner of the room where Gordon previously materialised and of whom there is currently no sign.

Beth (*softly, rather nervously*) . . . don't you dare . . . don't you bloody dare come back to haunt me, do you hear? Gordon? I know you're there . . .

Unseen by her during this, Martin, who is still dressed, appears silently in the doorway.

I can see you, you know . . . I know you're there . . . I know there's someone here. I know there is . . .

Martin (*tentatively*) Knock-knock . . .

Beth (*startled*) Oh, God! Martin! (*Gentler*) Listen, love, try not to do that too much, would you?

Martin How do you mean?

Beth All that knock-knock business . . .

Martin Sorry. I didn't realise . . .

Beth It's just a tiny little bit irritating, love. That's all. Either knock on the door properly or come into the room. One or the other.

Martin Right. Dad always used to do it, didn't he?

Beth Yes, he did.

Martin Sorry. You alright then, Mum?

Beth Yes, yes. Still a little – shook up . . . you know . . .

Martin You sure you won't take something?

Beth No, no . . . I'm fine now . . .

Martin Ella's got some sleeping pills. She says you're welcome to one of those, if you . . .

Beth No, no. You know me and pills. Never take them unless there's an emergency.

Martin I think that was an emergency. Fainting like that. I've never known you to –

Beth Well, I'm over it now.

Martin If you're sure . . .

Beth I'm fine, Martin, you're not to worry about me, do you hear? It's very sweet of you but . . . Go on upstairs to bed now. Ella will be wondering where you are –

Martin No, well, I didn't want to disturb her. Let her get to sleep. She's taken a couple of pills. Bit shaken up by all of this, you know . . .

Beth Sleeping pills? Ella takes sleeping pills?

Martin Well, relaxants, you know. Now and then. To relax her. Things tonight made her a bit tense . . . not just the – you know – apparition . . . I think she was a bit hurt that no one ate much of the dinner . . .

Beth I was lying there flat on my back in the middle of the floor, Martin. I was hardly going to tuck into a pile of mixed salad, was I?

Martin No, no. No one's to blame. I ate it. I ate two and a half of them, anyway, but it wasn't the same. She was just, you know, a bit hurt, you know . . .

Beth It was alright for her. She wasn't the one who saw something, was she?

Martin You really . . . saw . . . . thought you saw . . . Dad? You saw him . . .?

Beth I thought I did. Clear as day. Sitting there in his own chair, you know. Just like he used to. With his arms folded, waiting for his dinner. It was weird . . . I could have sworn he . . . really weird.

Martin I think you should have a check-up, Mum.

Beth Possibly.

Martin In the New Year. They say grief, you know, like you've got, can have profound side effects . . . trick the mind into . . . I'm going to try, Mum . . . it'll be difficult but – I'll try to take his place. Make up the difference.

Beth You don't need to do that, Martin. I've said.

Martin But there must be such a hole in your life now. Such a gap where Dad used to be. I mean, it's like you've lost a whole half of you. I know you're very clever at hiding things, always have been, but I can see how you're feeling.

Beth It'll heal over. Eventually. Life goes on. Hopefully. (*Slight pause*) Auntie Connie back, is she?

Martin Not yet. I was half waiting up for her . . .

Beth What time is it?

Martin (*consulting his watch*) Just gone twenty to two . . .
Oh. Happy Christmas, by the way . . .

Beth Happy Christmas. That's odd. She should be back
by now. Carol service doesn't go on for two hours, surely.
Maybe she's – gone on . . .

Martin Where's she gone on to after a midnight service?
Run off with the vicar, has she?

Beth Now you mention it . . .

Martin What?

Beth . . . Nothing.

Martin I hope she's alright. She was well away before she
went, wasn't she?

Beth She was . . .

Martin (*looking to the ceiling*) Well, I think Ella must be
asleep, I'd better get up there. I left the reindeer on by the
way. In the front garden. Hope it won't keep you awake.

Beth Can't you switch it off?

Martin I've tried. But there's a timer. Which must have
an override, somewhere, but I can't seem to figure it out.
Full of safety features.

Beth Well, it can't keep flashing on and off all night . . .

Martin The only solution is to take the whole thing
down again . . . and after the trouble it took to . . . I'll
sort it out in the morning, Mum, don't worry . . .

Beth It'll keep people awake though. We'll get
complaints . . .

Martin Yes, the bloke next door did pop round . . .

Beth What, Bill Chambers . . . ?

Martin He was very pleasant, considering. It was just his kids were waking up every ten minutes apparently, thinking Santa'd arrived . . . I hope it won't disturb you.

Beth It might disturb you two. You're just above here. It's right outside your window.

Martin No, that's alright. Ella has a sleep mask.

Beth Sleep mask?

Martin She has a – touch of insomnia. Occasionally. Anyway, I managed to get these lights on again. Fixed the fuse.

Beth (*gently*) Yes, you did, son. With a little bit of help from me.

A loud knock on the front door. The door bell rings simultaneously. They jump.

Martin God! That'll be her! Auntie Connie!

Beth Or more neighbours.

Martin (*hurrying out*) I hope to God she hasn't woken Ella . . .

More knocking.

I'll deal with it, Mum. Coming, I'm coming . . .

Martin goes out.

Beth (*sighs*) Oh, dear . . . I'm really so tired . . . .

She lies back. Outside in the hall, the sound of voices. Martin's and two others, a male and a female. Connie's drunken groans and slurred protests can also be heard. Then the sound of feet coming downstairs and Ella's voice joins the mêlée.

This goes on for quite some time, and should go as follows. Connie groans and mutters under all this.

Man Good evening, sir. Can you confirm this lady lives here?

Martin Oh, my God! What's happened to her?

Man Can you verify this is her current address? She's not sure.

Martin Oh, yes, that's my Auntie Connie. What's happened to her? What's she done?

Man Your Auntie Connie's just assaulted this officer . . .

Woman When apprehended as she was attempting to climb the statue in the town square . . .

Martin Oh, my God!

Woman . . . trying to get on the horse. She's very lucky we don't press charges.

Man I should put Auntie to bed, if I were you. She's lucky not to be locked up –

Ella (*coming downstairs*) Martin? What's happening? What the hell's going on? What the bloody hell's happening?

Man Hallo, who's this then, your fairy godmother?

Woman Here! Will you take her from me, dear? Watch yourself, she scratches.

Ella I don't want her. Don't give her to me! Why don't you take her, Martin?! She's your bloody auntie!

Martin Ella! Ella! Ella! Please! I will, I'll take her in a minute, love.

Man She can just consider herself lucky we're too busy looking after serious drunks to bother with her. Take my tip, you'll put her to bed to sleep it off. You tell her in the morning she's old enough to know better and she ought to be ashamed of herself. Good night to you.

Martin Thank you very much. Merry Xmas.

Door closes.
Connie continues her noises.

Martin Wait there, Ella! Just one second. I'm just going to tell Mum what's happened. Then I'll come and help you with her.

Ella I can't hold her on my own, Martin! Hurry up!

Beth (*sometime during this, wearily, still lying back*) What's everyone doing? What's going on? What the hell's going on?

At length, Martin returns.

Martin Knock-kno— (*Remembering*) Sorry, Mum . . .

Beth (*wearily*) Yes . . . ?

Martin Not asleep, are you?

Beth No . . .

Martin Only, in case you were wondering, it was only the police.

Beth (*sitting up, alarmed*) The what?

Martin They just brought Auntie Connie back. She's a bit under the . . . you know . . .

Beth (*making as if to get out of bed*) Oh, God . . .

Martin No! No! Mum! Ella's seeing her into bed . . . You stay there, we're taking care of it, it's all under control.

Beth What was she doing?

Martin Ella? She'd just got off to sleep.

Beth No, Connie. What was Connie doing for heaven's sake?

Martin Apparently, she was trying to climb the statue . . .

Beth The statue? What statue?

Martin The one in the town square. The one with the bloke on the horse. Oliver Cromwell, isn't it?

Beth The Duke of Wellington . . .

Martin The good news is that they're not going to charge her . . .

Beth They're not?

Martin They said they were far too busy looking after serious drunks to bother with her and that she should go to bed and sleep it off and that she was old enough to know better at her age and she ought to be ashamed of herself.

Beth Well, if you need any help with her, let me know . . .

Martin No, she's calm now. She put up a bit of a fight, they said. Scratched the policewoman . . . Why don't you switch off the light, Mum? Try and get a bit of sleep. You'll need it. Busy day tomorrow, eh?

Beth Yes, yes. I'll try.

Martin Right. I'll go up, then. Give Ella a hand. You need anything?

Beth Just a bit of quiet would be nice.

Martin Well, there shouldn't be any more excitements. Night then, Mum.

Beth Good night, Martin.

Martin Want me to turn the light out for you?

Beth No, I'll do it. Martin, would you make sure, before you go up, that everything else is turned off, please?

Martin Will do, Mum. Night-night.

Beth Night.

Martin goes out.
   Beth, on her own again, stares round the room nervously.

You're still here, Gordon, I can sense you. I know you are. I don't want to see you again, do you hear me? They say if you don't want to see ghosts, they don't appear. Well, I don't want to see you, d'you hear? I'm turning this light off now. And I'm going to sleep. Alright? (*With her hand on the light switch*) One . . . two . . . three . . .

Her bedside light goes off. The room is comparatively darker. However the effect of the flashing lights through the window gets correspondingly brighter.

Oh, my God. It's like bloody Las Vegas! Still, at least I can see. I can see whether you're here or not.

She listens to the silence for a moment.

Right, then. Nothing. All quiet!

Suddenly the kitchen hatch bursts open and a shaft of light illuminates the room.

(*Alarmed*) Oh!

Martin's head appears through the hatch.

Martin (*whispering*) Sorry to startle you, Mum!

Beth What?

Martin She left the oven on.

Beth What?

Martin Ella. She went and left the oven on.

Beth Did she?

Martin Left it on low. Just turned it off. She's more used to industrial ones, you know. I'm going up now.

Beth Good.

Martin Night, then, Mum.

Beth Night.

Martin closes the hatch.

Oh, sleep. Blessed sleep . . .

A silence. The lights flash on and off for a moment or two.
    A faint scratching sound from the kitchen on the hatch doorway.

What's that?

She listens.

    The scratching sound occurs again, louder this time.

Sounds like . . . Wagstaff? Wagstaff . . . (*She clambers out of bed*) Wagstaff!

She opens the hatch.

(*Tentatively*) Wagstaff? Nothing . . . I'm being haunted by the cat now –

She closes the hatch doors and makes to return to bed.
    Gordon is again sitting at the table in his corner chair, facing her.

(*Seeing him, clutching her heart*) Aaah!

Gordon (*cheerily*) Knock-knock.

Beth (*drawing back*) Gordon? Is that you? Is that really you?

Gordon It is indeed. (*Jovially*) And who else did you expect to find in your bedroom at this time of night, may I ask?

Beth (*starting to lose her grip, slightly*) It can't really be you . . . I mean, it can't be . . . I mean, I sat by your bed when you . . . while you were . . .

Gordon While I was departing, yes, I do recall . . .

Beth And then we took you up to the . . . up to the . . .

Gordon Crematorium, yes.

Beth And then we . . . they . . . they . . .

Gordon Cremated me, yes . . .

Beth And then I took your . . . then I took your . . .

Gordon My ashes, yes . . .

Beth And I scatt— I scatt— I scatt—

Gordon Scattered them, yes, in the park, didn't you, in accordance with my final wishes. The Victoria Park. Though I did specify the other end, Beth, you know, the south-west end, by the lake. That north-east end you chose, they did tend to blow back a bit into the kiddies' playground which I did feel was a little unhygienic . . .

Beth (*still weak*) I'm sorry, it was very windy, I'm sorry. I was aiming for the rose beds. I know how you liked roses . . .

Gordon No, well, you did your best. You can't do better than your best. I always say that of you, Beth, you're always trying if not quite succeeding. You may occasionally fall a whisker short of perfection, but I can never fault you for trying. And that, when the chips are down, is what counts.

Beth Gordon, why have you come back? What are you doing here? What have I done? Why have you come back to haunt me?

Gordon I've not come back to haunt you, certainly not –

Beth . . . Because I don't know what more I could have done . . .

Gordon I'm back to keep an eye on you. Make sure you're coping without me.

Beth I can cope, don't worry about me.

Gordon Now where have I heard that before? 'I can manage, Gordon, don't worry I can manage' . . . and the next minute where are we? All sixes and sevens . . . Or in your case, as often as not, sevens and eights, eh?

Beth Listen, Gordon, I can't deal with this.

Gordon Ah well, there, you see. A case in point. There's one problem you can't deal with for a kick-off . . . now who says you don't need me here?

Beth Yes, but you're the problem, Gordon. Please go away.

Gordon I can't do that, Beth. I'm sorry.

Beth You can't?

Gordon No, this is an official visit, you see. Authorised as the result of a formal request.

Beth Who by?

Gordon I'm afraid I'm not at liberty to disclose that information.

Beth You're not?

Gordon I'm under oath. As a result of one or two small services I have been able to render, I have been granted official dispensation.

Beth Small services? What small services?

Gordon Again, I regret I'm unable to disclose that. Suffice it to say that, following my demise, when I arrived there, the place was little short of a shambles, as my father would have said. Since I arrived, I'm pleased to report that systems are gradually being put into place. I'm introducing flow charts, comparison graphs and optimum-attainment targets like there's no tomorrow, which as it happens up there, there isn't. By the time you get there, which I trust will be a little while yet, Beth, everything will be operating as smooth as clockwork. And not before time. But you'll be familiar with all this, Beth. I don't need to tell you, do I? You know me . . .

Beth Yes, I know you, Gordon. Only too well.

Gordon Like a red rag to a bull for me, all that.

Upstairs a door slams.
  They both look up, momentarily.

Beth You're still the same, Gordon. You haven't changed.

Gordon Oh, no, just the same. Take more than a – slight change of circumstances – to alter me. (*Smiling*) Frankly, they were simply amazed. Gobsmacked.

Beth Who were?

Gordon The – persons concerned. I can't reveal their identities. But they were amazed. 'Heavens above, Mr Timms, I don't know how we've managed without you, all these years.' I tell you they were open-mouthed. Jaws to their knees. I told them, all it takes is a fresh eye. I mean, the majority of the procedures there were outdated, some of them were downright dangerous.

Beth Oh, dear.

Gordon I told them that. I didn't mince words, I was perfectly blunt with them.

Beth I bet.

Gordon But don't you worry, Beth, I'm setting them straight. Little by little.

Beth Well done.

Gordon Confidentially, *entre nous*, I think the problem goes higher. Much higher. I'll sort that out next. Yes, they're glad of me.

> *A slight self-congratulatory pause.*
> *A bump upstairs from the bedroom.*

Gordon Just like old times this, isn't it?

Beth Yes . . .

Gordon Me chattering away. You listening agog.

Beth Yes . . .

Gordon How it always used to be, eh?

Beth Yes . . .

Gordon You know, I don't mind saying, I'm quite looking forward to getting back into the swing of things, you know.

Beth Where?

Gordon Here.

Beth You're planning on staying?

Gordon Oh, yes.

Beth How long for?

Gordon Well, just until.

Beth Until when?

Gordon Just until. (*He considers*) Listen, Beth, I just want to say something to you.

Beth Oh, yes? Something else?

Gordon It's this. Now, as I'm sure you recall, due to circumstances beyond my personal control, I underwent a work-related accident in my place of employment . . . from which I subsequently was forced to retire. Now, during those final few weeks in the hospital and here at home, I'm aware that my ill health prevented me from putting into place adequate safeguards and correct procedures sufficient to guarantee your future well-being and livelihood . . .

Beth I've got the pension . . .

Gordon Yes, allow me to . . .

Beth . . . and the insurance . . .

Gordon – allow me to . . .

Beth I had the compensation, too. From Twistletons. They paid up . . .

Gordon . . . Beth . . .

Beth . . . eventually, they did.

Gordon Beth. Would you allow me to finish, please . . . would you mind?

Beth (*meekly*) Sorry.

Gordon Never quite hear me through, do you? Never listen to the end of a sentence, do you?

Beth I never know when you've got there.

Gordon I'm not talking about the money, love. I know

there's enough money. Well, there should be, for your needs. I mean, there's never enough money but . . . No, what I'm talking about is how you manage it. How you manage the money, do you see? Now that was always left to me, wasn't it?

Beth Only because you wanted to, I could probably have . . .

Gordon Beth, come on, come on, be fair. Be honest, now. Not what you'd term a financial brain, is it, yours? Could you, hand on heart, could you possibly have dealt with all that side for thirty-three years? Investments? Variable rates of interest? The fluctuating pound? Mortgage rates? Retail price index? No, you left it to Gordon, didn't you? Quite sensibly. In the same way, be fair, fair do's, I left certain things to you. When you wanted to redecorate, say, the bedroom, did I interfere in any way? No, I did not. Never said a word. When we changed this carpet in here . . .

Beth You did with the bathroom. You insisted . . .

Gordon Well, the bathroom, yes. That's my area. That's plumbing. Tiling and grouting and so on . . .

Beth You didn't do that yourself. We got the plumber in . . .

Gordon And who, may I enquire, supervised him? Virtually stood over the man while he was doing it?

Beth . . . I was left with all the boring bits, wasn't I? . . . Toilet-roll holders and soap dishes . . .

Gordon Now, now, now, now . . . .

Beth . . . lavatory brushes . . . I could have chosen the tiles.

Gordon What is there to choose with tiles? White is white, isn't it?

Beth Why do they always need to be white?

Gordon All bathroom tiles are white!

Beth (*muttering*) I'd have liked pink. Greyish pink.

Gordon (*scornfully*) Greyish pink? Come on, how could you ever tell they were clean?

Beth I'd have known.

Gordon Well, I wouldn't.

Beth You'd never have cleaned them.

Slight pause.

Gordon I'm not sure I'm liking the sound of this, Beth. This sounds like the beginnings of an argument, if you ask me . . .

Beth Not really, I'm just saying . . .

Gordon Thirty-three years and never a cross word and then, hey presto, I'm out of the house for a couple of weeks and when I come back there's a palace revolution under way . . . Dear me! Things certainly do need organising, don't they? Dear, oh dear!

Another bump from upstairs and Martin's despairing voice.

Martin (*shouting, off*) Well, what do you want from me, for God's sake?

Beth You say this is an official visit?

Gordon It has been authorised, yes.

Beth As a result of a formal request, you said?

Gordon That is correct.

Beth Where did the request come from, then?

Gordon I'm afraid I'm not at liberty to –

Beth – to disclose that information. Well, I think I have a right to know, Gordon. I mean, it was a request made on my behalf. Did it come from you?

Gordon I'm not saying, Beth, I'm not saying. My lips are sealed.

Beth Oh, when you get like this, you can be so annoying, Gordon. I could strangle you, you know, if you weren't already dead.

    Pause.

You're not telling me?

    Pause.

Alright. See if I care.

    Another pause.

Gordon I'll simply say . . . your beloved partner . . . your rock . . . your protector . . . the companion and mainstay of your life . . .

Beth (*realising*) Oh. But it wasn't me who said that.

Gordon It was said on your behalf. By an intermediary. You approved it.

Beth I never knew he was going to say that . . .

Gordon Nonetheless it caught someone's attention . . .

Beth Who? Oh, you mean . . .

Gordon Well, possibly not. I believe the request was intercepted at committee level. They did feel, though, it warranted immediate action. They generously allowed me to step down temporarily from my duties there and here I am.

Beth Listen, I'm trying to tell you, Gordon. I'm alright.
I had the dreadful shock of losing you and for a week or
two I was . . . I was beside myself with grief, I admit it . . .
But I'm gradually getting over it, love . . . I'm coming to
terms with it, you see. With being alone. Listen, I hate to
say this to your face, it sounds so terrible, but I really
don't need you, Gordon, not any more . . . I'm very sorry,
but I don't. (*She pauses for breath*)

Gordon (*calmly*) If you could only hear yourself, Beth.
Now it's late and you're tired, and you're in an emotional
state . . .

Beth (*excitedly*) Of course I'm in an emotional state,
who wouldn't be in an emotional state? I'm holding this
conversation with my late husband, aren't I –?

Gordon Now, Beth, calmly, old girl . . .

Beth – who still won't listen to me, even when he's dead.

Gordon (*moving to her slightly*) Lie down now, lie down!

Beth (*drawing back and sitting on the bed*) Don't you
touch me!

Gordon Don't worry, I can't touch you, we're on
different astral planes, Beth . . .

Beth Thank God for that . . .

Gordon My hand would pass right through you. Now lie
down, close your eyes.

Beth does so, reluctantly.

We can't have this, can we? Disagreements? Thirty-three
years and never a cross word between us, was there? Was
there?

Beth No. Not out loud, anyway.

Gordon Oh, come on, old girl. I won't hear talk like that. Bite your tongue, woman! You know, when I was alive, I told everyone that I had married the perfect wife. Couldn't fault her. In my opinion we had the perfect marriage. And I hoped that she felt the same. In fact I know she did. It was a true meeting of two minds and, on occasions, two bodies.

Beth On occasions . . .

Gordon Now I'm telling them all over again up there. You were perfection, Beth. I couldn't have asked for better. If I was to have my life over . . . I would not have altered a single nano-second. Nary a one.

Beth (*sleepily*) That's nice, Gordon. I'm very happy for you. (*She yawns*)

Gordon That's it, why don't you get some shut-eye, old girl? You've had a busy day, haven't you?

Beth You can say that again.

Gordon I'll leave you now. I'll be back in the morning, don't worry.

Beth Oh. Will you?

Gordon Nighty-night, then.

Beth Gordon . . .

Gordon Yes.

Beth Have you seen Wagstaff at all? Do you know if he's still alive?

Gordon Oh, no. I'm afraid, once again, can't reveal . . .

Beth I couldn't bear to think of him still alive, injured or trapped somewhere . . . I just wanted to check he wasn't with you . . .

Gordon Oh, no, he wouldn't be with me . . . No. Cats go. . . cats go elsewhere.

Beth To another astral plane . . . ?

Gordon If you like . . .

Beth (*her eyes still closed, smiling*) Pussy-cat heaven . . .

Gordon Possibly. Or knowing that cat . . . somewhere completely other.

Gordon has withdrawn during this to a dark corner of the room.
From upstairs, the sound of Ella crying, followed by heavy footsteps across the floor and the slamming of a door. The sound of Martin's despairing voice:

Martin (*off*) Oh, God, no – no – NO!

On hearing this, Beth sits up, wide awake.
As she does so, Gordon steps back into the far corner of the room and vanishes.

Beth Now what? Oh, what a night!

Martin arrives in the doorway. He is still dressed but in his stockinged feet. He carries his shoes.

Martin Knock-knock!

Beth (*very sharply, for her*) Yes? What is it now?

Martin Sorry, Mum.

Beth Sorry, love.

Martin You weren't asleep, were you?

Beth No. I was talking to . . . to . . . (*Looking to where Gordon had been*) . . . just talking to myself.

Martin Oh. First sign of madness, isn't it?

Beth Possibly. What is it, love? What's the problem, then?

Martin It's – er . . . well . . . She's . . . she's . . .

Beth A problem, is it? With Ella?

Martin Ella? Oh, no, that's all fine. You know, couldn't be better . . . whoarr!

Beth (*a bit puzzled*) Good. I'm pleased to hear it. What's that there?

Martin Sorry?

Beth On your shoes?

Martin Oh, yes. That's why I came down. Auntie Connie's been sick on the landing . . .

Beth (*falling back on the bed again*) Oh, for God's sake! Happy Christmas!

Martin (*rather bemused*) Happy Christmas!

The lights finally fade to a:

Blackout.

SCENE TWO

The same. A few hours have passed. Around lunchtime, Christmas Day. The sofa bed is now reassembled. The presents, mostly unopened, are still piled up under the unlit Christmas tree.

Beth has dressed and is now sitting on her own in the middle of the sofa. Unsurprisingly, she looks pale and drawn from lack of sleep.

She is surrounded by scraps of wrapping paper from a present she has recently opened. The present itself, a

273

*stole which clashes alarmingly with the outfit she now
wears, is draped forgotten around her shoulders.*

*The TV is on again. The jolliest of Christmas
programmes carries on inappropriately in the background.*

*In a moment, Martin enters cautiously. He is dressed
for travelling.*

Martin Knock-knock . . .

Beth (*faintly, without looking at him*) Hallo. You both
off, then?

Martin Sorry about this. Emergencies happen. In Ella's
line, especially, you know. Specialist catering. Who'd
have credited it, eh? An emergency buffet for a hundred
and fifty. The day after Boxing Day. What's that about
then, eh?

Beth I hope she's got some bread in.

Martin Sorry?

Beth Over Christmas. For the sandwiches. She'll need a
lot of bread for a hundred and fifty.

Martin She's not going to be making sandwiches, Mum.
Not for a special buffet. Sandwiches?

Beth I was going to say she can take some of ours. Our
freezer's stuffed with sliced loaves . . .

Martin It's fine, Mum, not to bother. As I say, I should be
back this evening. In time for dinner, anyway. Traffic
shouldn't be bad, Christmas Day, roads'll be fairly clear.
Sorry to mess up the morning. You know . . . we'd stay a
bit longer and have a drink with you, only . . .

*Ella appears behind him in the doorway where she
lingers, red-eyed.*

Here she is! Here she is! The girl in demand. Right. We
must be off. It's a long drive . . . I was telling Mum, Ella,

you need to be back at work, don't you, love? . . . You can't afford to lose an order like that . . . not in freelance catering . . .

Pause.

The stole looks really great. Doesn't it, Ella?

Beth Yes . . .

She absently removes the stole from her shoulders and places it beside her on the sofa.

Martin Fabulous. She's got a great eye, you know. Real flair for colours, haven't you?

Pause.

Tell you what, why don't we open the rest of the presents later, Mum? This evening, soon as I get back. Don't start without me, will you? No peeping. Don't you cheat, now!

Pause.

Well. Behave yourself while I'm gone. Fridge is full of food. One thing, you won't go hungry. She's just sorry she couldn't stay and cook it for you, you know.

Pause.

Well. Right. That's it then.

Slight pause.

Beth See you later, love.

Martin Right. Yes. See you later. Auntie Connie still at church, is she?

Beth Yes.

Martin Say cheerio to her from Ella, then. Bye!

Beth Bye!

Martin Say goodbye to Mum, Ella.

Ella gives a tight-lipped smile in Beth's direction. She and Martin go out.
Beth sits for a moment.
She becomes aware of the TV Christmas party, still in full swing.

Beth Oh, shut up, just shut up, will you!

She points the TV remote at the set, which goes off.

(*Looking at her watch*) No, she'll still be at church. Probably praying for forgiveness. I don't know what she's done to that carpet. She must have been drinking neat bleach.

She rises and goes to the window. She waves to the departing vehicle.

(*Mouthing and miming*) Bye! . . . Bye! Bye! . . . . Bye! Don't for God's sake bring her back here again, will you? Bye! Oh, no, he's still left the reindeer on, hasn't he? It'll be flashing away all day now.

She stands for a moment in the middle of the room.

Well, I'd better get on, I suppose. So much for not lifting a finger all Christmas . . .

A clatter from the kitchen.

What was that? Hallo . . . Anyone there? It's him, back again. He said he'd be back. He said he would. (*Tentatively calling*) Gordon? Is that you? Gordon?

Another sound from the kitchen.

I can hear you, you know, Gordon. I can't bear this, I'm going to be haunted for ever. (*Listening*) It can't be him, he'd have popped up by now. Come through the floor or through the wall or something.

A faint scratching at the hatch.

Wagstaff? (*Running to the hatch and throwing it open*)
Wagsta— !

She comes face to face with a very subdued Connie.

(*Coolly*) Oh, it's you.

Connie (*humbly*) Sorry to disturb you.

Beth What are you doing scratching around in there?

Connie I was just getting a –

Beth (*brusquely*) There's more red wine in the cupboard
if that's what you're looking for.

Connie – a glass of water. I was just getting a glass of
water, if that's alright.

Beth That's alright, help yourself.

Connie Thank you. I'm so thirsty . . .

Beth Not surprised.

Connie's head disappears but the hatch remains open.

(*Calling*) You go to church, then?

Connie (*off*) Yes.

Beth Enjoy it, did you?

Connie (*off*) Yes. I asked God to forgive me.

Beth Oh yes? And did He?

Connie (*off*) He's very understanding . . .

Beth That's good of Him. Then it wasn't His carpet,
was it?

Connie (*reappearing at the hatch*) Oh, Beth, I'm sorry.
I'm mortified. I'm really mortified.

Beth Well, I'm sure you are, Connie. But this happens every single year, doesn't it? Year after year, love?

Connie Not every year. I'm not sick every year.

Beth No, to be fair, you're not. Last year you had a nose bleed all down the new wallpaper, didn't you?

Connie Look, I've said, I'm sorry . . . what more can I say?

Beth There's nothing more to be said, Connie, is there? Nothing that hasn't been said a thou— Look, could we stop talking to each other through this hatchway, it's like visiting you in prison – either you come in here, or I'll come out there.

Connie It's alright, I'll come in there . . .

Beth Please do.

Connie It's the least I can do.

Connie closes the hatch.
 Beth kneels on the floor by the tree and begins to sift through the presents.

Beth (*pausing to glare at the tree*) And he never did get this thing working, did he?

Randomly she twists one of the bulbs. The tree lights up.

Oh. Right. That's fixed. Things are suddenly looking up . . .

Connie appears tentatively in the doorway with her glass of water.

Connie (*timidly*) Knock-knock . . .

Beth (*wincing*) Come in, Connie.

Connie Thank you. (*Moving to a chair*) May I sit down?

Beth Oh, for God's sake . . . Sit down, Connie. Not having you tiptoeing around all Christmas, are we?

Connie I'm just so mortified, Beth. I don't know what gets into me.

Beth Connie, what gets into you are several bottles of red wine . . .

Connie I know . . .

Beth If you're planning to start again, could you please switch to the white.

Connie I can't drink white.

Beth No?

Connie It makes me ill.

Beth Oh dear heaven. (*Still among the presents*) Who's this one for, it's got no label on it? – Oh, yes, it's for you. Want to open it?

Connie No thank you.

Beth Here. Open it. Cheer yourself up.

Beth slides the parcel across the floor in the direction of Connie.

Connie No, honestly I can't, Beth. I couldn't open a single present, not today.

Beth Don't be so stupid, why ever not?

Connie I'm unworthy. I promised Jesus I wouldn't. As a punishment for my behaviour, I promised him I wouldn't open a single present. I'm giving them to the poor. They were given in love and as one who is not worthy of love –

Beth (*angrily*) Oh, Connie, shut up, will you? Just shut up, you stupid woman!

A silence. Connie is stunned.

Sorry, I –

Connie You've got very hard, Beth. Since his death you've grown into a hard woman, did you know that?

Beth I don't think I have. I think I'm just growing out of being soft. I'm sorry I shouted at you, Connie. There's never an excuse for shouting, especially on Christmas Day, but . . . Now, open your bloody present.

Connie obediently unwraps the gift.

Connie (*staring at the contents, her voice trembling*) It's a pair of gloves . . .

Beth Oh, yes, they're nice . . .

Connie (*starting to cry*) . . . a pair of gloves . . . somebody's gone and given me a pair of gloves . . .

Beth Oh, Connie! Come on! For heaven's sake . . . pull yourself together.

Beth hugs Connie for a moment.

God, you're a mess, aren't you?

Connie continues to cry.

Connie! Come on, now, it's just a pair of gloves . . .

The doorbell rings.

Connie (*ceasing her crying*) What was that?

Beth Front door.

Connie Quarter past two. Who can that be?

Beth Oh, I know who it might be. I asked him to look round as soon as he'd a moment. Never expected him today, I must say.

Connie Who?

Beth (*as she goes out to the hall*) David Grinseed.

Connie (*alarmed*) David Grinseed? (*Dabbing at her face feverishly*) David can't see me like this . . . he can't see me like this, can he . . .? I need to lie down.

> *Connie scurries from the room after Beth.*

> *In a moment Beth is heard returning with David.*

David (*as he enters*) . . . I came as soon as I could. As soon as I got your message . . .

Beth Thank you.

David I hope this is a good time. I tried to judge things just right, between the end of lunch and the start of the Queen's Speech, if you're at all into that, as I'm sure you are. Now . . .

Beth I'm so sorry, I feel rather guilty. I had no intention of dragging you out, not today . . .

David No, no, no. Not at all. Working day.

Beth Yes.

David Me and the Queen, both. Though I understand she tends to be pre-recorded.

Beth Oh yes, probably. Please sit down . . .

David Unfortunately, it's not possible to pre-record me, I'm afraid. (*He laughs*)

Beth (*smiling politely*) No, no . . .

David Much as I'd welcome it, especially come the middle of January . . .

Beth Yes . . .

David It gets very cold in that church . . .

Beth Yes, it must do.

David With so few people . . . Now, Beth. What can I do for you?

Beth (*suddenly shy again*) Well, it's a bit complicated . . . it's hard to put into words . . . (*She hesitates*)

David (*gently*) Carry on, I'm listening.

Beth Do you . . . have you . . . have you ever seen a ghost, David?

David No. I can't say I have, not personally.

Beth But you think they can exist?

David Possibly.

Beth I mean, you don't disbelieve in them?

David (*proceeding cautiously*) I believe some people honestly believe they've seen ghosts. I respect that. Although there's seldom concrete evidence to support or deny their claims. Not dissimilar, in a way, to flying saucers, I suppose. But then again, most of religious faith is lacking in concrete evidence – indeed that's why they're called faiths, isn't it? As a bishop I know once said – when it comes down to it, all of it's based, in the end, on a lick and a promise, isn't it?

Beth Only I believe I have seen one.

David A ghost?

Beth Yes. On two separate occasions.

David Recently?

Beth Oh, yes. The first time was yesterday evening at dinner, shortly after you left.

David That recently?

Beth The second time was in the night. Well, early this morning, really. About two a.m.

David Two a.m.? Weren't you asleep?

Beth No, that's the point. There was all this commotion ...

David Commotion?

Beth It doesn't matter.

David No, the point I'm making is do you think you could have been dreaming. I mean, the middle of the night – ?

Beth No, I could see him as clearly as I see you. He was sitting just there –

David He?

Beth Yes.

David It was a man?

Beth It was my husband.

David Your husband?

Beth Yes. Gordon.

David Your late husband?

Beth Yes.

David The one with the – ladder?

Beth Yes.

David Did you – did you converse with him, at all? Have a wifely chat?

Beth Oh yes, we talked for quite a time.

David That must have been nice for you. Reassuring.

Beth Not very, no. He kept threatening to come back, telling me that I couldn't possibly manage on my own without him, that he'd been summoned as a result of a formal request and he was here officially.

David Summoned?

Beth Yes. As the result of a formal request.

David And where did this formal request come from, did he say?

Beth Well, as far as I could understand it, from the way it was put, you know, from the wording and so on, it came from you.

David Me?

Beth Yes.

David Goodness.

Beth So what I'm saying is, I'm asking you, can you somehow reverse it?

David Reverse it?

Beth I don't want him back, you see.

David You don't?

Beth No. Not at all. I realised as soon as I saw him that it was never going to work. His dying was very sad at the time, of course it was, but it was the end of a chapter, wasn't it? Not just for him – he'd moved on to other things, hadn't he? – but for me, as well. I've got to move on. If you stay set – you know, fixed in one point, then in a way you die as well, don't you? It's just the same as dying only worse. I have to carry on as me, don't I? Do you see?

David Yes, I – think I do.

Beth I mean, don't get me wrong, I'm not suddenly going to be playing the violin or start tap dancing, but it's like, in myself, moving on. Seeing things differently. Looking at different things, differently.

David Yes. (*Tentatively*) Is Gordon here still?

Beth He's around. Somewhere.

David Can you see him at the moment?

Beth No. But he won't be far away.

David I think what you're asking me to do, Beth, is some sort of exorcism.

Beth Not really, I don't think –

David Now, that is rather specialist stuff, you know, and not really my field. In fact, in certain quarters these days, it's quite frowned upon.

Beth No, I think we can do without all the bells and the books and the candles. All I need you to do is to reverse the prayer.

David Reverse it?

Beth Say, you know, like sorry, I made a mistake, she doesn't want to see him, after all. She doesn't miss him that much. It was a great marriage while it lasted but now she's just relieved to get shot of him.

David Beth, I can't believe you feel that. Look into your heart and ask yourself, do I really and truly believe that? Relieved to get shot of him?

Beth Well. Maybe that's putting it a bit strongly but – yes. He was a wonderful man in many ways, he was – yes, he was a rock, in a way. On which I felt safe to stand at first and, later, when times got hard, under which I could even shelter . . . But rocks, you see, well, if you're not careful, they can roll on top of you, can't they, if you let them. Last few years really and truly, David, I felt – suffocated . . . Please.

David (*quite moved by her plea*) Yes. Perhaps we should – perhaps we should simply sit together for a minute and share a silent prayer, Beth.

Beth Right. (*Indicating the table*) Over here be alright?

David Yes, yes. That'll be fine. Perhaps we could – sit opposite each other perhaps and –

Beth and David sit either side of the table.

Now, if we join hands, perhaps –

Beth allows him to take both her hands.

(*Closing his eyes*) That's good. Now, I want you to concentrate, Beth. Try and think of Gordon. Try to think of saying goodbye to Gordon. Waving him a fond, a loving farewell . . . Thanking him for the joy he's brought into your life, for the happiness you've shared together . . . and above all for the selfless love, over the years, he's given to you, to your family, your fine son, his lovely girlfriend, your sister-in-law . . . Let's both spare a minute, shall we, to concentrate on that . . .

Beth closes her eyes, too.
Gordon slowly rises up, till he's sitting at the end of the table in his chair.
He watches them.

Gordon You're committing a serious error, Beth. If you go through with it, this will be the last you'll ever see of me, old girl. Just ask yourself, quite frankly and honestly, Beth, can I really manage the rest of my life, without old Gordon? Can I, hand on heart, honestly say yes to that?

Beth (*in a firm, defiant, whisper*) Yes!

Gordon's chair sinks down again. He goes.

David (*opening his eyes again*) Yes?

Beth Yes. Thank you.

They both rise a little awkwardly as a result of the experience.

David (*moving to the door*) Well, I must – oh, look at the time. Must get home in time for the Speech – my mother would never forgive me if I – She's eighty-eight, you know. Still going strong. Amazing how some of them keep going, isn't it? Give my regards to your – to Connie, will you?

Beth Yes, I will. Thanks again, David.

David Don't bother, I can see myself out. Don't bother. Goodbye. Happy Christmas, Beth.

David goes out.

Beth Happy Christmas. (*Gazing round the room*) Well, now. What next?

From behind the hatch, the scratching sound again.

Oh, for heaven's sake, Connie. Would you kindly stop lurking, woman.

She crosses to the hatch, impatiently.

He's gone now, you can come out, you stupid thing. What on earth's the point of –?

Beth starts to open the hatch. Something invisible causes the doors to fly open sharply.
Beth is knocked aside as it brushes past her and, simultaneously, we hear a cat's miaow, loud and indignant.

The invisible cat then does a joyous circuit of the room. We and Beth are able to follow its progress due to the items that are dislodged or knocked over, as the creature does this. These include the Christmas tree which topples over on its base, the fire tongs which go over with a crash into the hearth, and the occasional ornament.

(*During this, incredulously*) Wagstaff? Wagstaff! You stop that, do you hear?

The circuit eventually brings Wagstaff round to his basket. There is a brief silence as the mayhem ceases.
The cushion in the cat basket gently flattens into an indentation as a feline body apparently settles on to it contentedly.
Beth approaches the basket tentatively, one hand extended.

Wagstaff . . . Wagstaff . . .

Another more pleasurable miaow from the basket followed by a loud purring.

(*Sighing*) Oh, dear God . . .

Beth sits amongst the debris staring at the basket, shaking her head. As the invisible Wagstaff walks towards her, she scoops him up into her arms as the lights fade to a:

Blackout.

End of play.

MY WONDERFUL DAY

My Wonderful Day was first performed at the Stephen Joseph Theatre, Scarborough, on 13 October 2009. The cast was as follows:

Winnie Barnstairs Ayesha Antoine
Laverne Petra Letang
The Man (Kevin) Terence Booth
The Wife (Paula) Alexandra Mathie
The Secretary (Tiffany) Ruth Gibson
The Friend (Josh) Paul Kemp

Director Alan Ayckbourn
Designed by Roger Glossop
Lighting by Mick Hughes

This production was given its American premiere at 59E59 Theaters, New York, on 11 November 2009, and was presented at the Yvonne Arnaud Theatre, Guildford, on 20 January 2010.

Author's Note

It is appreciated that one of the difficulties of this play is in casting Winnie the right age.

She may be played by a young actor of a similar age with all the ensuing legal and logistical problems which casting an under-age performer entails.

Alternatively, the role may be played by a slightly older actor who is able to create a truthful and credible impression of the character's age. This, after all, is theatre!

In either case, it is vital that the role is not in any way 'up-aged'.

Winnie is a child and this play is told through a child's eyes.

Characters

Winnie (Winona) Barnstairs
aged nearly nine

Laverne
her mother, late twenties–early thirties

The Man (Kevin)
forties

The Wife (Paula)
late thirties

The Secretary (Tiffany)
twenties

The Friend (Josh)
forties

Place and Time

Mainly in and around the Man's house on a
Tuesday in November in North London,
during the course of that day

EIGHT-THIRTY A.M.

*The partial downstairs areas of a modern town house
belonging to the Man.*

*What we see is perceived through the eyes of a nine-
year-old girl, Winnie (Winona) Barnstairs, thus each area
is lit as she enters it and correspondingly darkens as she
leaves.*

*Sometimes it will be part of the hall/living room,
especially the immediate area around the sofa and coffee
table. This hall is the carpeted, open-plan ground-floor
hub of the house. Leading off it are ways to the front
door, the stairs, the office and the kitchen.*

Other areas skeletally represented are:

*The office, also carpeted, represented by (at least) an
easy chair, a small desk and a swivel desk chair.*

*The kitchen, represented by a table with a minimum
of three chairs around it and a separate easy chair,
possibly a modern-style rocker.*

*The play starts in blackout. The house doorbell
sounds. After a moment, November morning light comes
up on the hall area through slatted blinds. It is still
comparatively early. The Man is leading Laverne and
Winnie from the front door where he has just let them
in.*

*He is about forty, still in his shortie dressing gown and
barefoot having recently got out of bed. He is unshaven
and tousled and appears to have had a rough night.*

*Laverne is late twenties, second-generation Afro-
Caribbean south London and heavily pregnant.*

*With her is her daughter, Winnie, nearly nine years
old, a silent watchful child. She carries her school bag.*

Throughout this next exchange, the Man gives both of them barely a glance, particularly Winnie whom he ignores completely. He is uneasy with children.

Laverne (*as they enter*) . . . I'm so sorry, Mr Tate, I arranged all this with Mrs Tate, you see. Last Friday. She kindly agreed I could come and clean this Tuesday instead of tomorrow. Wednesday, I have this doctor's appointment, you see . . .

Man (*only half listening*) . . . yeah . . . yeah . . . that's OK. No problems.

He moves away from them into the kitchen and glances in.

Laverne . . . I did warn Mrs Tate on Friday that I couldn't come Wednesday, that I'd have to come Tuesday. I mean, I did offer her Thursday or even possibly Monday. But Mrs Tate seemed to think Tuesday would be more convenient . . .

Man (*calling in the kitchen*) Paula!

Laverne . . . I mean, it's just for my regular check-up. But I daren't miss it. They don't like it if you miss it . . .

Man (*frowning*) . . . right, right . . . (*Calling, louder*) Paula!

Contenting himself there is no one there he leaves the kitchen, and moves to the office.

Laverne (*continuing regardless, following behind him*) . . . it's only my regular Wednesday check, you see. I mean, I did try having them move it to Thursday but they were adamant for Wednesday and you don't like to miss them, do you? And then this morning, I had to phone Mrs Tate – oh, an hour ago, it must have been – I had to ring her on her mobile . . . I couldn't get no reply from this number . . .

Man . . . no . . . (*Now in the office, calling*) Paulie!

Laverne . . . just to warn her I'd be bringing Winnie with me as well 'cause she was feeling little bit under the weather and she wasn't really up to going to her school. Nothing serious, a little bit throaty, weren't you, darling . . .? Bit throaty, aren't you . . .?

   Winnie nods.

Man Oh, dear . . . (*He returns finally to the hall*) Paulie! (*Muttering*) It's unbelievable . . .!

Laverne (*still trailing behind him with Winnie*) . . . and Mrs Tate ever so kindly said it would be alright if I was to bring Winnie with me just for an hour or so, while I did round. Just while I was working . . .

Man (*moving briskly towards the front door and yelling*) PAULIE! (*Muttering*) I don't believe this . . .!

Laverne Winnie's promised me she's going to sit nice and quiet, aren't you, Winnie?

   Winnie nods.

She's got her books and her homework, she's promised me she won't be in anyone's way. It'll be alright for her to sit here on the sofa here . . .?

Man What time is it?

Laverne Just gone eight thirty.

Man (*going up the stairs*) I must get dressed.

Laverne She's not here then?

Man Who?

Laverne Mrs Tate?

Man Apparently not.

Laverne Oh. Must have gone to work, then.

Man So it would appear . . .

The Man goes off upstairs.

Laverne (*after him*) Winnie's promised she'll be very quiet –

Upstairs a door slams.

(*Tailing off*) – she won't disturb you . . . (*Turning her attention to Winnie*) Now, quiet as a mouse, understand? You finish that homework first, alright? Before you do anything else. You write your essay you should have done last night.

Laverne busies herself removing both their coats, scarves, etc. Winnie sits herself on the sofa. She starts to unpack her school bag producing, among other things, an exercise book and various pens and pencils.

Remember what Mrs Crackle told you to do, don't you? You're to write about 'My Wonderful Day'. So you write that at the top of the page first – 'My Wonderful Day' . . .

Winnie I know . . .

Laverne 'My Wonderful Day', by Winnie Barnstairs.

Winnie Mum . . . !

Laverne Tell you what, you could write it about today, couldn't you? Instead of yesterday? Today, it might be more interesting than yesterday. You could start by saying how we came here on the bus . . .

Winnie (*squirming*) Mum . . .

Laverne Besides, you didn't do nothing yesterday except lie on your bed . . .

Winnie I was ill, wasn't I?

Laverne . . . and then you could write how we just met Mr Tate . . .

Winnie Mum, I can do it! Let me do it.

Laverne I'm just starting you off . . .

Winnie I'm alright, leave me, I can do it . . .

Laverne Alright, alright! I'm only helping . . . Use the pencil. Don't use the pen! You'll get ink on her sofa.

Winnie I've got to use the pen . . .

Laverne She thinks the world of this sofa . . .

Winnie . . . we're not allowed to use pencil . . .

Laverne . . . you can use pencil . . .

Winnie I've got to write in pen. Mrs Crackle says we have to use pen . . .

Laverne Yes, well. Just don't get ink on their sofa, will you? Mrs Tate's pride and joy, this sofa . . .

Winnie I won't.

Laverne I know you and pens. All over your sheets, wasn't it? Be careful, that's all.

> *Laverne goes off to hang up their coats by the front door. Winnie pulls a face and then starts to write. Upstairs, footsteps are heard from the bedroom, which causes her to look up briefly.*
> *Laverne returns.*

Oh, isn't this a beautiful house, Winnie? Didn't I tell you, it was beautiful? Isn't it gorgeous?

Winnie (*absorbed*) Yes.

Laverne She's got lovely taste, Mrs Tate. Lovely little touches. You should see the bedrooms . . . Maybe one day, darling, we'll live somewhere like this, won't we? If I can get a nice job and if your dad starts sending the money again. Well, maybe not quite as big a place as this. But somewhere smaller, nice and cosy – tasteful – just you and me – no, well, three of us by then, won't there be? You, me and your baby brother.

Winnie (*staring at her mother's bump apprehensively*) Yeah . . .

Laverne And when we look out of our window, we'll be looking at this beautiful bluey-green sea and the sunshine and the palm trees. And maybe little white boats bobbing about. It won't be like this, will it? Looking at the road and the houses opposite. It'll be even nicer than this.

Winnie (*muttering*) If we go.

Laverne What?

Winnie (*who's heard this a number of times*) We've got to get there first, haven't we?

Laverne We're going to get there. Don't worry, Winnie. Soon as I've had this baby, we're off, girl. We're going, I promise you. Trust me.

> *Winnie doesn't answer. During the next, Laverne changes out of her boots and into her work shoes. Because of her current state, Winnie has to help her mother.*

Winnie, I mean it, trust me. Trust your mum. I've promised you, haven't I? You know what I feel about promises, don't you? You know when I promise something, I always keep it, don't you?

Winnie Sometimes you can't.

Laverne Can't what?

Winnie Keep them. Promises. Sometimes you can't keep them.

Laverne If you can't keep them, you shouldn't make them. You should never make promises you can't keep, either.

Winnie You promised Dad.

Laverne What?

Winnie (*as she ties Laverne's laces*) When you married him. You promised Dad.

Laverne Yes. Well. That was different. He promised me too, didn't he? Till he broke it.

Winnie Yeah.

Laverne I didn't break that one, he did. Anyway, we're not talking about him, not this morning. Don't get me started on him . . . He gets talked about enough as it is . . . I must get on. I'll start on the kitchen, I think . . .

Winnie You just go carefully . . .

Laverne I'm alright, I'm alright. I feel fine. Another ten days yet.

Winnie After you nearly fell over. Mrs Copthorne said to be careful –

Laverne When I had you I was working right up till the day before you popped out almost –

Winnie That was different. You weren't doing all this cleaning then though, were you? Sitting behind a desk then.

Laverne I was right as rain. Felt perfectly fine. Now, you just get on.

Laverne makes a move towards the kitchen. Winnie shrugs and gives up. Her mother is impossible.

Laverne goes out briefly but returns almost at once, attempting to tie an apron, stretched impossibly tightly around her increased girth.

Oy! Oy! Yes, Miss! Talking of promises . . . what day is it today, then? *Quel jour est-lui aujourd'hui?* Tuesday. *C'est mardi, n'est-ce pas?* And what do we do every *mardi?*

Winnie Oh, Mum . . . No.

Laverne Tuesday is French day. We practise our French today, don't we?

Winnie I can't. Not here!

Laverne Yes, you can.

Winnie What about you?

Laverne I'm working. There's an excuse for me. No excuse for you. Day off school.

Winnie I'm ill.

Laverne No, you're not.

Winnie I got this terrible throat. I can't talk in French.

Laverne You're not ill.

Winnie I am . . .

Laverne (*still struggling to tie her apron*) Soon as we got on the bus, you forgot all about it.

Winnie (*going to Laverne's assistance*) I didn't want to go to school, I was worried about you.

Laverne That's very kind of you. But you worry about me in French.

Winnie I don't know how to say it.

Laverne Well, look it up then. You've got your dictionary with you, haven't you? If you don't know a word for something, you look it up. That's the only way you learn, Winnie. Soon as I'm done here, I'm switching to French as well. You know what we said. We'll learn together, won't we? That's what we agreed. We both promised. We'll be glad of it later. When we get there. Very few of them speak English there, you know. My grandmother, she couldn't speak a word of English – did you know that?

Winnie Yeah, yeah. You told me.

Laverne (*in rather dodgy French*) *Ah! Ah! Ah! En français s'il vous plaît, ma chérie.*

Winnie (*only slightly better*) *Oui, maman.*

Laverne *Bien! Bien! Je retour bientôt. Attente là, ma fille.*

Winnie (wearily) *Oui, maman.*

> *Laverne goes off to the kitchen.*
> *Winnie stares after her.*

(*To herself*) She's mad! Mad! (*After a moment's consideration*) *Elle est fou. Ma mère est une loonie!*

> *Winnie continues with writing. This is the first of several occasions when we see her on her own. She concentrates on her essay, writing slowly and laboriously with her pen. She takes in events occurring around her without reaction or comment, only sneaking a covert glance when she thinks no one sees her, which in general they don't. As a result, she becomes the child in the corner whom no one notices.*

Winnie (*to herself slowly, as she writes*) My . . . Wonderful . . . Day . . . by . . . Winnie . . .

NINE A.M.

The Man comes downstairs, now dressed. He is talking on his mobile. Hearing him, after a quick glance, Winnie gets her head down and concentrates on her writing.

Man (*as he enters . . . on the phone, not even glancing at Winnie*) . . . yes . . . yes . . . where are you at present, Tiffy? . . . What, in her office? In *my* office? . . . June's in there with you, then? . . . Is she listening? . . . (*Laughing sarcastically*) I bet . . . I bet she is . . . no, no . . . Paula's not here. Definitely . . . I don't know, do I? . . . I've tried it. Dozens of times. She's not answering . . . no . . . She talks to the bloody cleaning woman, she refuses to talk to me . . . Look, we can't – Listen, Tiffy darling, we can't – Look, come round here. Hop in a taxi and come round here straight away. We can't talk on the phone – not with you in the middle of the office, can we? . . . Not with June earwigging . . . No, there's no one here at present . . . nobody . . . Look, Tiffy, just grab a taxi, darling . . . Oh, yes, has it? Has it? I'll be keen to see that – see how that's turned out . . . Yes . . . Listen, grab a copy, bring it round with you, darling. We can have a look at it here . . . Yes. See you, darling. Yes see you soon, babe . . . love you, precious. (*He rings off. To himself*) Right, coffee, coffee, coffee . . .

He goes off into the office, briefly.
Winnie continues to write.

(*Off from the office*) Oh, shit!

The Man returns with an empty Cona jug.

(*Seeing Winnie for the first time*) Alright there, kid?

Winnie *Oui, monsieur. Merci beaucoup.*

The Man goes out to the kitchen, staring at Winnie,
puzzled.
    Slight pause.
    Winnie continues to write.
    Voices from the kitchen.

Laverne (*off, from the kitchen*) . . . oh, no, that's quite
alright, Mr Tate. You carry on in here.

Man (*off, from the kitchen*) Won't be second, Mrs . . .
er . . . Just making some fresh coffee . . .

Laverne (*off*) Would you like me to make you some?

Man (*off*) No, no. It's alright. I'm just topping up the
machine in the office . . .

Laverne (*off*) I could easily make you some. It's no
trouble . . .

Man (*off*) No, no. I can manage, Mrs . . . er . . .

In a moment, the Man returns from the kitchen with
the jug now filled with water and a bag of fresh ground
coffee. He goes off again to the office, whistling under
his breath.
    Winnie writes on.
    From the kitchen the sound of crockery clattering
and cutlery clinking as Laverne tidies away.
    The house phone rings loudly.
    In the office, the Man answers it.

Man (*off, answering*) . . . Hallo . . . Brian, mate! . . . how
did it go then? . . . yes . . . yes . . . no . . . yes . . .
(*Bellowing with laughter*) . . . She what? . . . (*He laughs*
again at length) . . . She didn't? . . .

The Man gives another huge laugh. Whatever it is
whoever she is did, it is evidently hilarious.

yep . . . yep . . . *fucking* hell! . . . never . . . fuck me –! . . .

Hang on a tick, Brian, just a tick . . . Don't go away,
I want to hear the rest of this . . .

He laughs again. The office door is heard to close.
The Man's laugh is heard again faintly now, muffled.
From time to time we hear his laugh again through the
door.
Winnie, who has reacted to none of this, continues
to write her essay, concentrating deeply on her task.
After a moment, Laverne returns from the kitchen in
kitchen gloves.

Laverne Alright, darling?

Winnie *Oui, maman. Je suis très content.*

Laverne Good girl. *Est ce que quelques choses que tu*
desire, cherie?

Winnie *Non. Rien, maman, merci.*

Laverne (*inspecting Winnie's work*) *Ah. Bon! C'est bon.*
Bravo!

Winnie (*instinctively covering her work with her hand*)
Merci, maman.

Laverne makes to move back to the kitchen then, seeing
her bag where she left it, stops, remembering something.

Laverne *Ah, Winnie, ma chère. Ici.*

Laverne rummages in her bag and produces a
crumpled travel leaflet.
. *In the office, the Man laughs again.*

Winnie *Quoi?*

Laverne (*putting the leaflet next to Winnie*) *Là.*
Regardez. Martinique.

Winnie (*without great enthusiasm*) *Ah. Oui.*

Laverne *C'est belle, non?*

Winnie *Oui.*

Laverne (*opening the leaflet*) *Tu regarde. Les montagnes . . . les plages . . . les voitures . . . les –* (*unsure of the word*) *– les palm trees – les arbres de palmes – c'est très belle, non?*

Winnie (*trying her best*) *Oui. C'est trop belle, maman.*

In the office, the Man laughs again.

Laverne puts the leaflet down beside Winnie.

Laverne (*as she does this*) *Ici. Là. Pour tu, ma chérie.*

Winnie (*without touching it*) *Merci, maman.*

Laverne moves back towards the kitchen.

Laverne *Cinq minutes. Je retourne. Bien?*

Winnie *Bien.*

Laverne goes. Winnie glances briefly at the leaflet.

Ma mère est complètement weird.

NINE FORTY-FIVE A.M.

Winnie puts down the leaflet and returns to her writing.
In the office, the Man laughs again.
A pause.
The doorbell rings.
Winnie ignores it. After a second, it rings again.
Laverne comes from the kitchen.
As she does so, the office door opens briefly.

Man Can someone get that?

Laverne (*calling*) Yes, I'm going, I'm just going, Mr Tate. I'll get it.

Man (*off, calling*) Probably be Miss Cavendish . . .

The office door closes again.
     Laverne goes out to the front door. In a moment she returns with Tiffany, smartly dressed for work, in her mid-twenties. She is holding the morning post which she's just picked up from the mat and a brown envelope containing a DVD which she has brought from the office.

Laverne (*as they enter*) Please come through. Mr Tate's just through here . . .

Tiffany (*cheerfully*) Thanks. Hi, I'm Tiffany, by the way. Just in case you were wondering who you were letting through the door . . . I work with Mr Tate.

Laverne How do you do? I'm Mrs – Laverne. Laverne Barnstairs. I'm the cleaner. Doing a little bit of cleaning for him.

Tiffany Yah, jolly good. You carry on, don't let me interrupt. Through here is he?

Laverne In the office, there. I think he's just on the phone, I think.

Another bellow of laughter from the office.

Tiffany (*hearing this*) Yes, well, I'll – wait a – (*Seeing Winnie for the first time*) Oh, hallo. Who's this, then?

Laverne This is my daughter.

Tiffany Oh, isn't she pretty! Hallo, there! And what's your name?

Winnie hesitates, uncertain how to reply.

Laverne Say hallo, Winnie.

Winnie *Bonjour, mam'selle.*

Tiffany (*enchanted*) Oh! (*To Laverne*) Isn't that lovely? (*Crouching down, to Winnie*) What's your name, then?

Winnie *Je m'appelle Winnie, mam'selle.*

Tiffany Winnie! And how old are you, Winnie?

Winnie *J'ai neuf ans, mam'selle.*

Laverne Nine. She's nine next month.

Tiffany Enchanting. Does she always speak in French?

Laverne On Tuesdays, she does. I encourage her every Tuesday.

Tiffany (*mystified*) Oh.

Laverne We both do. (*To Winnie*) *Nous parlons le français toutes les mardis, n'est-ce pas, ma petite?*

Winnie *Oui, maman. C'est vrai.*

Laverne We're not that good, but we're getting better, aren't we?

Tiffany How brilliant. What a brilliant idea! Every Tuesday, you say?

Laverne Every Tuesday, yes.

Tiffany What do you speak on Wednesday? German?

Laverne – er . . .

Tiffany I think that's truly a brilliant idea. Brilliant! What a fantastic way to learn languages, isn't it? We could use a different one every day, couldn't we? Thursdays, Spanish. Fridays, Dutch –

Laverne Possibly, yes . . .

Tiffany (*enthused*) I mean, we're generally dreadful in this country, aren't we? Never bother to learn anyone else's language, do we? And they're always learning ours.

During the next Tiffany removes her coat and goes off to the front door to hang it up. Laverne takes the opportunity to smarten Winnie up a little.

(*Off*) I mean, you go to somewhere like Holland, they practically all speak English, don't they? Even little kids. Or Germany. Germany's the same. I mean, even, *even* let's face it, the French – they at least have a go. No, they all put us to shame.

Tiffany returns, still talking.

Golly. I really think you're on to a winner. Now all you have to do is to persuade everyone else to join in. (*To Winnie*) *Bon! Bien! Excellente! Encore! Bravo!*

Winnie *Merci, mam'selle.*

Tiffany Oh, she's just enchanting. So sweet. How old did she say she was?

Laverne (*proudly*) She's just coming up to nine. She'll be nine next month.

Tiffany You must be so proud of her.

Laverne (*modestly*) Yes, well . . . I don't tell her that, though!

Tiffany I bet her daddy's proud of her, too. (*To Winnie*) I bet you're your daddy's pride and joy, aren't you?

Winnie *Non, mam'selle.*

Tiffany No? *Non?*

Winnie *Mon père n'est pas ici. Il depart depuis quelques mois.*

Laverne Her dad's gone.

Tiffany Oh, I am sorry. Was he very young?

Laverne No, but she was. The one he went off with.

Tiffany Oh. (*Realising*) Oh, I see. I'm so sorry, I thought you meant he was . . .

Laverne He was old enough to know better.

Tiffany (*of Laverne's condition*) And now you're – ? Oh dear, how difficult for you. When's baby due?

Laverne Another ten days.

Tiffany Oh, dear. Shouldn't you be . . .? I mean . . .?

Laverne I can manage. Soon as he's arrived, we're off, aren't we, girl? Soon as he's arrived . . .

Tiffany Your husband?

Laverne No, the baby! Not my husband, not him. We're best off without him, aren't we, Winnie?

Winnie does not reply.
A short silence.

Tiffany So you know it's a boy, then?

Laverne Oh, yes.

Tiffany How exciting! And have you settled on a name yet? That's always the tricky bit. Isn't it?

Laverne Three. I've settled on three.

Tiffany Oh, what are those?

Laverne Jericho, Alexander, Samson . . .

Tiffany Golly!

Winnie rolls her eyes.

What made you chose those? Jericho? That's terribly unusual. What made you choose Jericho?

Laverne After my grand-dad. I've chosen three, that way he gets a choice. When he's little, he can either be Jerry or Alex or Sam. Then once he grows up if he wants to, he can choose one of the big ones . . .

Tiffany How frightfully sensible. So he'll have masses of choices. I wish I'd been given choices when I was little. All I got was Tiffany Louise. Which left me with Tiffy or Tiff or Lou. Which always makes me sound like a cross between a quarrel and lavatory. (*To Winnie*) What about you? Did your mummy give you a choice of names as well?

Laverne She's just the two, she has. Winona Marguerite.

Winnie scowls.

Tiffany Marguerite? Wow! That's a great one! Marguerite!

Laverne She's not too fond of that one, are you, Winnie? I've told her she might when she grows up. When she grows into it.

Tiffany Yes, I know what you mean. You do need a bit of a cleavage, don't you, before you start calling yourself Marguerite? It's the sort of name that goes with breasts, isn't it?

Tiffany laughs. Laverne smiles politely. Tiffany remembers there is a child present and checks herself. A slight pause.

(*She slaps her own face*) Sorry. Where are your family from originally?

Laverne They came from Martinique. My mother came over with my grandma nearly thirty years ago. We're planning to go back soon aren't we, Winnie?

Winnie again does not reply.

Tiffany Ah! Hence the French! *La belle Martinique*. All is clear. How terrific! That's off the coast of Africa, isn't it?

Laverne No, it's in the Caribbean.

Tiffany Oh, yes, of course it is. (*Slapping herself*) Come on, Tiffy!

Laverne Fifteen-point-five miles south of Dominica and twenty-three miles north of St Lucia.

Tiffany Oh, yes. Got it! I think I was probably thinking of Mozambique.

Laverne No, no, not Mozambique. Martinique.

Tiffany Or possibly Madagascar? One of those. (*Laughing*) *God*, aren't we *hopeless* in this country? We don't know where anything is, do we? Not just abroad, but anywhere. You know, I don't think I could even find my way to Scunthorpe.

Laverne I don't think I could.

The two smile at each other.

Tiffany (*laughing*) Hopeless, aren't we? Absolutely hopeless. God, when I think of the fortune my parents splashed out on my education. Honestly!

Laverne Mine didn't.

Tiffany Well, good for them. Save your money, I say! (*She laughs*)

Laverne I still don't know nothing. (*She laughs*)

Tiffany laughs with her.
The Man has entered from the office. The women look a bit guilty.

Man (*to Tiffany*) Ah, you're here.

Tiffany Morning.

Man How long you been out here?

Tiffany Just a couple of minutes.

Laverne Well, I must get on. Finish the kitchen. Excuse me.

Man Yes, you carry on, Mrs – er . . .

Tiffany Sure you can manage?

Laverne Oh, yes . . .

Tiffany I mean, don't, for God's sake, don't try lifting the stove or anything, will you?

Laverne I can manage.

Man She can manage.

Laverne Nice talking to you, Tiffany. See you later.

    Laverne goes off to the kitchen.

Tiffany See you later, Laverne.

Man (*softly, to Tiffany*) What were you doing?

Tiffany Just chatting.

Man (*smiling, though he means it*) I don't pay you to chat, you know. Either of you.

Tiffany Sorry, I thought you were on the phone.

Man Come in here, then. We need to talk . . .

    He starts to move back towards the office.

What did you call her just then?

Tiffany (*following him*) Who?

Man Mrs Whatsname? What did you call her?

Tiffany Who, Laverne?

Man Laverne? What sort of name's that?

Tiffany It's her name.

Man How do you find that out?

Tiffany She just told me.

Man She's worked here for ages, I've never known her name's Laverne. Laverne?

Tiffany (*aware of Winnie*) Shhh!

Man *Laverne?* What sort of name's that for a cleaner?

Tiffany (*to Winnie*) You'll be alright there, will you, darling?

Winnie *Oui merci, ma'mselle. Je suis très content.*

Man What's she talking in? French?

Tiffany Yes.

Man Why's she talking French?

Tiffany She does on Tuesdays.

Man Why the hell does she usually talk in French – ?

His mobile rings. He checks it.

(*Seeing the caller ID*) Shit! It's her.

Tiffany (*indicating the office, furtively*) You want to take it in there?

But the Man has already answered.

Man Hallo, Paula . . . yes . . . what? . . . who? . . . no, she's not here . . . of course she's not . . . what makes you think she'd be here, for God's sake? . . . Bollocks . . . Paula, that is plain bollocks, darling . . . you are talking bollocks . . .

During the next:
   Tiffany indicates that Winnie is in the room.
   The Man indicates that Tiffany should take Winnie into the office.

Tiffany (*under the phone call, softly, to Winnie*) Come with me! This way! Come on we can wait in here, Winnie . . .

   Tiffany bundles up Winnie, helping her with her belongings, and steers her into the office.

Man (*as this happens, pacing*) . . . listen, Paula – Paula – Paula – where are you now? . . . no . . . no . . . because I was worried . . . I was, I was worried . . . about you, who else? . . . yes, I was . . . I *was* . . . Paula . . . Paula . . . Quieten down, love . . . will you just – QUIETEN DOWN, WOMAN! (*Kicking at the furniture, quieter*) Shit!!!

   He moves towards the front door as his conversation starts to hot up.

Yes! . . . YES! . . . of course I was worried . . . well, why shouldn't I be, for God's sake? . . . you suddenly piss off in the middle of the bloody night, I've every reason to be fucking –

   Winnie has been propelled by Tiffany into the office. The door slams behind them, cutting off the Man's voice. Simultaneously the lights change abruptly to indicate the office area.

TEN THIRTY A.M.

Tiffany tries to make everything appear normal for Winnie.

Tiffany He's just talking with someone . . . He gets quite excited sometimes but you musn't worry about it. He doesn't really mean it. Not really.

A further bellow of anger from the hall.
   Pause.

(*Indicating the easy chair*) You want to sit there, darling.

Winnie sits obediently, still holding her possessions.

He's a very clever person. He's brilliant. He's actually quite famous. Did you know that? Have you ever seen him? On television. He has his own programme. Have you ever watched his programme? No? Surely you must have seen him? He was actually on the front cover of the *Radio Times*. No?

Winnie (*shaking her head*) *Non, mam'selle. Je ne vois pas le TV.*

Tiffany You don't watch television?

Winnie (*shaking her head*) *Non, mam'selle. Jamais.*

Tiffany What, never? You never watch it? Well, you are a funny little girl, aren't you? I thought all children watched television. Does your mother not let you watch it?

Winnie *Oui. Mais je ne l'apprécie pas.*

Tiffany What? You don't like it? None of it?

Winnie (*shrugging*) *Non. Je le trouve être ennuyeux plutôt.*

Tiffany What do you like to do then?

Winnie *J'ai lu les livres. J'effectue mon travail d'école. J'écris parfois.*

Tiffany *Écris?* Oh, you write?

Winnie *Oui, mam'selle.*

Tiffany What? Poems?

Winnie shakes her head.

Stories?

Winnie nods.

Is that what you were doing just now? Writing?

Winnie nods.

Tiffany (*reaching towards her*) May I see?

Winnie clutches the exercise book to her more tightly.

No? Is it secret? Your special secret? Is it about private things? Do you like to keep secrets, do you? I used to have secrets when I was a little girl. Things I would never, ever tell anyone. But the important thing to remember is, if you do write them down, to make sure no one never, ever sees them except you. It's good to have secrets when you're young. Maybe, as you grow up, they're not quite as magic . . . (*She tails off*) Yep.

Pause.

When I was at school, you know, I used to keep a diary. Do you keep a diary? No?

Pause.

But I never let anyone see my diary. It was my most special, special secret book. And I used to keep it locked up. With a key. Until some boy went and . . .

Pause.

I was at boarding school, you know. Do you know what a boarding school is? It's when you go away from your home, when your parents send you away – even though they tell you they still love you – they send you away to live with lots and lots of other children. But you're there all on your own.

Pause.

And to start with you feel terribly, terribly sad being away from home but in the end you get used to it. And then you even start to like the school a little bit and some of the people there become your friends. And you may even start to love some of them, just a little. But it's a different sort of love, you see. It's what I call lonely love. There's all different sorts of love, you know. Did you know that?

Winnie nods.

But with lonely love, you see, it can never take the place of real love, however hard you try to make it. And the saddest thing of all is that in the end maybe because of it, you even start to love your parents a little tiny bit less. Do you see?

Pause.

So don't ever, ever let your mummy send you away. Because you love her very much, don't you?

Winnie nods.

And I can see she loves you very much, doesn't she?

Winnie nods.
    From outside the door, another yell of anger from the Man.

Man (*off, yelling*) OH, COME ON!!!

Winnie stares at the door. Tiffany searches round for something to distract the child. She snatches up the envelope she has brought.

Tiffany (*with the tone of a frenetic children's TV host*) Tell you what. I've got a great idea. While Mummy's busy, let's you and me watch this together, shall we?

She rips open the envelope and produces a DVD. It's a commercially mass-produced copy of a corporate video, labelled FANTACITY!

This is something we've just finished. It's very exciting. Would you like to watch this with me? Would you?

Winnie nods.

Yes! Now, how do we work this thing. It's complicated. Everything he has is complicated, nothing's ever simple. Where does this go? Oh, yes. Then we can watch it on that big screen, can't we? (*Slotting the disc into the console on the desk*) Be like going to the movies, won't it? You enjoy going to the movies, don't you?

Winnie *Non, mam'selle, je ne vais pas au cinéma beaucoup.*

Tiffany *Non?* No? Never?

Winnie *Ma mère dit qu'il coûte trop d'argent.*

Tiffany (*half to herself*) Weird kid. Weird.

She pulls out the desk chair to sit beside Winnie, grabbing the remote as she does so.

There. That's a plasma screen. Have you ever seen one that big? The man who has everything, honestly! Every gadget under the sun, he's got it.

Tiffany points the remote. After a second the (unseen) screen lights up and there's a burst of cheesy music. Winnie stares at the screen increasingly unimpressed.
Tiffany, on the other hand, is in a state of considerable excitement.

(*Over this introductory music*) I helped him on this, you know. Mainly typing the script and a little bit with the continuity. You know, if we're terribly lucky and watch very carefully, we might just catch a glimpse of me. Ever so briefly. If they haven't cut me out. (*Indicating the screen*) There! Just look at that! Isn't it fantastic?

On the disc the music fades down slightly and the Man's voice is heard.

Man (*his voice*) Hi! It's my pleasure to introduce a new experience in the art of living. Welcome to the amazing world of FANTACITY. I'm Kevin Tate and for the next few minutes, I'd like to show you around so you can see for yourselves some of the incredible features FANTACITY has to offer you – yes, and that means *you*, Mr and Mrs Business Person.

Tiffany (*to Winnie*) He's charismatic, isn't he? The camera adores him . . .

Man So, hey, tell you what, why don't you and I stroll around a little so I can point out just a few of the extra special features FANTACITY has to offer.

A short peak in the music and then: –

(*In another acoustic*) FANTACITY has been described as being part business park, part shopping mall. But, you know, neither of those descriptions can do FANTACITY real justice. I prefer to describe it as a place where business and retail are free to meet and integrate with the consumer. It's a place where, at the end of the day, everyone goes home happy – and for those who prefer to stay on, well, FANTACITY stays open 24/7, catering for your every need.

Another brief music peak.

(*In another acoustic, again*) FANTACITY offers workspace such as this for the business which thinks big – right down to the smaller scale – such as this – for smaller specialist firms and for those just starting up . . .

Another brief music peak. Winnie, already bored, is beginning to slide down in her seat. Tiffany remains glued to the screen.

(*In yet another acoustic*) And OK, retailers, in case you're feeling neglected, how about this for floor space? Imagine how your display would look in an environment like this. Or perhaps this? Or this?

The music peaks again.

Alright, alright, I hear you saying, it's all very well but these are just offices and shops, I can see those anywhere, any time. What's so special about FANTACITY? What on earth is someone like Kevin Tate getting so excited about? Well, I'll show you. Come with me to see the pleasure side of FANTACITY.

Music peak.

(*In another acoustic*) Just take a look at this.

Tiffany (*excitedly*) This is my bit, this my bit coming up! I'm a film star!

Man Here's what really caught my attention, what definitely got the five-star, gold-plated Kevin Tate diamond seal of approval. This is one of the three magnificent swimming pools FANTACITY has to offer. This is the largest of them, open free to all FANTACITY users – shopper or salesperson, typist or tycoon . . .

Tiffany That's me! That's me! That's me! There on the sun lounger!

Man . . . all absolutely free! (*With a little laugh in his voice*) Though that doesn't, I'm afraid, include the young lady!

Tiffany God! That costume makes me look huge! So fat!

Man Moving along – if I can tear you away – moving along –

The soundtrack stops abruptly. There's a brief blip and then Paula's voice interrupts.

Paula (*her voice, different acoustic, briskly*) Sorry to interrupt your tour of this ghastly little development, everyone. Hallo there, my name is Paula Hammond and I'm currently married to that deceitful little shit Kevin Tate.

Tiffany (*aghast*) Oh, my God. It's her!

Winnie has sat up again and taken notice.

Paula . . . yes, that's him, the forty-something year old, seen there drooling over Tiffany Cavendish – she's the tubby superannnuated teenager on the sunbed. But what you might also be interested to learn, dear business people, is that those two are currently fucking each other's brains out – if that is even remotely possible – considering that neither of them has a solitary brain cell –

Tiffany has grabbed the remote and feverishly fumbles with the stop button.

Tiffany (*finally freezing the disc*) Oh, my God! Oh, my God! Oh, my God!

She rushes out of the room, forgetting Winnie.

(*Calling as she goes, in panic*) Kevin! Kevin! KEVIN!

Winnie sits for a moment, digesting what she has seen. She then takes up her note book and continues writing. Agitated voices outside.

ELEVEN-THIRTY A.M.

After a moment, Tiffany returns with the Man following her.

Tiffany (*pointing at the screen, in panic*) Look! It's her! She's on it! Look!

Man (*staring at the screen*) What's she doing on there?

Tiffany I told you, she's on our DVD.

Man What DVD?

Tiffany I keep telling you. The one we did for FANTACITY.

Man She can't be. (*Grabbing the remote from her*) Give me that –

Tiffany No! Don't play back any more of it!

Man Why not? I want to see it . . . I want to see what that bitch has done!

Tiffany Not in front of – (*Indicating Winnie, mouthing*) – the kid!

Man (*aware of Winnie*) Oh, yes. (*To Winnie*) You want to sit in the other room for a minute, kid? Just while we have a look at the DVD. We just discovered it may have . . .

Tiffany helps Winnie up.

Tiffany . . . adult content.

Man Wouldn't want you to see that. Your mum might not approve. Off you go! Chop! Chop!

Winnie (*as she goes*) Oui, monsieur. Merci beaucoup.

Tiffany brings Winnie back to the living area with all

*her gear. As she does so the lights cross-fade briefly to
the Hall again.*
    The Man exits into the office during the next.
    A clinking of plates from the kitchen.

Tiffany (*registering this sound*) Listen, darling, perhaps
you'd like to sit in the kitchen with Mummy? Keep her
company. Would you like to do that? Jolly good.

She propels Winnie through the kitchen doorway.

That's it, straight through here. Good girl.

Tiffany brings Winnie into the kitchen.
    The lights, again, follow them to the area.
    *This is represented by a solid plain wood table and
one or two chairs around it.*
    *Laverne appears, looking weary and rather
breathless.*

Brought Winnie to see you, Mummy. She thought you
might be lonely.

Laverne I hope she's not been getting in people's way.

Tiffany No, no, no. Not at all. We've been having a
lovely chat, haven't we, Winnie?

Laverne Have you been getting under their feet, Winnie?

Winnie *Non, maman. J'ai été tranquille comme souris.*

Tiffany She's been as good as gold.

Man (*off, angrily*) Tiffy! Tiffy!

Tiffany Excuse me, must get back. Masses to do.

Tiffany hurries out.

Laverne Sit there then. Don't get under my feet either.
I've nearly finished in here.

Winnie sits at the table and lays out her stuff once more.

It was like a hurricane had been through this kitchen. God knows what they were up to last night, those two. Hurling food at each other, that's what it looked like. I'm going to give this a final wipe, then I'm off upstairs to do the bedrooms.

Laverne moves out of view to clean something.

Winnie You alright, Mum?

Laverne (*off*) I'm alright. Why shouldn't I be?

Winnie You look tired.

Laverne (*off*) I'll have a sit down in a minute.

Winnie You better had.

Laverne (*off*) Have you been practising your French?

Winnie Yeah.

Laverne (*off*) *Pardon? Qu'avez-vous dit?*

Winnie (*wearily*) *Oui, maman.*

Laverne (*off*) That's better! *C'est bien!*

Winnie sighs.
    Laverne reappears with a half-finished mug of tea and an opened can of Coke, which she plonks in front of Winnie.

Laverne *Voilà!*

Winnie (*automatically*) *Merci, maman.*

A silence between them.
    From off, an angry yell from the Man, a crash and a cry from Tiffany.

Laverne What they up to now then, for heaven's sake?

Laverne sits at the table to finish her tea.

You see? What do I always say to you? What did that man tell us in church the other day? All this money and they're still not happy. Let that be a warning to you, Winnie. It can't bring you happiness, darling. Be warned, darling.

Winnie is silent, drinking her Coke.

When your grandad and grandma, when they first got here, when they first arrived in this country, my mum told me they were the happiest two people in the whole world. And you know why she said that was? They were like Adam and Eve, she said, who had nothing in the world, no possessions, no money, nothing. Who'd just walked out of Paradise. And from then on, he found work, she found work, they made a bit of money, bought a little house, filled it with things, worldly possessions and everything went downhill from there. The more they had, the more miserable they became. Well, we'll soon be walking back to Paradise, darling, you, me and little Jericho. Any day now. I've nearly saved enough. Then the three of us – off we'll go – on that plane. You'll see.

Winnie (*softly*) Not if you die, we won't.

Laverne (*startled*) What?

Winnie Not if you die.

Laverne What are you talking about? Die? I'm not going to die, you stupid thing.

Winnie You might do.

Laverne hugs Winnie to her.

Laverne Who said anything about dying? Don't worry, I'm not dying not yet. No way.

Winnie You might if you don't take care of yourself, you might.

Laverne Be a few years yet, I can promise.

Tiffany bursts into the room, distraught. She has apparently forgotten that Winnie and Laverne are in there.

She slaps her face a couple of times, in an attempt to control herself. Looking round the room, she runs out of view briefly and returns with a length of hastily torn-off kitchen roll.

She runs out again, attempting to mop her eyes and blow her nose simultaneously.

The Man is heard calling her.

Man (*off, conciliatory*) Tiffy . . . Tiff! Come on, now! Don't be silly!

Laverne (*significantly gesturing after Tiffany*) There! You see. Be warned. (*Finally draining her mug and rising*) Well, I can't sit around here, can I? (*Indicating Winnie's can of Coke*) Finished with that?

Winnie swigs the last mouthful.
The doorbell rings.

Oh. Somebody else arriving. I hope someone's going to answer it.

Laverne promptly scoops up the empty can. She momentarily disappears from view, getting rid of the empties.

(*Off*) How are you getting on with your homework, then? Finished your essay yet?

Winnie Not quite.

Laverne (*off*) 'My Wonderful Day'. How's it getting on?

Winnie It isn't finished.

Laverne (*off*) You'll have Mrs Crackle after you if you don't finish your essay.

Winnie Not the essay, the day. The day isn't finished yet, is it?

Laverne (*off, not hearing her*) You'll be in all sorts of trouble, you don't hand it in first thing tomorrow morning.

Winnie I will. (*Muttering*) Soon as today's finished, I will.

Laverne re-emerges with the vacuum cleaner.

Laverne Right, you sit here quietly. Don't move. Don't get in nobody's way. I'll be back in a minute, then I'll take you home, alright?

Winnie OK.

Laverne Tell you what, you can read me it tonight, your essay. How about that?

Winnie Probably.

Laverne (*as she makes to leave*) And keep practising your French, too. Promise is a promise.

Winnie (*wearily*) Oui, maman.

She pulls a face behind her mother's back.

TWELVE THIRTY P.M.

As Laverne leaves, she nearly collides in the doorway with the Man and his newly arrived visitor, Josh, about the same age as the Man.
Laverne steps back to allow them to pass.

Josh Whoops! Mothers and children first.

Man (*waving Laverne through*) Alright, Mrs . . . er . . .
you come through first, come through . . .

Laverne Thank you, Mr Tate. (*To Josh*) Good morning.
Finished in here. All clear now.

Josh (*a bit the worse for wear*) Morning.

Laverne goes out with the vacuum.

Man Sorry to drag you out, mate.

Josh No, as I say, it was Colin's leaving do last night and
one thing led to another, as you'll well know . . . (*Seeing
Winnie*) Hallo, hallo, who's this then? Where did this
little thing spring from? Who are you, then?

Man Her kid. The cleaner's kid.

Josh Hallo. You're pretty, aren't you? Like your mummy.
Your mummy's pretty, too. Hallo. Want to say hallo, do
you?

Winnie *Bonjour, monsieur.*

Josh Eh?

Man She doesn't speak English.

Josh Really?

Man She only speaks French.

Josh Does she?

Man Apparently.

Josh Her mum speaks English.

Man Oh, yes, she does.

Josh How come she has a kid who only speaks French?

Man (*slightly impatiently*) I don't know, do I?

Josh She must speak English if her mum does.

Man I've never heard her speak English, anyway.

Josh Do you speak English? *Parlez-vous Anglais?*

Winnie *Non, monsieur. Je ne parle pas l'anglais, pas aujourd'hui. Je parle seulement français le mardi.*

Josh What did she say?

Man There you are, what did I tell you?

Josh I never heard of that before. A mum who speaks English and a kid who –

Man So, anyway. What did you find out, then?

Josh Do you mind if I get that glass of water . . . ?

Man Yes, go ahead, help yourself.

Josh (*disappearing from view momentarily*) I'm that dehydrated after last night . . . No, as I was saying, as soon as I got to your office, the minute you called me – which of these buttons do you press to get water –?

Man Either one. Green one's for ambient. Blue one's ice cold.

Josh (*off*) Oh, yes – there you go – what's wrong with good old fashioned taps? – yes, I say – I fast forwarded through the first two or three DVDs in the batch, just to check whether they were corrupted as well – and . . .

Man What, all of them?

Josh (*returning with a glass of water*) As far as I could tell, every single one. Good job you didn't send them out, wasn't it?

Man (*pounding the table*) Shit! Shit! Shit!

331

Josh (*admonishingly*) Kev!

Man What?

Josh (*indicating Winnie*) Better watch the language.

Man What bloody language? She doesn't even speak it. No, truth be told, I should have chucked Paula out of the bedroom window last night when I had the chance.

Josh (*sitting*) Bad?

Man Terrible.

Josh Where's she now?

Man I don't know. Walked out. Finally.

Josh When?

Man Last night, early this morning. I was asleep. Woke up, she'd taken off . . .

Josh Well . . .

Man Finally. At long last. And I pray for ever. (*Reflecting*) You know, I think she must be slightly mad.

Josh Paula?

Man Genetic, you know. Faulty genes. Violent streak. There's a streak of violence in her which is unnatural. I mean, in a woman it's not natural, is it? I mean a woman's natural nature is not a violent one, is it?

Josh I've known violent women. Very violent ones.

Man No, but they were unnatural. That's my point. I mean, with men violence is a natural ingredient, it's germane in their nature. But women. I mean, take the phrase 'feminine qualities' – what are they? – gentle, quiet spoken – submissive – agreeable – soft – don't argue with you . . .

Josh (*doubtfully*) Yes . . . I don't think I've met many of those. Maybe I've been unlucky. I mean, they may start out that way – but then they – you know – go off . . .

Man Paula went off. Like last week's milk. She always agreed with me to start with. Always. Even when I had to talk her round first. No, she's mad. Certifiable. I wed a lunatic, Josh.

Josh So. That's it then?

Man Marry an angel, divorce a monster. That's what my dad used to say. He should have known. Got through four of them, didn't he, before we buried him.

Josh Well. I have to say it's been a long time coming.

They reflect gloomily.

I was your best man.

Man Yes.

Josh She looked lovely, then. She did, she looked like an angel. Beautiful. I really fancied Paula then. Not that she'd have . . . with me. Only had eyes for you in those days.

Man Did you try it then? With her? With my wife? What, on our bloody wedding day? You're joking!

Josh Well . . . I may have hinted to her. In a roundabout way. You know, jokingly, like. You know, if you ever get bored of him . . .

Man What did she say to that?

Josh She told me to – (*with a brief glance at Winnie*) – you know – get stuffed.

Man Quite right, you cheeky berk! (*Slight pause*) You're welcome to her now, mate.

They laugh.
  A silence.
  Winnie watches them covertly.
  Josh notices this.
  Winnie resumes her writing again.

Josh (*regarding her suspiciously*) You sure that kid doesn't speak English?

Man Why?

Josh I get the feeling she does.

Man No. She doesn't. Unless she's lying.

Josh Lying? Why should she be lying?

Man I don't know. She's a woman, isn't she? They're all bloody liars.

  Pause.

I'm going to have a beer. Want some more of that?

Josh God, come on, be fair. *Two* glasses of water in one day? I'm already over my limit.

  The Man goes off momentarily.

Man (*off*) Tiffy went crazy as well,

Josh Tiffany?

Man (*off*) She was the one that saw it first. Ran upstairs. Howling her eyes out.

Josh Why she do that? What made her react like that?

Man (*returning with a can of beer*) Search me. Paula calling her fat, probably.

Josh Fat?

Man She calls her that on the DVD.

334

Josh What? Fat? Tiffy's not fat, is she?

Man (*sitting*) Try telling her. Anyway she's upstairs now, lying on the bed. Texting. Stupid kid. (*Sinking his head in his hands*) Gawd! What a mess!

Josh becomes aware of Winnie again.

Josh What's she writing there?

Man What?

Josh What's that kid writing? What's that you're writing, kid?

Winnie *Pardon, monsieur?*

Josh (*reaching out for her book*) Here. Show me. (*Grabbing it*)

Winnie and Josh tussle with it momentarily.

Man Look, Josh, leave her, for God's sake. We'll have the mother suing us for molestation next, won't we? That's all I need.

Josh draws back.

Josh (*to Winnie*) Sorry. *Pardonnez moi.*

Pause.
The Man takes a swig of beer.

Man So. You reckon Paula may have corrupted the whole batch?

Josh So far as I could tell.

Man How could she do that? How the hell could she have managed that?

Josh She's a resourceful woman, isn't she?

Man (*bitterly*) Oh, yes.

Josh Film director, isn't she? Knows about these things. Didn't she used to edit?

Man Oh, yes.

Josh There you go then. Piece of cake for her. Won that BAFTA, didn't she?

Man Don't remind me. She keeps it by the bed. Every time I wake up, I'm reminded of it, staring at me . . .

Josh Probably she's proud of it.

Man Probably to piss me off.

Josh Yes, well, whatever. She most probably got at the original tape. It was shot on video originally, wasn't it? And then copied to DVD.

Man Well, didn't anybody notice while they were copying it, for God's sake?

Josh Why should they?

Man Calling me a deceitful little shit and all that? Somebody must have noticed, surely?

Josh They run these things off by the hundreds, Kev. High-speed copying. Takes a matter of seconds, that's all . . .

Man (*rising*) Well. They'll all have to be withdrawn, won't they? Cost us thousands. Not to mention the good will. Well, she's won. She's got what she wanted, hasn't she? She's shafted us.

Josh At least she didn't cut up your shirts.

Man (*laughing*) I should be so lucky.

Josh My wife did. Before she kicked me out.

Man I'm going to look in on Tiffy, see how she is. See you in a minute.

Josh Right.

Man Tell you what, it's nearly one o'clock. We'll all nip round the corner for some lunch, if Tiff's up to it. Fancy a bit of lunch?

Josh I'm up for that. I'm ravenous. We had this huge Indian meal at Colin's leaving do, I woke up this morning I was starving. Mind you, I did lose most of it during the night.

Man Yes, well. See you in a minute.

The Man goes out, swilling the last of his beer. Josh and Winnie sit together silently for a second. Winnie crouching over her exercise book, writing. Josh sips water. In a moment, he gets restless.

ONE P.M.

Josh Hey – hey, kid. What's your name, then? Eh? What's your name? (*In quite appalling French*) *Quel nomme? Vous?*

Winnie *Je m'appelle Winnie, m'sieur.*

Josh Winnie. That's nice. Winnie the Pooh, eh? (*He laughs*) That what they call you at school, then, is it? Winnie the Pooh?

Winnie *Non, m'sieur.*

Josh No? Hey, Winnie, do you want to see a magic trick, then? I'll show you a magic trick, shall I? You don't have to speak English for this. I'll show you. I bet you can't guess how I do this? Bet you can't guess. Now then, first thing is, do I have a coin? (*Fumbling in his pocket and producing a coin*) Yes, yes, I do. I've got one here. Now watch very carefully. *Regardez*, s'ivvous play.

Winnie watches him politely.

(*Making magical gestures with the coin*) Now, watch . . .
regardez carefully . . . are you watching?

*Josh does a piece of sleight of hand (possibly a 'French
drop') to make the coin apparently disappear.*

Voilà! Say disapparay! *Oui!*

*Winnie nods solemnly. She does not seem that
impressed.*

Say magic, eh? Where's it gone, then? Where's it gone?
Shall I make it come back? Come back again? Yes?
Retourneray? *Oui?*

More gestures.

And . . . *un, deux, trois* . . . *et* . . . *voilà!* (*Producing it
from behind her ear*) How did it get there? Magic! How
did it get there, then? Eh? Eh?

Josh laughs, shakes his head.
*Winnie is silent. She smiles faintly and politely, the
way children do when humouring an adult.*

My little girl used to love that. How did you do that,
Dad? How did you do that? Do it again? Do it again?
That's what she used to say.

Pause.

I think she was probably a little bit younger than you,
Winnie, when I used to do it for her. My little girl. Her
name's Amber. You like that name? Amber. Unusual. Her
mum chose that. Amber.

Pause.

Little Amber. I think the world of her. She adores me. I go
round to visit her every other weekend, regular like

clockwork. She's always waiting there for me. Just inside the front gate. Looking out for me. Eager little face. Waiting. Little matching hat and coat. Waiting for me to take her out somewhere special. Give her a treat. A boat ride on the river. Or the zoo. Amber loves the zoo. Especially the gibbons. You know, the little tiny monkeys. They make her laugh and laugh. Yes, gibbons . . .

Pause. He smiles.
Winnie watches him.

Yes, she means the world to me. Little Amber. She adores me. Worships the ground I walk on. Whenever I bring her home again to her mum, you know, after we've both been out together for the day, she never wants to come home again. She kicks and screams. Clinging on to the gate. Her mum has to drag her inside. Terrible.

Pause.

Enough to break your heart, really.

Pause.

All the same, they're great days. Wouldn't miss them. Either of us.

Pause.

(*Suddenly tearful*) God, I miss her some days that much. I don't mind saying.

From the hall, the vacuum starts up.

(*Wiping his eyes*) Yes, well. Not that you'd understand any of that, would you, kid? Even if you could talk the language.

Josh rises suddenly rather depressed.

(*As he moves to the door*) You'll have to wait till you grow up for that, won't you?

339

Josh goes out.

Winnie sits alone for a moment. Then resumes her writing with fresh zeal.

The vacuuming continues for a second or two.

Then there is a cry from Laverne.

(*Off*) You alright there, my love?

Laverne (*off*) Yes, thank you. It was just a – I'll be fine.

Josh (*off*) You sure?

Laverne (*off*) Yes, it was just a – little – I get them from time to – (*As she has another one*) Wooh!

Winnie rises and tentatively moves to the doorway.

Josh (*off*) Just a second I'll get some help, my love. I think you may need a bit of help . . .

Laverne (*off*) No, please don't bother people. It's really nothing –

Josh (*off, calling*) Somebody! Can we have some help here, please? (*To Winnie*) You wait in there, darling!

Laverne (*off*) Stay in there, Winnie. I'm alright, darling, Mummy's alright!

Winnie obediently lingers reluctantly in the doorway. The kitchen remains lit.

Tiffany (*off, approaching*) What's happened? What's going on?

Man (*off, simultaneously*) Somebody calling?

During the following section the voices overlap as they cope with the emergency. Throughout this Laverne alternates between reassuring people she's fine and sudden little cries as she experiences early labour pains. Sometime during this the vacuum gets switched off.

Laverne (*off*) . . . I'm fine, I'm fine, please don't bother to . . . Ah! . . . I need probably to get to the . . . Wooh! (*Another spasm*) . . . hospital . . . *etc.*

Josh (*off, over this*) Sit down, now. You sit down here.

Tiffany (*off, simultaneously*) What's happening? Is she alright?

Josh (*off*) I think she might be going into labour . . .

Tiffany (*off*) She certainly is . . .

Man (*off*) I'll phone the ambulance. Hang on, I'll phone the ambulance . . .

Winnie (*in the doorway, apprehensively*) Mum . . . Mum!

Laverne (*off*) You're to wait in there, Winnie! I'm alright! I'm OK. (*Another cry*) AH!

Josh (*off, suddenly alarmed*) Oh, my God! Tiffy! Tiffy? What's happening here?

Tiffany (*off*) Oh, no –

Josh (*off*) Is she having it?

Tiffany (*off*) Wait there! Wait there!

Josh (*off*) What's happening?

Tiffany (*off*) It's just her waters . . . her waters . . . wait!

Josh (*off*) Jesus! Look at that!

Laverne (*off*) Oh, I'm sorry, I'm terribly sorry . . . it's your sofa, your lovely sofa . . .

Tiffany comes rushing into the kitchen, nearly knocking Winnie over.

Tiffany (*as she rushes in, slightly panicked*) Whoops! Sorry, love! Out the way! Out the way!

Winnie Mum?

Laverne (*off, calling after Tiffany*) Tell Winnie she's to
wait in there!

Tiffany It's alright, love, nothing to worry about . . . wait
here . . .

Josh (*off, calling*) Oh, God. Tiffy!

Tiffany (*as she goes*) . . . it's all perfectly natural . . .

Laverne (*off*) Aaah!

> *Tiffany disappears from view within the kitchen and
> returns swiftly with an assorted armload of hand
> towels, tea towels and paper towels, anything she can
> find that's remotely absorbent.*

Winnie (*calling through the door, again*) Mum? Mum?

Laverne (*off*) You wait in there, Winnie, do you hear me,
you're to wait in there! Don't worry, I'm alright! Aah!!

Tiffany (*as she returns*) You're to wait in here, darling.
Your mother's just – she's just been taken a little bit . . .
unawares . . .

Josh (*off, yelling*) TIFFY! Quickly!

Tiffany (*as she rushes out*) She's going into labour, that's
all! Stay there! It's perfectly natural! It happens to
everyone!

Man (*off*) She wanted to know if it was a genuine
emergency. Stupid cow. Of course it's a bloody emergency.

Laverne (*off*) I'm terribly sorry. I'll clean it up later, don't
worry!

Tiffany (*off, to Laverne*) For God's sake sit still, woman!

Josh (*off*) You sit still now, Mrs – er . . . You sit still.

Winnie reluctantly loiters in the kitchen.

The sounds from the other room continue but more quietly now as things calm down a bit.

Winnie sits down at the table while she waits. She is too distracted to return to her writing. She fidgets in her seat, waiting, rocking to and fro.

ONE FORTY-FIVE P.M.

Laverne, with Tiffany, appears in the doorway. Josh, in attendance, hovers behind, seemingly ready to catch Laverne if she falls.

Winnie rises.

Laverne is obviously very shaky but doing her best to hide things from Winnie.

Winnie (*anxiously*) Mum?

Laverne (*uncertainly*) Now, I'm alright, darling. You're not to worry. Mum's just off to have her baby. And then as soon as she has, you can come and visit at the hospital. Now, if I need to stay in overnight – they may want me to stop in – I'm arranging for you to sleep over at Mrs Copthorne's, alright? With her Sophie. You get on well with Sophie, don't you?

Winnie nods.

Now, Mr Tate's very kindly said that for the rest of this afternoon just until Mrs Copthorne gets home from work, Mr Tate says you can stop here with them. Isn't that kind of him? Ooo!

Laverne gets another contraction.

Another one! They're getting quicker! Now, you're to be big and grown up while I'm gone, do you hear? Don't you get under people's feet. Finish your essay. Practise your French. Promise, me? Promise your mum?

Winnie nods.

Tiffany We'll look after her, Mummy, don't worry.

Laverne Soon as it arrives, I'm going in the ambulance. You be a good girl. I'll see you very soon, darling.

Winnie runs and clings to her mother.

Winnie (*softly*) You take care of yourself, Mum.

Josh (*to Tiffany*) I knew it! The kid speaks English!

Tiffany (*to Josh*) Of course she does!

Josh (*vindicated*) I said she did! I said!

Winnie (*still clinging*) Mum?

The doorbell rings.

Laverne I'll be fine. Don't worry. (*Another contraction*) Woo! That's your little brother. Can you feel him? Little Jericho jumping about in there?

Man (*off*) It's here! Ambulance is here!

Winnie continues to cling on to her mother.

Josh (*mystified, to Tiffany softly*) Jericho?

Tiffany (*to Josh*) Shhh! (*Softly, to Laverne*) It's here.

Laverne gently prises Winnie from her.

Laverne (*kissing her gently*) Bye-bye, darling. See you soon. *Au 'voir.*

Winnie *Au 'voir, maman. Soin de prise.*

Laverne goes out, Tiffany and Josh following her. Winnie, on her own again, mooches round the

*kitchen. Despite her mother's reassurances, she
remains a little anxious.*

*From the living room, the sound of further voices,
farewells and the front door closing.*

Further muffled voices.

*A pause, then the Man, Tiffany and Josh all enter
together. They stare at her.*

*Winnie stares at them. They appear to be something
of a deputation.*

TWO FIFTEEN P.M.

Man (*rather formally*) Right. Winnie . . . that is your
name, isn't it? Winnie?

*Winnie nods. The Man is clearly not comfortable
talking to a child for any length of time.*

Now, Winnie. I understand you speak English perfectly
well, so . . . Now, while your mum's gone, we're all here
to look after you. So – I've got some work to do. And –
once she's tidied up in there, Tiffany's going to be helping
me with that in the office. In the meantime – Josh – Uncle
Josh will sit with you in the kitchen here. So – anything
you want . . . you've only got to ask him for it. Preferably
in English. So, anything you want right now, kid?

Winnie shakes her head.

Tiffany (*softly*) She might want something to eat, Kev.

Man You want something to eat, do you?

Winnie shakes her head.

Man No?

Tiffany It's after two o'clock. She hasn't had her lunch,
has she?

Josh I haven't had lunch yet, either.

Man Nor have I.

Tiffany Wouldn't you like a little bite of lunch, darling?

Winnie shakes her head.

No? You sure?

Winnie shakes her head.

Man No. She doesn't want lunch.

Tiffany She probably hasn't had anything since her breakfast. She might like a little bite.

Man She doesn't want any.

Tiffany She's probably starving. I am.

Josh I'm ravenous. I'd like some lunch.

Man I wouldn't mind a spot of lunch, either. Tell you what, we'll all of us go out and have lunch! How about that?

Tiffany Lovely!

Josh Great!

Tiffany (*to Winnie*) You'd like that, Winnie, wouldn't you? Come out and have lunch with us all?

Winnie shakes her head.

No? (*To the Man*) She doesn't want to go out.

Man No?

Tiffany No.

Man Why not?

Tiffany I don't know. She just doesn't.

Man (*irritated*) Why the hell doesn't she want lunch?

Josh Maybe she's not hungry.

Man Well, she can just sit there, then. She doesn't have to eat, does she? If she doesn't want to? She can just sit there, can't she, watch us while we three eat.

Josh (*to Winnie*) Would you like to do that, then? Come out and watch us eat? You'd enjoy that, wouldn't you?

Winnie shakes her head again.

Man I'll pay. (*To Winnie*) Don't worry, I'm paying.

Winnie shakes her head again.

(*Frustrated*) Jesus! Well, we'll just have to leave her here, won't we? (*To Winnie*) Stay behind here, sit on your own then.

Tiffany We can't do that!

Josh We couldn't do that, Kev!

Man Why not? She doesn't want to come with us! She can stay here!

Tiffany We can't go off and have lunch and leave the kid on her own?

Man Why not?

Tiffany She's nine years old!

Man Well, what are we going to do, then?

Josh We can't go out without the kid, Kev.

Man She'll be alright. Writing her bloody novel, isn't she?

Tiffany We cannot leave a nine-year-old child alone in this house, I'm sorry.

Josh No, that wouldn't be right, Kev. She might start playing with matches or something.

Man Matches?

Josh You know. Sharp objects. Razor blades.

Man Great. Not only are we now glorified babysitters, we're also looking after a bloody juvenile suicide risk, are we?

He glares frustratedly at Winnie.

Well, I tell you this, I for one am not going to starve because of her. I am going round the corner for some lunch. Anyone wants to come with me, I'll see you there. If not then bugger you! (*Angrily to Winnie*) That includes you, Emily Brontë!

Tiffany For God's sake, Kev . . . Don't yell at her like that. She's a kid.

Man Well. She drives me bloody nuts. First she's French, then she's English. First she wants lunch, then she doesn't want bloody lunch. I hate kids, I loathe them. I'll be in the office. (*He goes out*)

Tiffany (*calling after him*) I thought you said you were going out?

Man (*off, angrily*) I'm not eating on my own, am I?

A silence.

Tiffany (*after a pause*) I'll tell you what, why don't I rustle together something for us here? For those that want it.

Josh That'd be nice. I'm starving.

Tiffany (*moving out of view momentarily*) If I can find something . . . (*Off*) There ought to be something here to nibble on . . .

A slight pause then Tiffany reappears.

(*Returning*) No. There's absolutely nothing in the fridge, it's completely empty.

Josh Yes, that sounds like Paula. Never the great provider, was she?

Tiffany I'll go out and try and buy us all a sandwich, shall I?

Josh That'd be nice.

Tiffany There should be somewhere round here, even in this area . . . I'll see if he wants one. (*To Winnie*) Would you like me to bring you back a sandwich, darling?

Winnie shakes her head.

Josh No. She doesn't want a sandwich.

Tiffany (*as she goes out, concerned*) She ought to eat something . . .

TWO FORTY-FIVE P.M.

Winnie sits down again.
  Josh wanders round the kitchen, aimlessly.

Josh Well, I'm starving. I don't know about you, kid.

He disappears momentarily.

(*Off*) No, she's quite right. Nothing. Couple of cans of beer and a clove of garlic. The cupboard is bare.

Winnie gropes in her schoolbag and produces a chocolate bar which she opens and starts to eat.
  Josh returns and stares at her. He sits and watches Winnie as she eats.

Nice? Is that nice, then? It looks nice.

Winnie nods.

My daughter, Amber, she adores those. I've seen her eat, what, four or five of those, straight after the other. Why she isn't the size of a house, I do not know.

Winnie munches on.

(*Eyeing the remains of her bar, longingly*) Mind you, can't blame her. Bit more-ish, those. Know what I mean? They're a bit more-ish. One is never enough, is it? I bet you can't eat just the one. I bet you can't. I bet you've got another one hidden away somewhere. I bet you have, haven't you?

Winnie nods.

Yes! I knew it. Got another one, haven't you? Sneaky!

Winnie nods.

Yes. Tell you what. Want to share your other one, do you? With me? Want to share it, eh?

Winnie shakes her head.

No? Come on. That's a bit mean, isn't it? Bit selfish. Ah! I know! I bet your mum told you not to share sweets with strangers, is that it?

Winnie nods.

Right. She's quite right. Fair enough. That's what I always say to Amber. Never trust strangers. They may look friendly . . .

Winnie finishes the bar and, scrumpling up the paper, looks for somewhere to put it.

(*Indicating*) There. The bin's just under there, do you see it?

Winnie moves to the unseen bin and disappears from view momentarily. Josh hesitates, trying to avoid temptation. He licks his lips and then, swooping on

*Winnie's schoolbag, starts to rifle through it searching
for the other chocolate bar.*
Winnie returns and catches him at it.
Josh stops guiltily, his hand half inside the school bag.
Winnie stares at him blankly.
*Josh withdraws his hand to find he is holding a
book which has a bookmark sticking out.*

(*Covering his tracks*) Just having a look to see what
you're reading. What's this, then? (*Inspecting the cover*)
The Secret Garden. Oh, yes, that sounds exciting. This
what you're reading then? It's a good thick book, isn't it?

*He examines it and then opens the book at its marked
place.*

You read this far, then? Well, I'm impressed. I'm very
impressed. Small print, too. Not a lot of pictures. I think
this might be a bit beyond Amber, even though she's
older. The longest book she's ever read is the leaflet for
her mobile phone. You enjoy reading then, do you?
That's a good thing. Stand you in very good stead when
you're older. Reading. Broadens your mind. Ruins your
eyesight but broadens your mind. I regret never reading.
I never read as a kid. My dad used to say to me, for
God's sake, son, stop leaping about, sit down and read a
good book. But I never did, never took heed of him. Now
look at me, perfect twenty-twenty vision and ignorant as
buggery. (*Slight pause*) Sorry.

Pause.

Tell you what. While we're waiting, why don't you read
me a bit? Could you do that? Out loud? In English?
Would you like to do that?

*Winnie nods an 'if-I-must' sort of nod. We get the
impression that she'll agree to anything just to shut
Josh up.*

(*Returning the book to her*) Here you are. Hang on!
Hang on! Just get comfy.

> *He settles in the easy chair. Winnie continues to sit at
> the table.*

There we go. That's better. Right, away you go, kid.
Broaden my mind.

Winnie *Je commence à partir du commencement?*

Josh What's that? No, I said, you can read it in English.

Winnie Do you want me to go from the beginning?

Josh No, no. Just from where you got up to, darling. I'll
soon pick it up. Don't worry. I'm like lightning, me.

> *Winnie starts to read slowly and carefully at first.
> Then, as the narrative takes hold, with slightly more
> speed and gusto.*
> *Josh sits back listening with his eyes closed. Soon he
> falls asleep.*

Winnie (*reading*) 'Chapter Four. Martha. When she
opened her eyes in the morning it was because a young
housemaid had come into her room to light the fire –'

Josh Ah! Those were the days, eh?

Winnie (*reading*) '– to light the fire –'

Josh Gone are the days of waking up to young
housemaids, eh?

Winnie (*reading*) '– and was kneeling on the hearth –'

Josh – it's all alarm clocks and Radio Two these days,
isn't it –?

Winnie (*fairly politely*) M'avez-vous laissé lire ceci, s'il
vous plaît?

Josh Yes, yes, sorry. Carry on, kid.

Winnie (*reading*) '– and was kneeling on the hearthrug raking out the cinders noisily.'

Josh No central heating in those days . . .

Winnie (*shooting him a look, then continuing*) 'Mary lay and watched her for a few moments and then began to look about the room. She had never seen a room at all like it, and thought it curious and gloomy. The walls were covered with . . . (*an unfamiliar word*) – tape-stry with a forest scene . . . (*another one*) – em – embro-idered – embroidered on it. There were fanatic-ally – fanatically dressed people under the trees and in the distance there was a glimpse of the turrets of a castle. There were hunters and horses and dogs and ladies. Mary felt as if she were in the forest with them. Out of a deep window she could see a great climbing stretch which seemed to have no trees on it. And to look rather like an endless dull puplish – purplish – sea.

"What is that?" she said, pointing out of the window.

Martha, the young housemaid, who had just risen to her feet, looked, and pointed also.

"That there?" she said.

"Yes."

"That's th' moor," with a good natured grin. "Does tha' like it?"

"No," answered Mary. "I hate it."

"That's because th'art not used to it," Martha said, going back to her hearth. "Tha' thinks it's too big an' bare now. But tha' will like it."

"Do you?" enquired Mary.'

Josh is asleep. Under the next, he starts to snore softly.

(*Continuing, unaware of this*) '"Aye, that I do," answered Martha, cheerfully polishing away at the grate. "I just love it. It's none bare. It's covered wi' growing things as smells sweet. It's fair lovely in spring an'

353

summer when th' gorse an' broom an' heather's in flower.
It smells o' honey an' there's such a lot o' fresh air – an'
th' sky looks so high an' th' bees and skylarks makes
such a noise hummin' an' singin'. Eh! I wouldn't live
away from th' moor for anythin'" –'

> *Tiffany has crept in and Winnie breaks off her reading.*
> *They notice that Josh is asleep, snoring slightly more
> loudly now. Tiffany slides a wrapped sandwich bag on
> to the table and indicates that it is intended for Josh.*
> *Tiffany, anxious not to wake him, puts her finger to
> her lips and mouths to Winnie, pointing to the office to
> indicate that that's where the Man and she will be if
> they're needed.*
> *Winnie nods and Tiffany creeps out again.*
> *As Winnie continues to read, Josh's snoring
> increases in volume.*

(*Continuing, also with increased volume*) Mary listened
to her with a grave and puzzled exp— expression. The
native servants she had been used to in India were not
in the least like this. They were obs— obsqy-obs . . . and
serv— servil –'

> *She tuts and gives up. The combination of difficult
> words and the competition from Josh, are too much
> for her. She reads on silently for a bit, her lips moving
> slightly.*
> *She gets absorbed in the book. As she reads, she
> absently reaches out for the sandwich and, sliding it
> out of its wrapping, takes a bite or two.*
> *Josh stirs noisily in his sleep and shifts in the chair.*
> *Winnie realises guiltily she is eating his sandwich.*
> *Josh slumbers on.*
> *Winnie carefully puts the half-eaten sandwich back
> in its wrapping.*
> *She attempts to start reading her book again but
> after a second or two, gives up.*

*She returns to her notebook and writes a little more.
Josh's snoring gets louder, causing Winnie to frown.
No longer able to concentrate on her task, she
gathers up her things and, leaving the half-eaten
sandwich on the table in its wrapper, tiptoes out of the
kitchen past the noisy Josh.*

THREE FIFTEEN P.M.

*As we follow Winnie back into the hall, the lights follow
her. Out here, daylight is fading and the room is darker
in contrast with the brightness of the kichen.*

*Josh's snoring fades. He remains, now unlit, in the
kitchen chair.*

*Winnie moves initially to the study door, but hears
Tiffany crying in there and draws away and goes to the
sofa and sits on it. She springs up smartly and suspiciously
examines the cushion feeling it tentatively. It is apparently damp. She seats herself well away from this damp
patch at the extreme other end.*

*She places her belongings on the coffee table and sets
up camp again. She makes to resume her writing but has
difficulty in seeing properly because of the fading light.
As she is debating whether to be daring and switch the
lights on, from the office comes the sound of Tiffany
crying, then the Man's voice soothing her.*

Man (*off*) . . . Tiffy, come on, come on, darling. It's not
the end of the world, is it?

Tiffany (*off, tearfully*) It's all my fault. I've ruined
everything for you . . . You should never have met me . . .

Man (*off*) . . . it's never your fault, darling. How the hell
can it be your fault . . .?

Tiffany and the Man come into the office doorway, she retreating from him. A patch of light spills from the room behind them.

Neither notice Winnie in the gloom, absorbed as they are with each other. The following is all but whispered between the two.

Winnie, while making no attempt to hide, instinctively draws back slightly into the sofa.

Tiffany (*quietly*) . . . it's all my fault. I should never . . . I'm so sorry . . .

Man (*quietly*) . . . Tiffy . . .

Tiffany (*burying her head in his shoulder*) . . . I'm sorry! I'm so, so sorry . . .

Man (*holding her, cooing*) Tiffy! I keep saying, if it's anybody's fault, it's hers. It's Paula's. She was the one that caused it, darling. It's all Paula. She's a vindictive bitch . . .

Tiffany It'll be all round the office now, won't it . . .?

Man Well . . . What the hell! I can live with that, if you can . . .

Tiffany It'll probably be all over the internet as well . . . we'll be on Facebook.

Man (*stroking her*) Probably. Come on, Tiffy, come here, girl . . .

Tiffany Mmmm!

Man That's good, isn't it?

Tiffany (*wriggling from his grasp*) No, Kev! We can't, not now.

Man Why not? She's long gone. Paula's long gone, darling. She won't be back. Come on then, upstairs, come on, Tiffy . . .

Tiffany You sure?

Man Course I'm sure. I love you, don't I, darling? You know I love you. Come on, this way . . .

The Man draws Tiffany gently across the hall and towards the stairs. Neither notices the seemingly invisible Winnie on the sofa.

(*As if to a child*) Come on then, little Tiffy, this way. That's it . . .

Tiffany (*in little-girl mode, still a little tearful*) I love you, Big Bear . . .

Man I love you, too, darling. Big Bear loves Ickle Tiffy, you know he does . . .

Tiffany Ickle Tiffy loves Big Bear, too . . .

Man (*drawing her up the stairs*) . . . course she does . . . Big Bear's here to look after his Ickle Tiffy, you know he is . . . You know that, don't you?

Tiffany (*in a baby voice*) . . . yeth . . .

Man Ickle Tiffy's special. She's a very special Ickle Tiffy, isn't she?

Tiffany Yeth.

Man Anything happens to Ickle Tiffy, Big Bear would cwy and cwy . . .

Tiffany (*giggling*) . . . yeth . . .

Man He'd get cwoss. Good girl, that's it, mind the stair now – come on, Ickle Tiffy, nearly there . . . Big Bear will kiss it all better, won't he . . .?

Tiffany . . . yeth, he will . . .

The two go upstairs. Winnie watches them disbelievingly as they go.

Soon, when she's certain they've gone, she gropes in her schoolbag and finds another of her chocolate bars which she opens and sits munching happily. She seems unaffected and altogether unconcerned by the previous events. She considers starting to write again, but realises it is now even darker. Enterprisingly, she moves into the crack of brighter light in the office's half-open doorway, holding up her exercise book and starts to write again, eating as she does so.

THREE THIRTY P.M.

After a moment, Paula enters silently through the front door. She is an elegant, well-groomed woman in her late thirties, dressed in a dark business suit. She switches on the hall lights.
Winnie jumps guiltily.

Paula (*sharply*) Who the hell are you?

Winnie looks up startled. We haven't seen Paula before but Winnie has and recognises her from the DVD. She gapes.

What are you doing here?

Paula approaches Winnie, examining her more closely. Winnie nervously retreats.

Paula (*remembering*) Oh, yes, of course. You're Mrs Barnstairs' daughter, aren't you? What's your name? It's Winnie, isn't it? Winnie Barnstairs, yes?

Winnie nods nervously. Eventually she retreats to the safety of the sofa where she resumes her original seat.

Your mother isn't still here, is she? She should have gone hours ago, surely? Don't tell me she's still here, it's getting on for four o'clock. What time did she come, for God's sake? Winnie, what time did you get here? What time did you arrive, you and your mother?

Winnie (*nervously*) *Nous sommes arrivés à huit trente ce matin, Madame Tate.*

Paula (*somewhat startled*) I beg your pardon?

Winnie . . . *à huit trente ce matin* . . .

Paula Eight thirty? What on earth's she been doing all this time. Where is she?

Winnie *Je ne sais pas, Madame Tate.*

Paula Well, I'm certainly not paying her for all these hours. Costs us a fortune as it is. Where is she? Is she upstairs?

Winnie (*squeaking*) *Non! Elle n'est pas en haut!*

Paula Why are you talking in French all the time? *Pourquoi parlez-vous en français?*

Winnie *Parce que ma mère veut que je pratique mon français, madame.*

Paula Oh, I see. Excellent. Good for Mrs Barnstairs. Wish my wretched mother'd made me practise French instead of packing me off on a cookery course. Far more use. Is my husband here? *Est mon mari ici?*

Winnie (*shrugging*) *C'est possible, Madame Tate.*

Paula (*amused*) Well, you are a shy little thing, aren't you? What are you so nervous about? You don't need to be frightened of me, you know? I'm very fond of children. Unlike my husband. Children seem to bring him out in a rash for some reason, whenever the topic is raised.

She sits beside Winnie on the damp patch of which she seems initially unaware.

Paula (*gently, but rapidly*) Je suis fanatique des enfants. Il n'y a aucun besoin d'avoir peur de moi, Winnie. J'aimerais avoir des enfants de mes propres. Rien ne me rendrait plus heureux. Seulement mon mari ne les aime pas. Mais j'aimerais avoir une petite fille comme toi, Winnie. Tristement il obtient un peu en retard dans ma vie pour le tout cela – vous me comprenez?

As she speaks, Winnie searches in her bag for her French dictionary.

Winnie (*clutching her dictionary*) Non, madame. Je ne parle pas français vite –

Paula (*patiently, slower*) J'ai dit que j'étais fanatique des enfants et je . . .

She becomes aware that she is sitting on something damp.

(*Jumping up*) God, what's happened here? What the hell has happened to my sofa?

She examines the cushion.

It's soaking wet! It's *soaked*! What have you spilt on here? Have you spilt your drink on here, you little horror? Do you know how much this sofa cost me? Have you any idea?

Winnie Non, madame . . .

Paula It's ruined, absolutely ruined, you realise that? What is this you've spilt on it? (*Examining the fabric more carefully, sniffing*) Christ, it's smells like pee. Have you been peeing on my sofa, you horrendous creature?

Winnie (*terrified*) Non, madame, ce n'est pas pee . . .

Paula (*fiercely*) Then who did, if it wasn't you? Tell me how this piss got on my sofa. Come on!

Winnie *Ma mère . . . elle . . . ma mère, elle est . . .*
(*Searching her dictionary for the word*)

Paula Your mother? Don't tell me your mother peed on
the sofa, because, I don't believe you . . .

Winnie *Ma mère etait –* (*Finding the word*) *– etait –
enceinte . . . enceinte . . .*

Paula *Enceinte?* Yes, I know she's pregnant, you stupid
girl . . .

Winnie *. . . et elle entrée dans le travail. Et ses eaux s'est
cassée . . .*

Paula (*fiercely*) What? What the hell are you talking
about?

Winnie (*excitedly*) *. . . le cascade . . . tout à coup!
Comme ça! Deluge! Sur le couche! Soudainement!*

*Winnie gives up on her French and tosses the
dictionary aside.*

(*Rapidly, yelling*) My mother's waters broke and she
came and went all over your sofa!

Paula (*digesting this*) Your mother . . . came . . . and
went . . . on my sofa?

Winnie (*quietly*) *Oui, madame. C'est vrai.*

Paula (*immediately penitent*) Oh, dear God, you poor
child. You poor, poor child! What an ordeal! (*Staring
intently into Winnie's eyes*) Winnie, I apologise. I am
so sorry. Will you forgive me? (*Pausing to gather her
composure*) Ever since I was your age, I've had this
appalling temper. My mother used to say to me, Paula,
when you grow up if you carry on with that temper of
yours, my dear, by the end of your life, no one's going to
bother to turn up for your funeral. You'll be lying there

all alone in that crematorium with only yourself to blame. It's unforgivable. I fly into these blind rages and then I say things . . . I hurt people. I lose them as friends, I lose them as . . . Now I've gone and shouted at you which is unforgivable. (*Dramatically*) God, you're a mere child! I've started shouting at kids! He's right! I'm a monster! Here you were sitting peacefully, innocently writing your little story . . . and I march in, jumping to all the wrong conclusions . . . bellowing and screaming . . .

    Paula, in a fit of contrition, embraces Winnie.

(*Holding her tightly*) Forgive me, darling? Please forgive me?

Winnie (*slightly muffled*) Oui, Madame Tate.

Paula God never forgives us, you know, any of us, if we harm a child.

    Paula kisses the top of Winnie's head.

(*Holding her at arm's length*) Winnie, you are to bear witness. You have seen the very last of my childish, thoughtless tantrums. No more of them, my darling. I promise. From now on, I vow, I solemnly promise. (*More briskly, her business self taking over*) Now, then, Winnie. What time did your mother go into hospital? Was she taken in an ambulance? I hope my husband had the sense to phone for an ambulance?

Winnie *Oui, madame.*

Paula What time did they take her in, do you know?

Winnie *Peu après douze heures, Madame.*

Paula (*glancing at her watch*) What time is it now? One – two – three . . . Well, in a minute or two, I'll drive you up there, shall I? We can check how she's getting on.

Winnie *Merci, madame.*

Paula Where's Mr Tate, do you know?

Winnie (*evasively*) *Non.*

Paula Is he here?

Winnie shrugs.

He's not here?

Winnie shrugs again.

Did he go with your mother in the ambulance? No, he'd hardly leave you here all alone, would he? Where is he?

Winnie *Je ne sais pas, madame.*

Paula Well, I'll tell you what, let's go on a hunt for him, shall we? You want to come with me on a hunt for Mr Tate?

Paula grabs Winnie's hand before she can protest.

Off we go. Where shall we start? Shall we start in the kitchen? Let's see if he's in the kitchen, shall we? Tippy-toes now, so we can surprise him . . . Tippy-toes . . .

Paula leads Winnie through to the kitchen.
Josh is still asleep, snoring gently as they enter.

Oh, no! What the hell's he doing here? Josh! Josh, wake up!

Josh (*waking up with a start*) Wah! (*His alarm bells immediately starting to ring*) Oh, my God! Paula!

Paula What are you doing here, Josh, for God's sake?

Josh (*still half asleep*) I just . . . I just . . . looked in . . . was passing through, you know . . . sort of thing . . .

Paula Have you seen Kevin? Do you know where he is?

Josh He's – he's . . . I don't know, Paula . . . I don't know if he's even here . . . He's not even here.

Paula But he let you in?

Josh Oh, yes.

Paula He's somewhere in the house then?

Josh has noticed the sandwich packet which is still on the table where Winnie left it.

Josh (*opening it now as he speaks*) Oh, yes. He's – he's – he's probably – somewhere – in the house . . .

He is holding the half-eaten sandwich that Winnie replaced earlier. He stares at it, puzzled. He looks at Winnie who avoids his look.

Paula Right, let's go and find him. Come along, Winnie. Let's look in the office.

Paula leads Winnie out of the kitchen and back into the hall. Josh hurries ahead of them.

Josh (*intercepting them*) No, no, Paula, you don't want to look in the office. He won't want to be disturbed. Kev said he was specially busy and no one was to disturb him.

Paula That doesn't include me.

Josh (*barring the office doorway*) Just a tick then, just a tick! (*Calling through the still half-open door*) Excuse me! Kevin! Kevin, mate! Bit of a surprise for you here, mate. Paula's popped back. (*He listens*) Kev!

Josh peers inside the office, cautiously.

(*With a shade of relief*) No, he's not in there.

Paula (*smiling*) Apparently not.

Josh They must have gone out for lunch. He. Must have. Gone out. To lunch.

Silence.

Paula They?

Josh They?

Paula You said they? Who's they?

Josh Kev – and – her mother.

Paula Her mother?

Josh Yes.

Paula Winnie's mother?

Josh That's right. You know. He thought he'd treat her. Sort of – thank you.

Paula By taking Mrs Barnstairs out to lunch?

Josh S'right.

Paula How lovely. They're both dining in the maternity ward, I take it?

Silence.

Josh (*coming clean*) I've no idea where he is, Paula. Unless he's upstairs having a lie down. He was a bit tired earlier. Yes. That's probably it. He's maybe having a kip. Don't want to disturb his kip, do we?

Paula (*dangerously*) Tell you what, we'll have a look up there then, shall we, Winnie? To see if Mr Tate's hiding upstairs. Perhaps he's crouching in a cupboard without his trousers on, you never know, waiting to jump out at us and shout 'Boo'. Let's go up and see if we can surprise him first, shall we? Then we can shout 'BOO!' at him. Come on, come with me.

Winnie (*pulling away from Paula's grasp*) Non, non, madame! Je ne veux pas monter là!

Paula What's the matter, Winnie?

Winnie Non! *Ma mère n'approuverait pas. Je ne dois pas voir des choses comme cela! Je suis trop jeune!*

Paula stares at Winnie.

Josh (*apprehensively*) What did she say?

Paula (*grimly*) Enough. She said quite enough. Wait there, Winnie.

Josh (*moving forward*) Paula!

Paula (*steely*) Both of you! (*To Winnie, pointing fiercely*) *Attends là!*

Paula goes upstairs.

Josh (*softly, to Winnie*) Are they really up there?

Winnie *Oui, monsieur.*

Josh What, both of them?

Winnie Yes!

Josh Oh, Jesus! (*As he goes*) KEV!!!

Josh hurtles up the stairs after Paula.
 Winnie remains watching in the hall.
 A succession of noises from upstairs.
 First, a blood-curdling bellow of rage from Paula.
 A cry of pain from the Man cut off abruptly by a sickening thud.
 A scream of terror from Tiffany.
 Ineffectual noises from Josh, vainly trying to calm the situation.
 In a second, Tiffany comes rushing downstairs, whimpering with terror. She has a sheet wrapped round her but appears to be wearing precious little else.

Pursuing her, close behind, is Paula, holding
Tiffany's bundle of clothes. Tiffany reaches the hall
and scampers like a terrified rabbit this way and that,
as Paula grimly closes on her.
Winnie scuttles back to her seat on the sofa.

Paula (*as she pursues her*) Come here, you greasy slut . . .
you dumpy bitch . . . you hussy, you shameless little
whore . . . you cheap tramp . . . you podgy strumpet . . .
you pathetic, half-baked tart . . .

Tiffany (*evading her, whimpering with fear*) . . . no, please,
please don't . . . I didn't mean any harm . . . please don't
hurt me . . . please . . .

Tiffany is finally forced to retreat through the front door.

. . . no . . . not out here in the road. I need my clothes, let
me get dressed first, please!

Paula You get dressed in the street where you belong,
you brainless little bimbo!

Paula follows Tiffany out and throws the clothes after
her.
The sound of the front door slamming.

(*Off*) And stay out!

Paula marches back to the stairs again. She is now
clutching Tiffany's sheet.

(*Muttering as she goes*) And don't you ever set foot in my
bloody house again!

She goes off upstairs, ignoring Winnie sitting there
quietly, who once again appears to have been
forgotten.
Winnie takes up her exercise book once more and
writes.

367

*Through the letter box, Tiffany's voice is heard
pleading.*

Tiffany (*off, slightly muffled*) Could someone let me in
again, please . . ? Somebody? . . . Please! . . . It's freezing
cold out here . . . (*Her teeth chattering*) I've got no
clothes on . . . Nothing at all . . .

*Winnie considering whether to help her, rises
tentatively.*

(*Giving it her last shot, in her baby voice again*) Ickle
Tiffy's out here in the cold!

*On hearing this, Winnie reconsiders, scowls and
promptly sits down again.*

Please . . . anybody? . . . Somebody help Ickle Tiffy . . .
please! (*After a slight pause, giving up, in her normal
voice*) Oh, Jesus! Let me in, you fucking bastards! (*Pause,
then seeing something*) Oh. I say! I say! Over here, please!
Taxi! TAXI!

*A squeal of brakes outside as the taxi does an
emergency stop.*
*The Man, clasping a cold flannel to his forehead,
comes uncertainly downstairs supported by Josh.
There is evidence of some blood.*
*Paula follows them, a pace or two behind. Her
manner is now slightly more subdued.*

Man (*in pain*) Oh, God!

Josh (*guiding him down the stairs*) Alright, easy, Kev,
easy. Careful! There you go. Steady!

Man My head! It's killing me!

Josh Yes, it looked fairly deep, mate, you ought to get
that looked at, Kev. It's a nasty gash –

Paula (*muttering*) Good.

Josh What did you hit him with? What did she hit you with, for God's sake?

Man With her BAFTA. She hit me with her sodding BAFTA.

Paula (*drily*) Came in useful for something.

They process to the front door.

Josh You may need a stitch or two. Probably not too serious.

Paula Pity.

Josh I'll run you up to A&E. I'll drive. Don't worry. I'll drive. We'll go in mine, Kev.

Man So long as she's not driving, I don't care. Just don't let her drive, will you? I don't even want her in the same car!

Josh No way . . . It's alright. Alright. I'm driving.

They go out.

(*As they go*) You'll have to give me a hand with him, Paula, just getting him in.

Paula (*off*) If I have to . . .

Josh (*off*) Just watch his head as he gets in . . .

Winnie is alone again, still sitting on the sofa writing in her exercise book.
She seems perfectly happy.
A car starts up outside and drives off.

FIVE P.M.

Paula comes back through the front door. Winnie looks up.

Paula Thought I'd forgotten about you, didn't you? Come on, I promised I'd take you up to the hospital, didn't I? To see your mum? Bring your things.

Winnie (*gathering up her stuff*) Oui, madame. Merci beaucoup, madame.

Winnie eagerly packs up.

Paula (*watching her, ruefully*) I'm afraid I broke my promise to you, didn't I? Lost my temper again. It's still not good to lose your temper but it's sometimes very, very difficult you'll find, Winnie. Especially if you go and marry a berk like that. Come on, love. (*Holding out her hand*) Off we go. *Nous nous voyagerons ensemble dans ma voiture. Oui? C'est bon?*

Winnie (*as they leave the house hand in hand*) C'est bon, madame. C'est très bon. Merci beaucoup.

A quick montage of appropriate sounds and a lighting change to a hospital room.
Paula and Winnie remain onstage as Laverne is wheeled on in a hospital bed.
Paula, still holding Winnie's hand, enters this new room.

FIVE THIRTY P.M.

Paula There she is! There's Mummy. There's your mum. We've found her at last!

Laverne (*rather weakly, happily*) Darling!

> *Winnie silently runs to hug her mother. Laverne strokes her daughter's head.*

(*Stroking Winnie's head*) Here she is! Here's my darling! Thank you so much, Mrs Tate. I hope she's not been too much trouble to you.

Paula She's been as good as gold, haven't you, Winnie?

Laverne I got really worried about you, darling, I really did.

Paula She's been fine. And they've just let us have a little peep at the baby. We had a look through the window just now, didn't we, Winnie? A quick peep at baby Barnstairs. He's gorgeous! Has he got a name yet?

Laverne Oh, yes. We're calling him Jericho.

> *Still clinging to her mother, Winnie gives a muffled groan.*

Paula Jericho?

Laverne Jericho. Alexander. Samson.

Paula (*taking this in*) Great. Fine. That should keep him out of trouble, shouldn't it? Well, I won't – hang about – leave you two – I must just go and – visit – another patient. Switch off his life support. Take care. See you soon. *Au 'voir*, Winnie.

Winnie *Au 'voir, Madame Tate.*

Laverne Bye-bye. Thanks again, Mrs Tate. Thank you for bringing her.

> *Paula goes.*

Laverne Oh, he's a little beauty. You've got a lovely baby brother, Winnie. Isn't that nice. God's been good.

Winnie Does he have to be called Jericho?

Laverne I like Jericho. It's strong. Good for a boy. Don't you like it?

Winnie No, I hate it. It's a stupid name, Mum. Everyone'll laugh at him.

Laverne They won't!

Winnie They will!

Laverne Oh. What do you think we should call him, then?

Winnie I don't know.

Laverne Well. (*She considers*) How about we call him after Mr Tate then? We could call him Kevin, couldn't we, after Mr Tate. Seeing they've both been so kind to us. She'd appreciate that as well. What do you think, Winnie? Shall we call him Kevin?

Winnie (*immediately*) Jericho.

Laverne Jericho?

Winnie Jericho.

Laverne Jericho it is. Now, I hope you've been good and well behaved today, Winnie. Been practising your French, like you promised me?

Winnie Yes.

Laverne What?

Winnie *Oui, maman.*

Laverne That's better. You keep practising now, won't you? It won't be long, Winnie, darling, I promise you. We'll be climbing aboard that great big plane, flying off into the sunshine. Eh? Any day now.

Winnie is silent.

Laverne (*smiling*) Any day now.

Winnie (*rather restless*) Can we go home now please, Mum?

Laverne Not just this minute, darling.

Winnie Soon.

Laverne Mummy's just a little bit tired. They may need to keep her in overnight. Little Jericho was in such a hurry to come out, you see, he was that keen to see you. You can stay here. Sit with me for a little while longer.

Pause. Winnie sits on the chair.

Have you finished your essay yet for Mrs Crackle?

Winnie nods.

Good girl. You can give it to her in the morning then, can't you?

Slight pause. Winnie fidgets in the chair.

Tell you what? Why don't we do like we said this morning? You could read it to me, how about that? Then I'll be able to hear all about your day, won't I? Your wonderful day. Wouldn't that be nice? Would you like to read it to Mummy, would you, darling?

Winnie produces her exercise book.

Alright. Off we go, then.

Winnie hesitates, uncertain whether her mother is ready for this.

Laverne (*gently encouraging*) Come on, Winnie. I'm listening, darling. I'm all ears.

Winnie (*reading*) 'My Wonderful Day by Winnie Barnstairs. At eight o'clock my mum and I caught the bus to Mr

Tate's house. Mum cleans it usually every Wednesday only today we had to come on Tuesday because my mum is expecting a baby and has to go to the clinic for a check-up on the Wednesday. When I woke up I wasn't feeling very well and my mum said I needn't go to school but to go with her instead. And when we got to Mr Tate's house we rang the bell and Mr Tate let us in. He was dressed in his dressing gown and no pyjamas and his bare feet even though it was half past eight and he seemed rather cross and I saw that he needed to cut his toenails.'

Music starts under.

'And Mum told me to sit on the sofa in the hall and to be quiet and to talk in French because we were soon going to be going off to Martinique, only I think she sometimes says this only because she is unhappy what with my dad leaving us . . .'

As the music builds, Winnie continues reading silently. Laverne lies back, initially smiling proudly as she listens to her child's detailed account of her day. As Winnie silently continues, Laverne starts to frown, eventually snatching the exercise book from her daughter and starting to read it for herself, with an expression of growing consternation. She continues to read, giving Winnie the occasional incredulous glance. Winnie moves her chair slightly further away as:
Music continues as the lights fade to:

Blackout.

LIFE OF RILEY

Life of Riley was first performed at the Stephen Joseph Theatre, Scarborough, on 21 September 2010. The cast was as follows:

Kathryn Liza Goddard
Colin Kim Wall
Simeon Jamie Kenna
Tamsin Laura Doddington
Jack Ben Porter
Monica Laura Howard

Director Alan Ayckbourn
Design by Michael Holt
Lighting by Jason Taylor

This production toured in 2011, opening at the Yvonne Arnaud Theatre, Guildford, on 26 January.

Characters

Monica
a teacher, George's estranged wife, late thirties

Simeon
a farmer, widower and Monica's new partner, forties

Jack
a businessman, George's oldest and best friend, forties

Tamsin
a former beautician, Jack's wife, late thirties

Colin
a doctor, forties

Kathryn
a dental receptionist, Colin's wife, forties

Place and Time

Four gardens, one year, between May and November

Act One

SCENE ONE

May.

*The stage is divided into four distinct garden areas,
each of which tends to reflect the personality or
personalities of their owners.*

*The first belongs to the Rileys, Monica and George
(whom we never see). It is a small suburban garden,
once lovingly tended by Monica but now wild and
overgrown. Perhaps, in part, the neglect is because
Monica no longer lives there and George seldom goes
out there. One entrance leads to the living room of the
unseen house. This area is currently deserted.*

*The second garden is a patio, part of a far larger
unseen garden, and belongs to Jack and Tamsin. Two
entrances to this, one to the kitchen doors of a big modern
house, the other to the rest of the garden. This is also
deserted.*

*The third is not strictly a garden but a rough part of
Simeon's farmyard, wild grass and weeds covering an
area originally paved or concreted. There is a hunk of
stone which now serves as an improvised seat. The area
is bounded on one side by a fence with a stile leading to
a meadow and countryside beyond. The other leads to
the farm entrance and the house itself.*

*Monica, George's estranged wife, currently occupies
this area alone. She is sitting on the makeshift seat, deep
in thought. She is casually dressed in jeans, muddy farm
boots and a sweater. In her late thirties with her hair tied
roughly back, she appears to have taken little trouble
with her overall appearance of late. She is currently*

toying with the idea of having a cigarette. She resists this for some time. It remains unlit in her hand.

The fourth area, belonging to Kathryn and Colin, is a neat suburban show garden in miniature. This also has a patio but, unlike Jack and Tamsin's, it is minute with barely room to accommodate the small garden table and the two chairs which currently occupy it. Kathryn sits here with Colin.

Both are dressed in coats as if they were shortly going somewhere. They are currently running lines from a script (Relatively Speaking). *This is not immediately apparent.*

Colin (*as Philip*) 'I can't say I'm very taken with this marmalade.'

Kathryn (*as Sheila*) 'No, nor am I.'

Colin (*as Philip*) 'Then why did you buy it?'

Kathryn (*as Sheila*) 'I couldn't tell by looking at it, could I?'

Colin (*as Philip*) 'Hmm'.

Slight pause.

Kathryn (*as Sheila*) 'They didn't –'

Colin (*as Philip, interrupting her*) 'I'd sooner have none than this.'

Kathryn (*coming out of character, impatiently*) Just a minute! Just a minute . . .

Colin What?

Kathryn I hadn't finished.

Colin Hadn't you?

Kathryn I've got more to say.

Colin Are you sure?

Kathryn (*producing her script*) Look. I say, 'They didn't have our sort' and *then* you say, 'I'd sooner have none than this'.

Colin I thought you'd already said that.

Kathryn Said what?

Colin 'They didn't have our sort.' I thought you'd already said that.

Kathryn No, I didn't. Because I didn't get a chance to, did I?

Colin You sure?

Kathryn No, because you came crashing in with 'I'd sooner have none than this'. Before I could say 'They didn't have our sort'. Which made absolutely no sense at all to the scene, did it? I do wish you'd listen, Colin. Why don't you listen? You never listen, do you?

Colin I was listening.

Kathryn You're the same in real life. You never listen to a word, do you?

Colin You'd stopped speaking. I thought you'd finished.

Kathryn That was a pause. It's in the script. I was leaving a slight pause . . .

Colin Well, how am I supposed to know? I thought you'd stopped altogether.

Kathryn If you'd only look at your script. Look . . . Here! (*She stabs a finger at the text*)

Colin You're always pausing, how am I supposed to know? If you stop speaking, I assume it must be my go.

383

There's only two of us in the scene. If you stop, I assume that's my turn to start.

Kathryn I don't know why you agreed to appear in this play in the first place, I really don't . . .

Colin Nor do I.

Kathryn I mean, if you're not going to take it seriously. You don't say half the correct lines. You walk through other people's pauses. I can't think why Peggy Parker picked you, I really can't.

Colin (*muttering*) I wish to God you'd pause a bit in real life.

Kathryn (*icily*) What? What did you say?

Colin Nothing.

From the house their phone rings.

Colin Saved by the bell . . .

Kathryn My God. That phone – it hasn't stopped ringing from the minute I got in.

Colin (*getting up*) I'll answer it.

From the house, a grandfather clock starts to strike six. Colin goes inside.

Kathryn We must leave in a minute – Peggy hates it when you're late for rehearsal . . .

Kathryn resumes her study of the script.
The lights cross-fade to Monica, sitting deep in thought, about finally to light her cigarette.

Simeon (*off, calling*) Monica! Monica! Where have you got to? Monica?

Monica hastily jams the unlit cigarette back in the packet and hides the evidence.

384

The lights cross-fade and come up on Jack and Tamsin's area. Tamsin enters from the garden, also carrying her script for the play. She glances at her watch. She mutters a few lines under her breath.

From the house, the front door slams. In a moment, Jack comes out, still with his coat on, having just arrived home. He carries his overnight bag.

Jack Oh, you're out here . . .

Tamsin (*slightly listlessly*) Hi!

Jack What you doing out here?

Tamsin Just tidied up the playroom. Switched on the heating.

Jack Oh, yes, of course. Your rehearsals. How's it going?

Tamsin Haven't started, yet. Just waiting for the others.

Jack (*hugging her, kissing her cheek*) Hi!

Tamsin (*responding faintly*) Good trip?

Jack The usual. Conference. You know. Bit boring.

Tamsin Oh.

Jack You know.

Tamsin Long way to go to get a bit bored.

Jack Yes, well . . . Tilly around, is she?

Tamsin At another of her parties.

Jack What? That's the second one this week, isn't it?

Tamsin The third.

Jack I didn't go to this many parties at her age. Not when I was fifteen.

Tamsin I did.

Jack Well. It's a girl thing, isn't it? Probably.

Slight pause.

(*Making to move indoors again*) I'll just unpack, then.

Tamsin Leave any washing there. I'll put it in with the rest.

Jack Thanks.

He puts his case down on the table, opens it and dumps a rolled bundle of overnight laundry on the table.

Tamsin (*as he does this*) Nice hotel?

Jack What?

Tamsin Your hotel? Nice, was it?

Jack Oh, one of those – chain places – you know . . . Cosy broom cupboard with a kettle. Packet of last year's biscuits. Narrow little bed . . .

Tamsin Oh, dear, you could have afforded somewhere better, couldn't you?

Jack What was the point? In and out, wasn't I? I'm not fussed.

Tamsin You could have at least had a room with a double bed.

Jack What would I need a double bed for? (*He laughs*)

A silence. Tamsin doesn't smile.
Jack laughs again. Another slight pause.

Oh, yes, hey, I was thinking on the way back – Tilly's big birthday coming up soon, isn't it?

Tamsin Not till September. Middle of September.

Jack We ought to be planning her party. Special one this.

Tamsin I seem to remember you said that when she was thirteen. How many special birthdays are you planning to give her?

Jack No, come on, fair do's, Tam. She'll be sixteen. Age of consent, eh?

Tamsin I think she's probably jumped the gun a bit there, Jack.

Jack (*frowning*) I don't know anything about that. That's not what she's told me.

Tamsin No, she wouldn't.

Jack I'll get changed, then.

Jack goes back into the house.
    Tamsin stares after him, troubled. She picks up his discarded washing, a bundle wrapped in yesterday's shirt. She unrolls the bundle.

Tamsin (*sniffing the shirt, reacting*) You bugger . . .

She goes back into the house.
    The lights cross-fade back to Colin and Kathryn's.
    From the house, a different grandfather clock starts to strike five.
    Kathryn has taken a small hip flask from her bag and is in the process of taking a swig when Colin returns from the house.
    He notices Kathryn as she hastily puts away the flask, but makes no comment.

Kathryn Was that for me?

Colin What?

Kathryn The phone? Was it for me?

Colin No. For me.

Kathryn Who was it?

Colin Oh, nothing. Work.

Kathryn You were talking for long enough.

Silence. Colin is troubled.

What's the time?

Colin (*abstracted*) Mmm?

Kathryn Only a few minutes ago, the clock in the hall struck six and now the one in the dining room just struck five.

Colin Oh, lord. They're out of step again.

Kathryn Well, I wish you'd sort them out, Colin. They're driving me mad.

Colin I will. As soon as I've . . .

Kathryn I mean, which one of them is right?

Colin Neither of them.

Kathryn Then what's the time, for heaven's sake?

Colin Seventeen and a half minutes to seven.

Kathryn We are, we're going to be very late. Very late.
(*Aware of his abstracted mood*) You alright?

Colin Yes. Yes, yes. (*Pause*) Yes . . . It was – er – this specialist from Manchester, that's all.

Pause. Kathryn waits.

He had some rather bad news . . . That's all.

Kathryn Oh, I see. Manchester?

Colin Chap called Hinchwood. Jeremy Hinchwood.

Kathryn Hinchwood? Do we know him?

Colin No. We've never met him. Cancer specialist. Rather good in his field. (*Pause*) Yes, I had to refer a patient of mine a week or so ago. Hinchwood's just come back with a rather negative diagnosis.

Kathryn Oh, dear.

Colin Yes. Oh, dear.

Kathryn That's life.

Colin Yes. Well. In his particular case, only a month or two more of it.

Kathryn A month?

Colin Well, six at the most.

Kathryn Dreadful. Do they know they've only got six months? This person?

Colin Hinchwood said he'd written to him. Followed up with a phone call this morning. Explained the situation and probable ramifications. Then I'm around to pick up the pieces.

Kathryn I'd hate to be told that. Six months? Hardly time to do anything. If someone told me that, I'd probably drop dead with shock.

Colin I don't think this chap will. Not the type. It'll probably all happen pretty quickly when it happens. He can look forward to a few good months, before he goes.

Kathryn Who is it? Do I know him?

Colin (*admonishingly*) Now, Kathryn . . .

Kathryn What does he do, then? What's his job? You can at least tell me that.

Colin Don't for heaven's sake start all this twenty questions business again. You're always doing this. I can't discuss it, I really can't. After all, I am the chap's GP and there is such a thing as patient confidentiality.

Kathryn You can tell your own wife, surely.

Colin No, I can't tell my own wife. Especially when she happens to be you. Because she'll promptly go and tell everyone else.

Kathryn What's the point of being married to a doctor if you can't hear these things first? If he won't share them? What's the point in being married to you, Colin?

Colin That's a separate issue entirely.

Pause. The first grandfather clock starts to chime seven. Kathryn closes her eyes in exasperation.

Why on earth does it matter what the blessed man does for a living?

Kathryn Well, if he were a bus driver, say, for instance, it could be very dangerous. If he dropped dead at the wheel with a bus load of passengers on board.

Colin I daresay the bus company would have Health and Safety regulations in place to cover such an eventuality. (*He laughs at his own rare joke*) I don't know whether that's the same in the case of schoolteachers. (*He laughs again*)

Kathryn Schoolteachers?

Colin stops laughing.

He's a schoolteacher, then?

Colin (*vaguely*) – er – possibly. No. Look, we should be going, Kathryn, we really should. It's nearly eight and a half minutes to. We're going to be dreadfully late for

rehearsal. Then we'll have Peggy in a stew, won't we?
I'll get the car out.

Colin starts to move off to the house.

Kathryn, I know you, you'll try and wheedle this thing
out of me, but this time my lips are totally sealed. You
mustn't mention a word about this, not to anyone –

Kathryn About what?

Colin About George's condition. Don't say a word to
anybody. Please. I'll be out in the driveway.

Colin goes off.

Kathryn (*thoughtfully*) George? Teacher? George Riley?
(*As the penny finally drops, stunned*) Oh, dear God! Not
George. Not George Riley, please!

*She dives into her bag and takes out her mobile
phone. She taps a number and waits.*

(*Rising, as someone replies*) Jack? . . . Kathryn . . . I've
got the most terrible news . . . I thought you should be
the first to know, you being so close to him . . . It's about
George. George Riley . . . yes . . .

Colin (*off, calling*) Darling!

Kathryn (*calling*) Coming! Just a minute!

She moves towards the house.

(*Talking into the phone as she does so*) . . . well, Colin's
just let slip – you know how hopelessly indiscreet Colin
is . . . he's just told me . . . now you're not to mention a
word of this to anyone, Jack . . . promise me . . .

*As Kathryn goes indoors, still talking, the lights cross-
fade back to the farm area. Monica is again on the
point of lighting a cigarette when Simeon enters from
the house. She hastily conceals the cigarette and lighter.*

Simeon (*concerned*) OK?

Monica nods.

(*Smiling*) Thought you might have been having a crafty smoke there.

Monica shakes her head.

We had an agreement about that, hadn't we?

Monica is silent.

Come on . . . Monica . . . come on, girl . . .

Monica I don't think I can cope with him. Eight years old, he really frightens me, Simeon, he does. He won't even acknowledge I'm in the room. He's been three months like this.

Simeon is silent.

Three months!

Simeon (*awkwardly*) Well . . . His mum meant the world to him . . .

Monica (*angrily*) Yes, well, she's gone, hasn't she? She was so fond of him, she walked out and left you both. So he'll have to get used to me now, won't he? (*Slight pause*) Till I run away as well.

Simeon touches her arm gently.

God, I spend my life running away, don't I? We both got on so well, too, when I used to teach him. My star pupil. Ridiculous of us to think he'd adjust to all this. That he'd ever accept me as his . . . No, we were in too much of a hurry. I was. I moved in here far too early – before he'd had time to – before he was ready. We should have waited.

Simeon (*tenderly*) I couldn't have waited.

*Monica, touched by this, touches his face and smiles
at him tenderly. Simeon makes to respond but she gets
up abruptly, moving back to the house.*

Monica Sorry, Sim. You can do without all this, can't
you? I'll go back inside. Check he's OK. Have another go.

Simeon You alright, then?

Monica (*unconvincingly*) Yes . . . yes . . .

*Monica goes off to the house.
    Simeon watches her and then, in frustration, makes
as if to kick the seat.*

Simeon Oh, bugger it all to buggery!

*He stamps off towards the house as the lights cross-
fade to Jack and Tamsin's.
    Jack comes out from the house, distressed. Tamsin
follows him, concerned.*

Tamsin Six months?

Jack That's what she just told me. According to Colin.

Tamsin Could they be wrong?

Jack (*stunned*) I don't know. I don't know. Maybe. (*He
sits*) Oh, God. George? Not George.

Tamsin (*concerned*) Oh, I'm sorry. You're both so close,
too.

Jack My best friend. Always has been. Oh, God, it takes
the wind out of you, something like this. The breath out
of your body. I haven't felt like this since I gave up
bloody five-a-side . . .

Tamsin They may have got it wrong. You read about
them getting it wrong all the time. Besides, you know
Colin. I wouldn't trust him, not as a doctor. He put Tilly

on those tablets when she first started her you-know-whats, didn't he? Remember? Made her constipated for weeks.

Jack (*in a daze, barely hearing her*) Yes . . . yes . . . yes . . .

Tamsin You want a drink? Can I get you a brandy?

Jack . . . yes . . .

Tamsin I'll get you a brandy. Wait there.

The doorbell rings.

Oh, this'll be them. I'll go. Sit still.

Jack (*fumbling for his mobile*) I ought to ring George, you know. Kathryn said Colin let it out by mistake. Do you think George even knows yet?

Tamsin I don't know. Maybe he doesn't . . .

The doorbell rings again.

. . . better be careful what you say to him. In case he hasn't heard. Terrible if you were the first to break the news to him, wouldn't it?

Tamsin goes indoors.

Jack (*listening to his phone*) It's ringing.

Lights come up on George's house for the first time. From inside the house, a phone starts to ring. It continues for a second or so and then loud rock music starts up from within as someone, presumably George, starts up his sound system. The phone continues to ring.
    In his own garden, Jack waits impatiently.
    Tamsin returns with Colin and Kathryn.

Tamsin (*as she enters*) He's just out here . . . he's on the phone . . .

Jack No reply from his house. (*He cuts off his mobile call*)

The phone stops ringing in George's house. The lights and the music cut off.

Colin (*cheerily*) Hallo, Jack. Good to see you. How are things?

Jack (*moving off to the house*) Excuse me one minute. Sorry, Colin, mate.

Kathryn Hallo, Jack . . .

Tamsin What are you doing?

Jack (*as he goes*) I'm going to try his mobile. In case he's out somewhere.

Jack goes off down the garden.

Kathryn Poor Jack. It must be especially awful for him . . .

Tamsin Yes, terrible news, isn't it? Jack's taken it very hard, of course.

Colin What news is this?

Tamsin The news about George.

Colin George?

Kathryn George Riley, darling.

Tamsin About his – you know – condition . . .

Colin His condition?

Tamsin Yes. He's dying apparently. Six months to live.

Colin Good God!

Tamsin Didn't you know? I thought you knew.

Kathryn Of course he knew.

Colin Yes, of course I knew. I just didn't know anyone else knew. How on earth did you know?

Tamsin Jack told me.

Colin How did he know?

Tamsin Well, from Kathryn. Kathryn told him.

Colin How on earth did you know it was George Riley?

Kathryn I guessed.

Colin There we go again. So much for patient confidentiality.

Tamsin Do you know if George knows yet?

Colin Oh, yes. The consultant wrote to him a couple of days ago. And then phoned him today.

Kathryn Why on earth's George not mentioned it to anyone?

Tamsin Probably doesn't want to upset people. Knowing George. Jack's trying to get hold of him. But there's no answer. It's awful. He's all on his own in that little house, isn't he?

Kathryn Since that wretched woman walked out.

Colin What wretched woman?

Kathryn His wife, darling. George's wife. What was her name?

Tamsin Monica.

Colin Oh, yes. Monica. She ought to be told, of course.

Kathryn Why should she? She walked out on the man, didn't she? She's probably not even remotely interested.

Tamsin I think that's slightly unfair on her. I think there were probably two sides to it.

Kathryn Anyway, sorry we're late. Rehearsals are in the playroom as usual, I take it?

Tamsin Oh, I'd almost forgotten we're meant to be rehearsing.

Kathryn Our director's no doubt already in there? Impatiently hopping up and down?

Tamsin No, Peggy's not arrived yet.

Kathryn Really? That's unlike Peggy.

Tamsin No, you're the first. I was beginning to think I'd got the wrong day.

Jack returns, slightly tearful.

Any luck?

Jack He's not answering his mobile either. I left a message. Just in case he picks up later. You know, I was thinking one of us ought to go round there, you know . . .

Tamsin Are you sure, Jack?

Jack George will be in a terrible state. He'll need our help. Need us to rally round him. All of us.

Kathryn If it was me, I don't think I'd welcome a coach party.

Tamsin No, he probably wants to be on his own. You've left the message on his mobile, Jack, that's all you can do for now. He'll call if he needs us.

Colin My advice is to leave him be. Let him come to terms in his own way. Perhaps a moment of quiet reflection.

Kathryn I can't imagine George ever quiet. Let alone in reflection.

Tamsin Was the answering machine on when you rang his landline?

397

Jack No, it wasn't switched on. It rang for ages.

Tamsin Well, there you are. He must be home. He's choosing not to answer.

Jack Unless he's lying there. Unconscious. Taken an overdose –

Kathryn Oh, Jack, really . . .

Tamsin He'll be fine, love. George would never do that.

Jack (*in sudden despair*) Why George? Why the hell did it have to be George? It's always the people who are full of life that go first, have you noticed? The miserable bastards live for ever, don't they?

Slight pause.

Tamsin Oh, I promised you a brandy, love, didn't I? Anyone else fancy a drink? I know we shouldn't before rehearsal, but . . . Tea? Or coffee?

Kathryn Brandy sounds lovely. Good for shock, don't they say?

Colin No, it's not. Complete fallacy.

Tamsin Really? I always thought –

Colin You're far better off with a glass of water.

Kathryn Try telling the St Bernards, dear.

Tamsin I'll get the brandy.

Jack (*rising*) I'll get it. You stay put.

Tamsin You sure?

Jack (*his tears welling up again*) I'm going to try George again . . .

Jack goes off, barely able to hide his grief.

Tamsin He's really taking this badly. They're such friends, of course.

Jack (*off, with a cry of grief*) Oh, God!

The others do their best to ignore this. Not wishing to intrude.

Tamsin (*rather too brightly*) Where on earth have Peggy and co. got to? This isn't like her at all, is it?

Jack (*off, wailing*) Why George? Why?

Tamsin I'm – I was in two minds whether to take this part, actually. It's only because Peggy – I think she couldn't find anyone else to play it . . .

Another burst of sobbing from Jack.

Kathryn You're perfect. You'll be a perfect Ginny.

Tamsin She's supposed to be twenty-something, isn't she?

Kathryn Where does it say that?

Tamsin She's supposed to be twenty-seven or something . . . Late twenties

Kathryn Where does it say that in the script? Listen, I've done this play three times before and I can tell you, you're a perfect Ginny. Far and away the best. Believe me, Tam, you're ideal casting. You look young – youthful. With just that little hint of knowingness behind the eyes. The tiniest bit worn round the edges . . .

Tamsin Thanks very much . . .

Kathryn No, you know what I mean. It's what the character needs. Innocence. With a suggestion that she's seen it all before.

Tamsin Please don't go on . . .

Colin (*gallantly interceding*) After all, she's meant to be having an affair with me, isn't she? In the play, I mean.

Kathryn Well, dramatic licence there, I think.

Tamsin Don't be so mean, Kathryn! (*Coming on to Colin slightly*) We could have a lovely affair, you and me, couldn't we, Colin?

Colin laughs nervously, drawing back.

Kathryn I rest my case.

Tamsin I mean, in the first scene I have to walk around with virtually nothing on.

Colin (*laughing*) Look forward to that . . .

Kathryn You're not even onstage. You'll be in the wings, I hope. Learning your lines.

Tamsin I mean, next to Jeff, I'm going to look like his mother, aren't I? I've got a daughter practically the same age as him.

Kathryn What nonsense! Jeff's much older than Tilly. He's twenty, isn't he? He must be.

Tamsin Nineteen. He's nineteen. He told me in the pub the other night.

Kathryn And how old's Tilly?

Tamsin Sixteen in September.

Colin Sixteen. I can't even remember being sixteen, you know.

Kathryn You may have skipped that age altogether, Colin. You probably slept through it.

Jack returns with a bottle of brandy and four glasses.

Jack (*sniffing*) Sorry.

Tamsin Did you get hold of him, love?

Jack (*setting down the tray*) No, he's still not answering.

Tamsin (*taking over*) I'll do this. (*She pours brandies during the next*) Kathryn?

Kathryn Thank you. Just a wee one. Little bit more. Whooaa! Easy!

Colin No, thank you. I'm driving. I'll have a sip of Kathryn's.

Kathryn No, you won't.

Tamsin (*passing a glass to Jack*) Darling?

She pours herself a glass and they settle.

(*Raising her glass*) Well, here's to . . .

Kathryn Yes, to . . .

Colin Yes . . .

Jack Listen, I've been giving things a bit of thought out there. We're all George's friends, aren't we? I know I'm a particularly special friend . . . his greatest friend . . . his oldest . . . I love the man . . .

He stops, in danger of breaking down again.

. . . but we all of us share that in our own ways . . . (*He falters again*) . . . love . . . I've known George since he and I were at school together . . . just down the road there . . . the same school, of course, he teaches in now . . . we were twins, really . . . that's what it amounted to . . . different parents, of course, but . . . living next door to each other . . . both only kids . . . sharing the same dreams, ideals to start with . . . brothers. Till George chose one path . . . and I – went off down another . . . did what I wanted to do. He stayed here – married a fellow

teacher, married Monica . . . whilst I . . . met Tam . . .
made a bit of money . . . had Tilly . . . came back here
then . . . get her away from London . . . But George – all
that time stayed here, he kept faith with the original
dream. He held on to the ideals. Whereas – I – sold off
my bit . . . like another chunk of real estate . . .

Tamsin (*quietly*) That's not actually true, you know . . .

Jack Well, that's what it feels like . . . not that George
ever . . . he's never criticised me for it . . . never accused
me, you know, of selling out . . . of not keeping . . . But
let me tell you, that is one very special person there. And,
at this time, he's going to need every bit of love we can
spare . . . And I think we, all of us, in our various ways,
we owe him that, at least.

Kathryn Hear! Hear!

Tamsin Agreed.

Colin Oh, yes.

Jack (*raising his glass*) To George.

All To George.

> *Pause.*
> *Jack is suddenly overcome with grief. With a*
> *convulsive sob, he suddenly rises and rushes into the*
> *far garden.*

Jack (*as he goes*) Excuse me . . . excuse me, please . . .

> *Another silence.*

Kathryn Where on earth's he gone now?

Tamsin I don't know. The tree house probably. Gone to
sit up in Tilly's tree house. Jack built it for her years ago.
They both still use it. Whenever one or the other of them
gets – upset.

Colin Oh. Do you ever go and sit in there?

Tamsin Me? Go and sulk in a tree house? God, no. I've got far too much to do down here on the ground. (*Slight pause*) I can't bear to think of George all on his own, you know, in that pokey little . . . semi.

Kathryn Perhaps you could rent him your tree house?

From the house, the phone rings.

Tamsin (*rising*) Oh, that could be him.

Tamsin goes off.

Kathryn On our way home, Colin, we really should look in on George. No matter how late it is. If we still haven't heard from him. Shouldn't we?

Colin Yes, possibly. I must say, Jack's taking this awfully badly.

Kathryn Well, he's known George for ages, you heard what he said.

Colin You've known George a long time too, come to that.

Kathryn Not as long as Jack has. Anyway, George and I are just friends. Small F. Whereas Jack and George – theirs is a Male Friendship. Capital M. Capital F. Nothing more sacred than a Male Friendship. I'm a mere female. With another equally small F.

Colin I don't think I've ever had a Male Friendship. Not like that.

Kathryn No.

Colin Well, not unless you count Basil.

Kathryn Basil? Who on earth's Basil when he's at home?

Colin Basil Bender. Before he died.

Kathryn Basil Bender? You can't possibly call that a Male Friendship. That wasn't even a friendship. You weren't even particularly friendly.

Colin We used to write to each other a bit. Went on walking holidays together a couple of times.

Kathryn You didn't even go to his funeral, poor man. I don't think Dorothy Bender's ever forgiven you.

Colin Well, I wasn't lugging all the way to Bournemouth. Not even for Basil Bender.

Jack returns, still a little red-eyed.

Kathryn Jack!

Jack Sorry. I can't seem to be able to control this. (*Another suppressed sob*) I'm sorry . . .

Kathryn Don't worry, grief is perfectly natural, Jack. Grief is a perfectly normal human reaction. In most people . . .

Tamsin returns.

Tamsin That was Peggy. She's just had Jeff round there. He apparently wants to quit the show. He's got a new girlfriend and they're moving to Wolverhampton in three weeks so she can start her new job.

Kathryn Well, thank you so much, Jeff, for telling us now . . .

Colin Oh, dear . . .

Kathryn . . . on the first day of rehearsal. Wonderful timing, I must say.

Tamsin Peggy's been trying to persuade him to put off the move until after the performances in September. But he's terrified of losing this new girl. She's apparently the best thing that ever happened to him and he wants to be with her every second.

Kathryn (*with a dry laugh*) Oh, God! I'll give that two weeks. Maximum. They'll be at each other's throats in a fortnight, dear. Young people, they've absolutely no commitment, have they, these days? None at all. Never mind, we'll manage without him, won't we? To be perfectly honest, I did find Jeff very unprepossessing. I don't for the life of me know why Peggy cast him in the first place. He had appalling acne. What made her choose him?

Tamsin One, he was young. Two, he was male. Rare qualities in societies like ours. No, I wasn't particularly looking forward to the love scenes, I must say. Anyway, Peggy's on a hunt for someone else. In the meantime, she says unless we want to start a four-handed play with only three of us, there's nothing more we can do tonight, is there?

A silence.

Kathryn (*thoughtfully*) Now, who do we know? There must be someone. Young and male?

Tamsin (*thinking*) Yes. Must be someone. Got any young patients, Colin?

Colin (*shaking his head*) No. Most of them are older than I am.

Pause.

Jack (*tentatively*) George?

Tamsin What?

Jack How about George? Could George do it? I mean, I don't even know this play but if you're stuck . . .

Kathryn (*doubtfully*) Well. He's a bit old.

Tamsin Well . . . look who he's up against.

Kathryn It's not a bad idea, you know . . .

Colin Can George act? Do we know if he can even act?

Kathryn That's not strictly necessary, not in Peggy's productions. It helps, but it's sort of an option.

Jack He was pretty good in that school play, wasn't he? We saw him in that, Tam. The one Tilly had a small part in?

Tamsin What, *Grease*?

Jack George can hold a tune.

Kathryn He doesn't need to sing in this.

Jack Well, there you are then. Even better.

Kathryn We mustn't rule him out, you know . . .

Tamsin With all this on his mind, he surely won't want to –

Jack Why not? Get him involved. Throw himself into something. Amongst friends.

Kathryn They've given him six months, haven't they?

Colin More or less.

Kathryn And we don't open till September, do we? He won't miss the first night.

Tamsin We could always ask him, I suppose. No harm in that.

Colin We'll need to run it past Peggy first, won't we?

Kathryn George is a trifle old for the part but . . . He does have all that long hair. Perfect for the sixties – I presume we're doing it in period – once he rinses out the grey bits.

Jack Something like this is just what George needs.

Kathryn What do you think, Tamsin? It's really up to you, isn't it? A lot of your stuff's with him. He'll be playing your boyfriend, after all.

Tamsin (*cautiously*) Let's see what George says first, shall we? Peggy may have found someone else by then, you never know.

The doorbell rings.

Jack (*springing up*) That could be George . . .

Tamsin Probably Tilly. Back from her party. She never remembers her key . . . (*Irritably*) She drives me mad sometimes, that girl. Why she can't ever remember to take her front door key with her . . .?

Jack (*as he goes*) Now, don't yell at her, love. She's only a kid . . .

Jack goes out.

Tamsin (*after him*) She's not a kid, Jack, she's nearly sixteen years old! (*Muttering*) When I was sixteen, I had . . . oh, forget it . . .

Colin (*after a pause, rising*) Yes, we must be . . . I think . . . mustn't we?

Kathryn Yes. (*Pointedly*) And we might on the way home . . . mightn't we, Colin?

Colin (*mystified*) What?

Kathryn Pass by . . .? On our way . . . look in on . . . (*Mouthing*) George.

Colin What? Oh, yes, we well might do . . . we very well might do that. We might – I might look in on George, Tamsin. See how he is.

Tamsin Oh, good, that'd be such a relief. Thank you. I mean, I was thinking we'd both go. But with Jack in his current state, I think it might do more harm than good – especially if George is . . . I mean, if he isn't upset now, by the time he and Jack have had a drink or two – the place'll be awash.

Colin No, as his doctor, I feel I need to look in . . . and say – reassuring things.

Tamsin That would be a weight off both our minds, especially Jack's.

Kathryn And I might – only if the subject crops up, mind you – I might just drop into the conversation this other business. About the play . . .

Tamsin (*doubtfully*) Oh, yes. But only if the –

Kathryn Only if the subject crops up, of course . . .

Colin (*laughing*) That way we can kill two birds, eh? (*Realising*) Sorry.

Colin goes out.

Kathryn He has this wonderful bedside manner. He saves patients' lives only to kill them off with his tactless small talk. Goodnight, I do hope Jack will be alright.

Tamsin Oh, he'll be fine. Now Tilly's home, he'll be perfectly fine. She'll sort him out. Better than I could, these days.

Kathryn Ah, well. Mothers and daughters . . . It can be a bit of a powder keg, can't it?

Tamsin (*anxious not to prolong this*) Yes, it can, it can. I'll see you out, Kathryn.

Kathryn No, it's alright, don't bother, Tamsin. Thank you so much for the brandy. Night, night.

Tamsin Night.

Kathryn goes out. Tamsin gathers up the glasses thoughtfully. She goes indoors with the tray. As she does so, the lights cross-fade to George's house. The lights are now on there as the loud rock music continues unabated as the lights fade to:

Blackout.

SCENE TWO

July.
   The same.
   Kathryn and Colin are seated in their garden as before. Colin has a prop newspaper which he rustles. Kathryn looks at him beadily.

Colin (*as Philip*) 'I can't say I'm very taken with this marmalade.'

He rustles his newspaper.

Kathryn (*as Sheila*) 'No, nor am I.'

Colin (*as Philip*) 'Then why did you buy it?'

Kathryn (*as Sheila*) 'I couldn't tell by looking at it, could I?'

Colin (*as Philip*) 'Hmm.'

Pause. Colin opens his mouth and then closes it again. Instead he rustles his newspaper

Kathryn (*as Sheila*) 'They didn't have our sort.'

Colin (*as Philip*) 'I'd sooner have none than this.' (*He rustles the paper*)

Kathryn (*as Sheila*) 'You say that now. You say that –'

Colin (*as Philip*) 'If you ask me we'd have been better off with jam.' (*He rustles the paper*)

Kathryn (*as Sheila*) 'You may well say that –'

Colin (*as Philip*) 'I do. I mean it.' (*He rustles the paper*)

Kathryn (*coming out of character, angrily*) Colin, will you please stop that!

Colin What?

Kathryn Rustling that wretched paper! Every syllable I utter. Rustle, rustle . . .

Colin I'm only doing what it says here.

Kathryn . . . rustle! It's driving me mad!

Colin It says it here they're both reading the Sunday papers.

Kathryn Well, you can do it quietly, can't you? You're drowning every word I say. Throwing all my timing. How can one possibly hold a comic pause with you . . . rustling away there.

Colin I was only filling in the gaps.

Kathryn What gaps?

Colin The gaps you keep on leaving. When neither of us is saying anything.

Kathryn They're not gaps, they're pauses. Pauses for laughs.

Colin Oh, really?

Kathryn Pauses for where the laughs come. At least they will eventually. We hope.

Silence.

Colin George is coming on a treat, isn't he?

Kathryn Yes. George is.

Colin I caught a bit of his scene with Tamsin yesterday evening. She's going to be terrific, too. Really – hurling herself into it. Both of them were.

Kathryn Yes. They're far too old for the parts, of course.

Silence.

(*Irritably*) Oh, it's too hot out here. There's no shade in this garden. I've told you, we need an umbrella, I keep saying.

Kathryn goes indoors.

Colin (*rising to follow her*) And I keep saying, I'm not lugging all the way out to Ikea just for an umbrella. Not for one sunny day per annum.

From the house, one of the grandfather clocks starts to chime eight. Colin, instinctively checking his watch, shakes his head.

Oh, dear.

He follows Kathryn indoors. As he does so, the lights cross-fade to Simeon's farm area.
    Jack enters. As he does so, his mobile starts ringing with a rather jolly ring tone.

Jack (*glancing at the screen, softly*) Oh, God, not again. (*Answering*) What is it, darling? . . . Yes . . . yes . . . no . . . I can't do that, my love . . . because I've got – because I've got too many . . . yes . . . yes . . . (*Sympathetically*) . . .

I know . . . I know it must do . . . it's the same for me,
darling . . . yes, I do . . . yes . . . Listen, I . . . listen, I . . .
I can't . . . (*Seeing someone in the fields*) Listen, I have
to go, darling . . . I'm in the middle of this meeting . . .
yes . . . yes . . . yes . . . I love you, too . . . Yes . . . 'bye . . .
'bye-bye . . . 'bye.

> *He rings off. As he does so, Monica enters from across*
> *the fields.*

Monica Sorry. You been here long?

Jack I thought you'd forgotten.

Monica I was . . . I was out for my walk. My new regime.
Every morning. Before school.

Jack How are you?

Monica Oh, pretty good. You know. Yes.

Jack Busy?

Monica Oh, yes. School's hectic. Paperwork gets worse
and worse. Scarcely any time for teaching these days.

Jack How's country life, then?

Monica Wonderful.

Jack You're well away from things out here. Quiet.

Monica Peaceful.

Jack Happy?

Monica Very.

> *Pause.*

This'll be about George, will it?

Jack Has he been in touch?

Monica No.

Jack Ah. He said he was going to.

Monica No. (*Pause*) How is he?

Jack Oh . . . All things considered. It's early stages, of course.

Monica Yes.

Jack With these drugs they've put him on. He's not physically in too bad a shape. Not in any sort of pain, anyway.

Monica I'm glad of that.

Slight pause.

Jack No. It's psychologically, you know . . . That's the problem. I can't even begin to guess what's going on inside his head.

Monica No. But that was never really possible with George, was it?

Jack (*puzzled*) Sorry?

Monica Even at the best of times. Trying to guess what the hell was going on inside his head. After eleven years I gave up trying.

Jack smiles faintly.

I did try and call him actually. Only . . . only . . . I kept missing him. (*Slight pause*) No. That's not true. I kept – hanging up at the last minute. As soon as I got the answering machine.

Pause.

I couldn't think what to say to him. Not at all. I thought of leaving a message. 'George, this is your ex-wife just calling to say sorry to hear the news and I didn't mean all the things I called you when I left you . . .' But then I thought, that would all sound a bit insincere – hypocritical, you know? Because I did mean all the things I called him. They were true. And I don't take back a single one of them.

Pause.

It's ironic really. You get to a stage in a relationship which starts out so passionately, so filled with love. Then, gradually over the years, you drive each other to a point when there are moments you actually do wish the other would simply drop dead. And then, when you hear they are dying . . . on the point of death. You think, was that partly my doing?

Pause.

Jack He's all on his own, Monica.

Monica (*shaking her head firmly*) No.

Jack He's got no one with him, since you left –

Monica I gave him every opportunity –

Jack – I mean, his friends are gathering round, as best we can –

Monica I stuck with him as long as humanly possible, Jack. God, I did!

Jack – but he needs *you*, Monica. George needs you back.

Monica Did he say that?

Jack (*a slight hesitation*) Yes.

Monica He needs me back? Or is that you saying it? Putting words into his mouth?

Jack He said – words to that effect. He might not have used that exact wording but he – I know George. I know in his heart he wants you back. In his heart, he –

Monica Yes, well, that's another mystery, isn't it? George's heart? I never fathomed that out either. Even more confused than his head.

Pause.

Jack If – if he were to call you, would you consider it?

Monica No.

Jack Not if he begged you – said he was sorry?

Monica I've got a new life here, Jack. It's too late.

Jack Just for a few months? George's few remaining months?

Monica I've found someone else to love. Who loves me, who does genuinely need me – And this time, thank God, a man I can read like a book.

Jack Well, you could take leave of absence from him just for a month, surely?

Monica What are you talking about? Leave of absence –?

Jack This bloke would understand that you need to put things on hold – temporarily –

Monica What the hell are you talking about? You sound exactly like George! You and he, you're as batty as each other. Put things on hold? It's not a bloody DVD, Jack! Pause, play . . . freeze-frame . . . fast fucking forward! Rewind! It's real life! That's what got me about living with George, you know. Whenever we had one of our frequent rows – our increasingly frequent rows – ten minutes later he'd come back in the room, head tilted on one side, that little boy look on his face, you know, the way he always does, and he'd say, 'Sorry, old love, let's forget that, shall we? Start again?' So we'd rewind the past few hours and we'd re-record over it again like it never happened. And you know what? Because of that, nothing ever changed between us. Nothing was ever learnt. Never even referred to again. Like it never happened. And we went round and round and round, day after day, month after month, year in year out, for eleven years, repeating the same mistakes all over again. Saying the same spur-of-the-moment, thoughtless, hurtful things to each other –

Silence.

(*Regaining her breath*) There's someone in my life now who simply loves me. No – rephrase that – loves me simply. Quite a lot, I think. I hope. Who's never said a hurtful thing in his whole life. He's gentle, he's kind and considerate and he wants to make me happy. And I feel the same about him. You're right. It is quiet here. Peaceful and calm. You could say it lacks excitement. Maybe. But at least I'm out of the war zone.

Slight pause.

There's also a very troubled little boy here who's badly in need of love.

A silence.

Jack I won't desert George, not now. Whatever it takes. He's my friend. I want his life to end happily. I won't give up, Monica. I'll keep trying.

Monica You do that, Jack. Good luck.

Simeon appears from the house. The men stare at each other.
A silence.

Jack Morning.

Simeon Morning.

Slight pause.

Jack Well, I'd better be . . . Good to see you again, Monica. Talk to you soon.

Monica Possibly.

Jack (*to Simeon*) Nice to have met you.

Simeon Yes.

Jack goes off towards the house. In a moment, his car starts up. Simeon and Monica watch him leave. They look at each other.

Monica (*taking his hand*) It's alright. Don't worry. It's alright.

As they go off towards the house the lights cross-fade to Tamsin and Jack's patio. Kathryn comes from the house. She stands impatiently. Tamsin enters from the garden.

Kathryn You mean they haven't even got as far as my entrance yet?

Tamsin Not quite.

Kathryn Well, I do wish someone had phoned to warn me. This is so unlike Peggy. Her rehearsals are usually bang on the dot. That's the best thing about her as a director. Not awfully helpful in times of artistic *crise* but at least you could rely on her rehearsals going like clockwork.

Kathryn sits.

Tamsin As I say, it's not Peggy's fault entirely. George was forty minutes late – Again.

Kathryn I hurtled home from work to be here. Which wasn't easy. This time of year we're snowed under in the

417

surgery with wretched people going on holiday, making last-minute appointments because half their fillings have fallen out . . .

Tamsin I've been sitting twiddling my thumbs out here for ages. Did you say lemonade rather than tea?

Kathryn Just the teeniest drop.

Tamsin Home-made. I think it's turned out rather well. You want to come and sit indoors to wait? Bit hot out here, isn't it? They said they'd call us when they're ready.

Kathryn No, I'm happy out here. Just a cool drink.

Tamsin (*as she leaves*) Think I'll join you.

Kathryn Just a *soupçon*. While I'm waiting.

Tamsin goes into the house.

I think the least someone could have done was to telephone.

Tamsin (*off, distant*) Yes . . .

Kathryn (*calling loudly*) I mean, what about that wretched stage manager woman? Anthea or whatever her name is?

Tamsin (*off, distant*) Who, Andrea?

Kathryn (*calling loudly*) That's her job surely? To inform the artistes? What else does she have to do? Except sit there like a useless dollop, doing absolutely nothing. Fiddling with her iPod or whatever it is. I mean, what is the point of even having her there? You set your own props, you move your own furniture, you even have to do your own prompting because she's never got the wretched book open at the right place. No, I'm sorry. I think that girl's utterly and completely worse than useless . . .

Colin comes from the garden, a little concerned.

Colin Kathryn, Peggy says could you keep it down a bit? Only we're trying to rehearse a scene in there.

Kathryn Have they got to me yet?

Colin Not quite. If you could just keep it down a bit, Kathryn. We've had to leave the windows open. We can hear every word in there.

Colin goes back.

Kathryn (*unrepentant*) Tell them to hurry up. Or I'm going home. I have better things to do with my time.

Tamsin returns with two glasses and a jug of home-made lemonade on a tray.

Tamsin Here we are. Might be a bit cold, it's straight out of the fridge.

She sets the tray down on the table.

Kathryn Oh now, doesn't that look tempting?

Tamsin Hang on, I'll get some napkins. Do help yourself.

Tamsin goes in again. Kathryn pours herself half a glass of lemonade. Swiftly she dives into her bag for her flask and tops her glass up with its contents.
As she finishes doing this, Tamsin returns with a couple of paper napkins.

Kathryn This looks so good. You must give me the recipe.

Tamsin Well. It's lemons, mostly. Lemons and water.

Kathryn Brilliant. How clever. (*Taking sip*) Mmmm! Delicious. Cheers!

Tamsin Cheers!

They drink.

Kathryn It's not good news to hear George was late for rehearsal again.

Tamsin No, I don't think George even owns a clock. God knows how he ever turns up for school on time. Nice they've kept him on, though, isn't it? Just till the end of term, anyway. Mind you, he's so popular. I don't think they'd have dared . . . The kids adore him, of course. That OK?

Kathryn Delicious.

Tamsin Was George always like that? Always late for everything?

Kathryn I can't remember. Probably.

Tamsin I mean, you've known him for years, haven't you? Almost as long as Jack has.

Kathryn Yes. Years.

A silence.
Tamsin waits for Kathryn to continue.

Tamsin No. Whatever you say about George, you can't accuse him of being a clock-watcher.

Kathryn No. I know. But then I do live with one. If ever there was a man who was clock-driven, it's Colin. Practically bordering on the anal.

Tamsin Well, being a doctor, I suppose he needs to be . . . I mean, appointments and so on . . .

Kathryn Colin has a clock permanently embedded in his arse. We lie in bed I can hear him. Ticking . . . One day he'll simply explode.

Tamsin (*laughing*) Well. Have fun when he does.

Kathryn God, I don't mean explode in that way, dear. I don't mean sexually. That's long gone. As they used to say in the westerns, it went thataway.

Tamsin Ah.

Kathryn Thank God. Not a problem with Jack, I take it?

Tamsin No . . . Not that . . . I . . .

Tamsin may be about to say more only Colin comes in from the garden.

Colin We've just got to Sheila's entrance . . .

Kathryn Oh, hooray. (*She rises*)

Tamsin Well done, you're making up on time, then?

Colin We're currently – slightly less than seventeen minutes behind schedule.

Kathryn Tick-tock, tick-tock, tick-tock . . .

Colin George is doing amazingly well. Knows most of his lines, already . . .

Kathryn I hope you do, too.

Colin Well, roughly. Roughly.

Kathryn Roughly?

They go off up the garden.
Tamsin makes to clear the glasses. She picks up Kathryn's glass and becomes aware of the odour from the contents. She sniffs it. She recoils at the alcohol fumes.
She cautiously sips and tastes it. Finding the result less than displeasing, she picks up her own script. She sits and studies it, Kathryn's glass still in her hand.
Jack enters from the house.

Jack Oh, hi.

Tamsin (*without looking up*) Hi.

Jack Thought you'd be rehearsing.

Tamsin They haven't got to my bit.

Jack How's George getting on?

Tamsin He's going to be good. Far better than me, anyway.

Jack You'll be great. You always say that. You always are.

Tamsin continues to stare at her script. Jack looks at her.

What's that you're drinking?

Tamsin (*without looking up*) Lemonade.

Jack Oh, lemonade. Well, I'll make a great effort and refrain.

Jack watches her. He fiddles restlessly. Tamsin stays concentrated on her task.

What you doing?

Tamsin Going over the lines for my scene.

Jack Oh, right. Sorry. Won't interrupt you. (*Slight pause*) I'll go over them with you, if you like. Your lines.

Tamsin It's OK.

Jack Sure? I don't mind. No trouble. No?

Pause.

Tamsin studies her script.

I was thinking, you know, we could have a marquee just out there. For Tilly's birthday. Just a small one.

Tamsin (*without looking up*) Is that what she wants?
A marquee?

Jack I don't know, haven't asked her.

Tamsin Why don't you ask her whether she wants a
marquee?

Jack It wouldn't be a surprise then, would it?

Tamsin She doesn't need a marquee.

Tamsin gets up.

Jack Where are you going?

Tamsin I'm going to sit in the tree house. I need to look
at these lines.

Jack I've said, I'll go over them with you –

Tamsin No, it's OK –

Jack Come on, you know, like I used to? Whenever you
did a show? I always used to help you with them,
remember? In the old days. Most of the time I knew the
lines better than the bloke you were acting with. I used to
sit there in the audience at the first performance saying
the lines along with him, under my breath. Better than
him most of the time.

Tamsin (*thawing faintly*) Not always under your breath,
either . . . Alright, then. Here. (*Handing him the script*)
From the top of the page there. You read George's bits.
You read Greg.

Jack Top of the page?

Tamsin Top of the page.

Jack (*reading, as Greg*) 'You know? I've been thinking –
it might be a good idea if we got married – pretty soon.'

Tamsin (*as Ginny*) 'When – now?'

Jack (*as Greg*) 'No.'

Tamsin (*as Ginny*) 'Oh, good. Going to say, I'd have to go and change my dress again.'

Jack (*as Greg*) 'No. Seriously.'

Tamsin (*as Ginny*) 'When did you suddenly get this idea?'

Jack (*as Greg*) 'I thought it might be a good thing.'

Tamsin (*as Ginny*) 'I take it you're proposing to me?'

Jack (*as Greg*) 'Yes, I suppose I am really. If you look at it that way.' (*As himself*) There you go! What did I say? As good as George, aren't I?

Tamsin (*as herself*) No, you're not as good as George. (*As Ginny*) 'Either you are or you aren't.'

Jack (*as Greg*) 'Yes, I am.'

Tamsin (*as Ginny*) 'I see. I'm just going out – actually.'

Jack (*as Greg*) 'The taxi won't be here for a second. It doesn't take you that long to make up your mind, does it?' (*As himself*) This bloke's an idiot, isn't he?

Tamsin (*as Ginny*) 'I'm afraid it does. If you're serious, I don't know what to say. I love you very much, more than I've ever loved anybody, I think.' (*As herself, pursing her lips and making a kissing sound*) Then we have a bit of a kiss – 'And I think I'll –'

Jack A kiss?

Tamsin Just a quick one.

Jack It's not in the script here.

Tamsin No, we put one in – (*As Ginny*) 'I think I'll probably say yes, one day. But not at the moment.'

Jack (*as Greg*) 'I see.'

Tamsin (*as Ginny*) 'Greg, have you really thought about this? I'm sorry to ask you – but you're not asking me away for a dirty weekend or something. Or even a dirty month.'

Jack (*as Greg*) 'A dirty great lifetime. I know.'

Tamsin (*as Ginny*) 'Who have you known apart from me? How many other girls?'

Jack (*as Greg*) 'Well –'

Tamsin (*as Ginny*) 'I mean really known – you know what I mean.'

Jack (*as Greg*) 'Well – I – well –'

> *Pause.*
> *Tamsin is staring at Jack directly for the first time. Jack becomes aware of this and looks up at her.*

Then she says, 'I'm the first, aren't I?'

Tamsin I know. I know what she says.

Jack You are. You know that, Tam. The first. Always will be. Number one.

Tamsin (*unconvinced*) Yes.

> *Colin comes from the garden.*

Colin Tam! Just coming up to you.

Tamsin Right. (*To Jack, indicating the glasses, etc*) Clear those away, would you?

> *Tamsin goes off with Colin.*
> *Jack sits for a second. His mobile rings.*

Jack (*glancing at the screen, savagely*) No! Not now!

He cancels the call.
He gathers up the jug and two glasses which he is about to place on the tray. He becomes aware of the whiff of alcohol from the glass Tamsin had been drinking from. He sniffs it and stares after her worriedly.

Oh, God. (*Shaking his head*) No, no, no . . .

He goes into the house with the tray.
The lights cross-fade to the farmyard.
Monica comes from the house. She stands looking out over the fields. Simeon comes from the house. He stops when he sees her.

Simeon Who was that, then?

Monica What?

Simeon On the phone? Just now? Anything important?

Monica No.

Simeon That bloke the other day? The one with the big car? What did he want? Again.

Monica Nothing.

Simeon (*putting his arms round her*) What do you mean, 'nothing'? If it's nothing, why's nothing upsetting you so much?

Monica It's not. (*Pulling away*) Just –

Simeon What? What is it?

Monica (*hurrying back to the house*) Nothing! Nothing! Nothing! NOTHING!

Monica goes back to the house.
Simeon stares after her. He makes to kick at the stone seat again. He checks himself and follows her

more slowly. As he does so, the lights cross-fade to George's garden. Kathryn, as if looking for someone, comes from the house. She stands puzzled. She picks her way into the garden a little.

After a moment, Tamsin, dressed in her jeans and a work shirt, also enters from the house behind her.

Tamsin (*stopping as she sees Kathryn*) Oh, it's you.

Kathryn, startled, jumps.

Kathryn What are you doing here?

Tamsin I promised George I'd collect his washing and bung it in our machine at home. His one here's not working.

Kathryn I wondered why the front door was unlocked.

Tamsin I was just upstairs. Why are you here, then?

Kathryn I came to see George, on the off-chance. Promised I'd run some lines.

Tamsin I see. He's not here.

Kathryn No.

Tamsin He's at the cricket. The one-day game.

Kathryn I didn't know George liked cricket.

Tamsin I don't think he does much. Jack persuaded him to go on his own. Lent him his season ticket. I think George just went along for the beer, really. I'm glad I came round, though. This house is disgusting. It can't have been cleaned since Monica left.

Pause.

Have you been following me, then?

Kathryn (*startled*) What on earth do you mean?

Tamsin Following me? Just now?

Kathryn Good heavens, no. (*Pause*) Why on earth would I want to follow you?

Pause. Tamsin continues to stare at her.

No, no, no. (*Slight pause*) No . . . I passed you – quite by chance – in town. And I guessed you were on your way here . . . And I – I – yes, I did, I followed you.

Tamsin To see if George and I were at it like rabbits?

Kathryn I thought you were about to do something extremely stupid. Something you'd regret.

Tamsin As you see, he isn't here. Otherwise we would have been.

Kathryn (*slightly shocked*) Really? Truthfully?

Tamsin No. Not really. (*Slight pause*) I must get on. Tidy up a bit.

Kathryn I'll give you a hand, shall I?

Tamsin God, no, look at you, you're hardly dressed for that.

Kathryn Oh, this thing's terribly old . . .

Tamsin You'll get filthy, I warn you . . .

Kathryn Then we'll both get filthy together, won't we?

Tamsin and Kathryn go into the house.

Cross-fade to Jack and Tamsin's patio.
Jack comes from the house with a glass of beer in a tankard.
Colin, without a drink, follows him.

Jack Thanks for coming round, mate, I really appreciate it. Giving up your afternoon. Sit down. Sure I can't offer you anything. Beer? Soft drink?

They both sit.

Colin No, no, thank you. I've just made myself a cup of tea back home. Catching up on things.

Jack Ah, the dreaded paperwork, eh?

Colin No, Sunday afternoon is my clock day.

Jack Sorry?

Colin The day when I go round trying to synchronise our clocks.

Jack Clocks? How many have you got?

Colin Well, principally the two grandfathers. One I inherited from my parents and the other one I bought Kathryn for our twelfth anniversary. But alas, neither of them are particularly good timekeepers, you see.

Jack That's important, isn't it? In a clock? Good timekeeping?

Colin It is. But one of them has a tendency to gain – oh, anything up to four or five minutes a week. And the other one tends to lose and occasionally, for no accountable reason, stop altogether. Which is irritating, of course, because then one has trouble with the chime.

Jack The chime?

Colin Yes. Getting out of step with the hour hand.

Jack Oh, yes, that'll be a problem.

Colin (*warming to his subject*) The hands are saying four o'clock but the clock chimes seven. Which means one often needs to crank through the chiming cycle, you see? Which can be anything up to nine or ten hours' worth. With the thing striking up to fifty-five times within the space of two or three minutes. Which drives Kathryn, of course, to distraction. So I usually try and time it when

429

she's out and the house is quiet. I think she must be out. Somewhere. I've really no idea where she is today.

Slight pause.

Well, that's quite enough of me and my clocks. How can I help, Jack?

Jack It's a – I'd just really appreciate your advice, Colin.

Colin As a doctor?

Jack No, no. No, it's more – as a friend. I'd like your advice, as a friend. It's a personal thing. Very personal . . .

Colin waits for Jack to continue. He doesn't.

Colin I see.

Jack Normally, if it's something this personal, the first one I'd discuss it with would be Tam. I mean, the wife's the first person you turn to, isn't she?

Colin (*slightly unconvinced*) Yes. I suppose so.

Jack Or your best friend. Which in my case, of course, would be George. In normal circumstances, George would be the first person I'd turn to. My number-one choice would be George. But in this case, I can't.

Colin Why not?

Jack In this case, it's to do with George.

Colin I see.

Jack And Tam.

Colin Tamsin?

Jack George and Tamsin. You'd not noticed?

Colin How do you mean? (*He considers*) Oh, I see. Well, I can't say I had. They seem to be getting on very well in rehearsals. Lots of laughter. Very friendly.

Jack Over-friendly, you think?

Colin Well, no, I assumed with this play, the roles they were playing, young lovers and so on – they were simply throwing themselves into their parts.

Jack You think I could be overreacting, then?

Colin I'm sure you are, Jack. I mean, Tamsin would never do anything like that, surely? She always seems to me a totally loyal wife.

Jack Yes.

Colin And ask yourself this question for a moment, Jack. What possible reason could Tamsin have for wanting to cheat on you?

Jack (*after a slight pause*) Right.

Colin None at all, surely? George has been your friend for years, hasn't he? I mean, he has a lot of faults has dear old George, but I don't think betraying his best friend is one of them. It would never cross his mind.

Jack Probably not. It's just I've known him a long time. As you say, he's loyal. Loyalty's his middle name. But now, of course – without Monica – he's a bit more, shall we say, more of a loose cannon. Rolling around the deck there. Pointing at all and sundry, threatening to go off at any minute. (*Laughing*) It's all hands and batten down the wife, mate, eh?

Colin (*laughing*) Yes. Point taken, Jack. Though I think Kathryn's safe enough! No need to batten her down.

Jack Cannonball proof, eh? These days. All safely tucked up and married to you, isn't she? No, I think those days are safely behind her, eh?

Colin Those days?

Jack The old days. The old wild oats and all that.

Colin (*smiling slightly incredulously*) Kathryn? Wild oats? What on earth are you talking about?

Jack (*back-pedalling*) Well – she's probably sowed a few. Oats. In her day. What woman hasn't, eh?

Colin No, not Kathryn. When Kathryn married me she was – I was the first.

Jack Were you? Oh, that's great. Great. Rare, too. Saved herself, did she, for you?

Colin Oh, yes. I certainly did. No rolling around the deck in my case, either.

Jack That's brilliant. (*Rising*) Look, I really mustn't keep you, Colin. You need to be getting back to your – clocks.

Colin (*rising*) I hope I've been of help, Jack.

Jack I really appreciate it, mate, I really do. Let me see you out.

Colin Good talking to you, Jack. I've enjoyed it. (*Laughing*) Kathryn? Wild oats? Really! I have to smile at that . . .

> *Colin and Jack go out, both laughing.*
> *The lights cross-fade to George's house as Tamsin and Kathryn come out, both slightly grimy from their labours, taking a break. They each hold a chipped mug of tea.*

Kathryn (*as they enter*) . . . get out of all that dust. God, the place is filthy.

Tamsin Now. Where can we sit? Hang on a tick . . .

> *She improvises a couple of seats from discarded objects in the garden and in due course they both sit down.*

Kathryn (*as this happens*) I don't know what it is about men who live on their own. How on earth do they survive, some of them?

Tamsin Is Colin as bad?

Kathryn No, in fact Colin's an exception. Quite the reverse. On the rare occasions I go away, I come back to a house which is ever so slightly cleaner than when I left. Certainly a lot tidier. Which in its way, of course, is equally unnerving. I have this image of Colin, as soon as I've gone, slipping into a little pink housecoat and prancing around the place in fluffy mules and a feather duster.

Tamsin (*laughing*) He's not into that, is he?

Kathryn God, I hope not.

Tamsin Jack's not too bad, I suppose. I've managed to civilise him over the years. Mind you, I'm never away for that long and – Tilly's usually around to look after him. (*Presenting Kathryn with an improvised seat*) There. Try that. It should be alright to sit on.

Kathryn Thank you. (*Gingerly sitting, dubiously*) I'm still not altogether convinced this tea is safe to drink, you know.

Tamsin I rinsed the mugs in boiling water. Shame there's no milk. Well, there was milk, but –

Kathryn (*squeamishly*) Don't remind me . . . Yeeuurr . . . yeeurr . . . yeeurrk! How can anyone leave a whole bottle simply . . .? George has always been like that. Even in the old days . . . My God, you know there was a possibility at one time – of the two of us getting together permanently.

Tamsin You and George?

Kathryn Oh, years ago. Back in the dark ages . . . when he and I we were both – babies . . . Well, he was. I was – slightly older than him. Long before I met Colin, of course. And years before George got together with Monica. But at one stage I seriously considered throwing in my lot and settling down with him.

Tamsin (*intrigued*) I had no idea you were that close.

Kathryn Very few people knew. Except my dear mother, of course. When I was forced to run home to her. Fled back home to Mummy.

Tamsin (*amused*) Why did you do that?

Kathryn I had to, darling, I was pregnant.

Tamsin Oh.

Kathryn We were never that careful, George and I. I knew precious little about it and he never bothered. I had to get rid of it, of course.

Tamsin Adopted?

Kathryn No, no, no.

Tamsin Oh, I see. Does Colin know?

Kathryn Certainly not. As I say, no one does. Except my dear late mother, of course. I don't think George ever mentioned it to anybody, except possibly to Jack. But probably not. You know men when they get together, they never talk about anything remotely important, do they?

Tamsin Did you ever consider having children with Colin?

Kathryn Briefly, in the early days. We talked about it. Once or twice. But then I found out, ironically, I couldn't have any more . . . And that was that.

Tamsin Oh, I'm sorry.

Kathryn Just as well, probably. We'd have made quite the most appalling parents.

Pause.

Do you find, Tamsin, with most men, they don't really listen to you, do they? After the first few minutes they become increasingly, selectively deafer. Hearing only the bits they choose to hear. Oh yes, when you're young they do, they hang on your every word. But then, of course, they sense there might be something in it for them, don't they? It's in their interest to listen. But as you grow older and less – overtly attractive – they hear less and less. They get that glazed, vaguely interested look, like you're both conversing through a sheet of glass. As if you're in prison or the post office. I've found that's generally the case with most men . . . But you know with George. He invariably does listen. He gives you his full attention, doesn't he? Have you found that? As a woman? Which is rare and wonderful. As if you're the only one . . . the only . . . what you are to him is important . . . vital . . . Those months I spent with him in that one-room flat – he could perform this magic – this magic trick – of slowing down time. Till it seemed to stand still in its tracks . . . whilst everything around you bustled on at the same mad, breathtaking pace – there we were, he and I, floating in this timeless limbo . . . (*Smiling*) 'Let it happen . . . let it all pass by, darling girl . . .' I suspect he can still do that, after all these years. The old magic's still there . . .

Tamsin (*softly*) Yes . . .

Kathryn I think that's what makes him a good teacher, too. Kids just love people who give them their full attention, don't they?

Tamsin Yes. When George taught Tilly, she adored him. She had this huge crush on him . . . Nine years old, she

435

used to cry her eyes out to me every night . . . (*Gently mimicking*) 'I love him . . . I love him . . . I love him.'

Kathryn How did Jack react to that, I wonder?

Tamsin Jack? He never knew. What? His beloved daughter? He could never have coped with that . . .

Kathryn Don't you go down that path yourself, dear, will you? Be warned.

Tamsin Yes.

Kathryn You've got a good husband, a beautiful daughter . . . Don't get your wings burnt, dear. Fly away home.

Tamsin Yes. No way.

Slight pause.

Kathryn Before much longer, I must do something with this sad little garden, too.

Tamsin Monica's pride and joy, wasn't it?

Kathryn Add that to the list, then! (*Sipping her tea*) This tea is utterly disgusting. He must have had these tea bags since Tetley was a boy. Well, onwards and upwards! Bedrooms?

Tamsin Bedrooms, it is!

Tamsin and Kathryn go indoors.
The lights cross-fade. It is dusk now.
At Colin and Kathryn's, Colin comes out thoughtfully. He has a half-filled whisky glass in his hand. He sits.
In the farmyard, Monica enters followed by Simeon.

Simeon Look, if he rings again and upsets you like this, I warn you, I'm pulling that phone off the wall.

Silence.

He can't do this to you. To us. It's harassment. (*Pause*) I'll have him arrested. (*Pause*) I'll go round there and hit him. I will. He can't keep doing this to you.

Monica (*softly*) I'm sorry.

Simeon You going to go back then? To this George? Well, are you?

Monica (*miserably*) I don't know . . . I don't know . . .

She rushes past him and back towards the house.

Simeon (*distressed*) Oh, buggering, blasted – buggeration!

He makes to kick at the stone seat again, thinks better of it and sits, his head in his hands.
The lights cross-fade to Jack and Tamsin's. Jack comes outside thoughtfully with his tankard.
In Colin and Kathryn's garden, Kathryn comes out.

Kathryn Oh. What on earth are you doing there, sitting in the dark?

Colin I was just – sitting in the dark. Thinking and drinking.

Kathryn Is that Scotch? You only drink Scotch when you think you've got a cold coming. You're not coming down with something, are you?

Colin Don't ask me, I'm only a doctor.

Kathryn Don't give it to me, whatever you do. I think I'll join you, just to be on the safe side. Have you done the clocks?

Colin Yes, I've done the clocks. For the time being.

Kathryn Only the one in the hall's stopped ticking.

Kathryn goes indoors.

Colin (*sinking his head in his hands*) Oh, God!

Tamsin comes out to join Jack.

Tamsin Hi!

Jack Where have you been?

Tamsin Up to George's place. Told you I was going.

Jack Oh, yes. Was he there?

Tamsin George? No. Of course not. You packed him off to the cricket, didn't you. Poor man.

Jack Oh, yes.

Tamsin I brought his washing back. His machine's not working. There's mountains of it . . .

Tamsin goes indoors. Kathryn comes out with a glass of Scotch.

Kathryn What have you been thinking about, all alone out here in the dark, anyway?

Colin Nothing much. Wild oats . . .

Kathryn Wild what?

Colin Oats.

Kathryn Oats? You mean porridge?

Colin No, not porridge. Just oats. Wild porridge? Might possibly have been wild porridge, I don't know. I don't know anything any more.

Kathryn I think you're going off your rocker, Colin. I'm going to have a bath. I'm filthy.

Colin Where have you been?

Kathryn Up at George's place. With Tam. We were giving the place a thorough clean. It needed it. Come indoors now, or you will, you'll catch a chill.

Kathryn goes indoors.
Colin rises and stares out into the gathering darkness, sipping his Scotch.
Jack stands and sips his beer.
Simeon rises and stares out across the fields.
Lights up on George's house as, from within, the usual loud rock music starts to play.
The lights fade to:

Blackout.

End of Act One.

Act Two

SCENE ONE

September.
The same. There is evidence that work has been done in clearing George's garden. Kathryn and Colin are at their table in their own garden as usual. This time it is set with the remains of their breakfast. Kathryn starts to clear this away during the next.

Kathryn I may need to take a brief holiday soon.

Colin Sorry?

Kathryn I said, I may need to take a brief holiday soon.

Colin What?

Kathryn Oh, for goodness sake, I said –

Colin Sorry, are we still running lines?

Kathryn No, we're not running lines –

Colin Oh, good. Because I didn't recognise a single one of them. Aren't you supposed to say 'I might go down to Kent for the weekend'?

Kathryn No, not Kent!

Colin Yes, Kent. Definitely Kent. It's Kent in the script.

Kathryn No . . .

Colin And then you go on to say that your cousin Natalie's written to ask you.

Kathryn Colin . . .

Colin Something like that. Unless we've changed it. I hope not. I'd just got that scene under my belt . . .

Kathryn Tenerife.

Colin Tenerife? We've changed it to Tenerife, have we?

Kathryn No. I'm telling you *I* may need to go to Tenerife.

Colin What, for the weekend? Bit extravagant.

Kathryn No, Colin. Listen. I, Kathryn, your wife – at this rate soon to be ex-wife – may be going for a fortnight to Tenerife.

Colin Your cousin Natalie's asked you to Tenerife?

Kathryn NO! Not Natalie! Will you listen, Colin? Listen! Listen to me!

Colin I am listening! Who has asked you, then?

Kathryn George.

Colin George?

Kathryn Yes.

A silence.

Colin Why on earth has he asked you?

Kathryn He's planning possibly the last holiday he'll ever take, as soon as the play's over and – he wanted someone to come with him. And he's asked me.

Colin What about his wife? What about Monica?

Kathryn Monica is long gone. She's out of his life. She's happy being a farmer's – woman. She's never coming back to George – despite all Jack's efforts. No, I'm the obvious choice.

Colin I don't see why.

Kathryn Well, I'm – he needs someone to take care of him, if necessary nurse him, if things get . . . Generally be on hand –

Colin You're not a nurse. You're a receptionist.

Kathryn – in case of emergencies.

Colin A dental receptionist.

Kathryn I have nursing experience. In the past. My mother.

Colin looks unconvinced.

It would all be above board. I mean, I'd be – I'd just be on hand. Nothing untoward. Nothing like that. Nothing . . . mucky –

Kathryn goes into the house.
Colin sits digesting this new development.

Colin (*to himself*) I sincerely hope not, for his sake.

He sits and studies his script. In a moment, he too goes indoors under the next. The lights come up on Jack and Tamsin's area. Jack comes on from the garden. He is calling back to someone out of sight.

Jack Yes, that's better. Little more this way . . . more . . . more . . . little bit more . . . That's it! That'll do nicely!

During this Tamsin comes from the house and watches Jack disinterestedly. She is spoiling for something. She is sipping a glass of lemonade.

(*Seeing Tamsin*) Just moving the end of the marquee slightly that way, so it'll be well clear of the beech tree. Not too close to the house, is it?

Tamsin remains silent.

(*Sitting, aware of her mood but soldiering on*) Ah, just watch those lads go – they'll have that marquee up in ten minutes. Professionals. There's something very restful about watching other people working.

Tamsin (*drily*) Yes. You must be quite exhausted this morning. After last night.

Jack What? (*Pause*) Oh, that. (*Pause*) I thought you were asleep.

Tamsin The phone rings by the bed at some ungodly hour. You immediately pick it up . . .

Jack I thought you were asleep.

Tamsin . . . you answer it. You say, 'Just a tick, love, I can't talk, I need to take this somewhere else.' You put down the phone and you creep downstairs . . .

Jack I thought you were asleep.

Tamsin . . . you answer the phone in the study. Then I hear you saying, over the extension, 'Hang on, darling, be with you in a second . . .'

Jack I didn't say 'darling' . . .

Tamsin . . . you creep back upstairs again . . .

Jack . . . I never said 'darling' . . .

Tamsin . . . you creep upstairs again and you quietly replace the receiver by the bed, so as not to wake me . . .

Jack I thought you were asleep.

Tamsin . . . and then you creep all the way back downstairs again. And you talk to the fucking girl for an hour and a half . . . before crawling back to bed, with freezing cold feet, at five a.m.

Jack I'm sorry if I woke you up. Did you listen in?

Tamsin I wouldn't lower myself. I wouldn't mind but why the hell don't you give her your mobile number, at least I'd get some sleep?

Jack I did give her my mobile number. I don't know why she didn't use it. I don't know why she keeps using the landline lately.

Tamsin For my benefit, Jack, that's why. Just to let me know she's still around.

Jack I'm – trying to sort it out, Tam. Sal's being a bit . . . unreasonable. Difficult, you know. Intransigent.

Tamsin Oh, dear. I am so sorry. Poor old you . . .

Jack Thanks.

Tamsin You don't think all this could have been the tiniest bit your fault in the first place, do you, Jack?

Jack Possibly . . .

Tamsin (*furiously*) Of course it was – YOU SELFISH BASTARD!!

She hurls her glass of lemonade in his face.

Jack (*reacting, springing up*) Hey, hey, hey! What you doing? What the hell are you doing?

Tamsin goes indoors.
Jack stands wiping lemonade from his face. Work on the marquee has stopped.

(*Calling into the garden*) OK, mate. No worries! Carry on, lads! Bit of a domestic here, that's all. Carry on! Keep up the good work! My God! Look at this shirt.

Jack goes indoors to clean up.
The lights come up on the farmyard.

Monica and Simeon enter from the house. She is dressed less casually than usual as if she were going somewhere.

Monica I'm not walking out. I promise.

Simeon stands miserably staring at the ground like a small boy.

I'll be back every night, Sim. Every night. I'm not moving back in with him. I'm just – going to look after him. A little daycare, that's all. You don't have to worry about Carl. Not now my mother's here. They both get on fine.

Silence.

I mean, at nights George'll – have to make his own arrangements, won't he? I'll be back home here with you. I'm not running away, Sim. I'm never running away ever again, I told you. Promise. But Jack was right. I'm still technically married to George. And now he's . . . what's it going to look like if I leave him alone there? In that . . . ? What are people going to . . . ? How am I ever going to . . . ? (*Suddenly moved*) Oh! (*She hugs him*) I love you so much.

She releases him and moves away.

I must go. See you this evening. Sure you don't need the car today? No? I'll miss you. (*Backing away still looking at him*) 'Bye! (*She gives a little wave*)

Simeon (*not moving, not looking at her, sotto*) 'Bye!

Monica (*as she goes*) 'Bye!

Monica goes off.

(*Off*) 'Bye!

Simeon stands watching her. Monica is apparently mouthing silent goodbyes to him which he responds to silently.

445

The car starts up and pulls away.
Simeon gives a little wave.
Slight pause.

Simeon (*taking a flying kick at the seat*) Oh, bollocks and hellfire buggery! Ow! I've broke my bloody foot now!

Simeon limps off.
    The lights cross-fade back to Jack and Tamsin's patio. Jack leads Colin back from the garden.

Jack . . . then we're siting the band – I've got a little local rock band, local lads, friends of Tilly's – just over there, d'you see?

Colin (*attempting a keen interest*) . . . yes, yes, I see . . .

Jack I've had them build that platform there, you see? To protect the rockery. What do you think? Impressive or what? All the bunting.

Colin Very impressive. It's a big marquee, isn't it?

Jack That's the smallest they had. They don't come much smaller. I mean, after that, you're into bivouacs. I'm not interested in small. Not for my little girl.

Colin I won't even ask what it cost you.

Jack No object. It only happens once, doesn't it? Sweet sixteen, my little princess.

Colin Lucky girl.

Jack (*smiling*) Tam says I spoil her, but what the hell, I'm her dad, aren't I? If a father can't . . . (*Remembering, suddenly*) Now, Colin, you came round for something, didn't you, mate? Sorry, got carried away with all this other. Sit down. Please sit down.

Colin (*sitting*) Thank you.

Jack (*also sitting*) Right. Fire ahead, mate.

Colin Well, it's –

Jack Sorry – can I get you anything? A beer?

Colin Oh, no. No, thank you. Rather early in the day –

Jack Sunday morning. Never too early for a beer, eh? No?

Colin No, thank you, really and truly. Thank you, Jack. (*Slight pause*) This is really something I shouldn't be bothering you with. It's something I should be discussing with my wife or indeed my best friend. But since Basil Bender passed away . . .

Jack (*mystified*) Who's Basil Bender?

Colin Jack, I had this curious conversation with Kathryn this morning. I – was wondering what you made of it –

Jack's mobile rings.

Jack Sorry . . . excuse me, Colin. One second . . .

Jack glances at the screen and instinctively moves away.

Hallo . . . yes . . . yes . . . no . . . (*He goes a little way up the garden, dropping his voice*) . . . yes . . . yes . . . yes . . . no . . . no . . . (*Loudly*) No! I've said, YES, I DO! YES! (*He disconnects*) Shit!

Jack returns to Colin, who has been sitting patiently.

Just business. Sorry, mate. Carry on. You were saying, Basil Bender, I'm listening. I'm all ears now, I promise.

Colin No, it's nothing to do with Basil . . .

Jack No?

Colin (*awkwardly*) You see, I was talking to Kathryn this morning and she – she said – she told me she was off on holiday . . .

Jack Oh, that's nice. You both going, are you?

Colin No, that's the point. She's going with someone else.

Jack Who's she going with? With this Basil, is it?

Colin No, no. Not with Basil. He died seven years ago.

Jack Oh, I'm sorry to hear that.

Colin No, she intends going with George.

Jack George?

Colin Yes.

Jack George and Kathryn?

Colin Yes.

Jack But not you?

Colin No. Apparently not. To Tenerife. For two weeks. She assured me it was all above board. Nothing – er – mucky.

Jack I wouldn't bank on that, Col.

Colin She assured me . . .

Jack Not with George. Even with him being – you know – less than a hundred per . . . I wouldn't count on it not getting a bit . . . you know . . .

Colin Mucky?

Jack If you want to put it that way.

Pause.
  Kathryn has come out into George's garden to continue her work with a small tray of bright bedding plants and a fork. She starts to plant these in a neat row during the next.

You going to let her go, then?

Colin I don't think I can stop her, once Kathryn sets her mind on something . . .

Jack I wouldn't let my wife go on holiday with George. I'd chain her up in the broom cupboard. I mean, he's my best friend, he's my oldest friend, but even so . . . Some things, they're taboo, aren't they? Know what I mean? Sacrosanct. A man's marriage is one of them.

Colin Kathryn says she's going in her capacity as a nurse.

Jack With George?

Colin So she says.

Jack Doctors and nurses, eh? (*Reflecting*) It's a tricky call, isn't it? I can't see a way round this one, Colin, mate. Unless you take a firm line.

Colin I don't think I could possibly chain Kathryn up in the broom cupboard.

Jack Figure of speech.

Colin (*rising*) Well, thank you, Jack, for – your advice . . .

Jack (*also rising*) Sorry I can't be of more help, Col . . .

Colin (*as they move to the house together*) No, no. That's all been very useful. Given me something to chew on, at least.

Jack If I get any further thoughts, I'll be in touch. I'll give you a bell . . .

Jack and Colin go off into the house.
 In a moment, Tamsin comes out of George's house. She carries a plastic carrier bag of clean washing.

Tamsin Hi.

Kathryn Hallo.

Tamsin Oh, this looks better already. Well done. Brilliant.

Kathryn Bit of an improvement, anyway. At least it won't be such a shock for Monica.

Tamsin She arrived yet?

Kathryn No. She said sometime this morning. She was rather vague.

Tamsin Those are pretty . . . Bright.

Kathryn They're just a gesture. I picked them up from the garage on the way.

Tamsin Where's George?

Kathryn Still asleep, I think. Haven't heard him yet anyway.

Tamsin Oh, well, I'll hold on breakfast till he wakes up, then.

Kathryn No, it's alright. I'm doing breakfast –

Tamsin No, I'll do it.

Kathryn I bought some eggs specially. I'll do it.

Tamsin No, you're busy doing that.

Kathryn I'm doing breakfast. Leave it to me. You drop the washing off and get back home to Jack.

Tamsin I've bought sausages, though.

Kathryn No, I'm doing breakfast. George isn't that keen on sausages.

Tamsin Really? He always eats them whenever . . . I bought the Sunday papers for him, anyway.

Kathryn So did I.

Tamsin (*shrugging, rather miffed*) Oh, well, he can read them twice, can't he?

She lingers, watching Kathryn at work.

He doesn't know he's born, does he, George? All these women running after him.

Kathryn Tam, please don't hang around on my account, will you? I'll let Monica in when she comes. If she hasn't clung on to her key, that is. You hurry home to Jack.

Tamsin No, it's OK. (*Slight pause*) I left a bit of an atmosphere back there.

Kathryn Oh, dear.

Tamsin I'm afraid I shouted at him. Threw lemonade all down his favourite shirt. Which was a bloody stupid thing to do, of course. Because now it's me who's going to end up washing it, isn't it? I mean, I was perfectly justified. Perfectly.

Kathryn Oh. Problem?

Tamsin Oh, the usual.

Silence. Kathryn works on.

He's been fooling around with this girl – he has been for months . . . and at first I was terribly hurt and upset. I wanted to go round and scratch her eyes out – but then I thought . . . well, these things . . . there're two ways they can end, aren't there? Either they'll simply fizzle out of their own accord or else she'll cling on and we'll have this huge public acrimonious divorce. And knowing Jack . . . and knowing what I do of her . . . I didn't think they could face all that . . . So it's fizzling out. But it's taking its time . . . she's clinging on by the tips of her tiny finger-nails . . . which, in the meantime, I'm finding extremely tedious. Not to say irritating.

Kathryn What does Tilly think of all this?

Tamsin Tilly? I don't think she even knows. She hasn't said anything. Even if she does, she'll probably side with Jack. Her precious father . . . can do no wrong in her eyes . . . On top of that, to crown it all, last week he more or less accused me of being a secret drinker. Which is bloody good coming from Jack, I must say.

Kathryn A secret drinker? You?

Tamsin It's true. Cheek! I said, I'm sorry, love, you must be getting me muddled up with – someone else. You know I was so angry, on top of everything else, I was almost tempted to . . . almost . . .

Kathryn Tempted?

Tamsin To take George up on his offer there and then.

Kathryn His offer?

Tamsin To go with him to Tenerife.

Kathryn Tenerife?

Tamsin He asked me, the other night after rehearsals, would you believe? Right out of the blue. 'Fancy a bit of a holiday, kid? When all this is over?'

Kathryn What did you say?

Tamsin What do you think? No way, George. No way.

Kathryn Quite right.

Tamsin But I was tempted. I have to admit it. No doubt a lesser woman would have jumped at the chance.

Kathryn No doubt.

Tamsin (*laughing*) God! Imagine if I'd agreed. Jack's face. His wife and his best friend. Can you imagine?

Kathryn (*smiling rather thinly*) Yes.

Tamsin Can you imagine Colin's face? If it had been you?

Tamsin laughs again. Kathryn forces herself to join in but her laughter is rather more strained.
Monica enters. They both stop as they see her.

Monica Hallo. Oh, you're both here. Enjoying yourselves?

Kathryn Hallo, Monica.

Tamsin Hi.

Kathryn Welcome back.

Monica Yes. Only briefly. Thanks for holding the fort. Sorry I'm late. I'm here now to take over. I've brought the Sunday papers and his favourite lambs' kidneys from the farm shop, so that's his breakfast sorted. Where is he, by the way?

Kathryn Still asleep.

Monica No change there, then. He sounded quite cheerful when he called me yesterday. He's really enjoying rehearsing the play, you know. It was a brilliant idea of you all to involve him in something like that, it really was.

Monica starts to move back to the house, talking animatedly as she does so.

Just what George needs. We have to keep him involved, that's the important thing. He mustn't be allowed to get bored and start to brood. That's the only thing that will drag him down. He's like a kid. He needs people constantly around him. I must say he seems very up at present. You know, he was even suggesting we both have a holiday together? Which shows he must be feeling reasonably strong. George loathes and detests holidays, normally. Madness! I told him, no way is he lugging me off on a holiday. No way . . .

Monica goes off. Kathryn and Tamsin exchange a look and then follow. As they do, the lights cross-fade to Jack and Tamsin's garden.

It is the day of Tilly's birthday and the party is in full swing. The main event is happening further down the garden in the unseen marquee and beyond. A local rock band is playing in the distance. What it lacks in expertise it more than makes up for in energy.

Jack comes from the house. He carries a carton of fresh plastic glasses. Colin enters from the garden.

Jack (*as they meet*) . . . This lot are certainly getting through the booze . . .

Colin So I see.

Jack You not dancing then, Colin?

Colin This music's all a little bit vigorous for my taste . . . Middle age, eh?

Jack Yeah, yeah. Bit loud. Then we probably had it wound up just the same when we were their age, didn't we? If not louder. I remember George and me, we had the occasional evening together. Put a few away. (*Nostalgically*) AC/DC, Whitesnake, Def Leppard, Pink Floyd . . . Into all that, were you, Colin? Stadium rock?

Colin No, no, no. Mainly folk music, I think.

Jack What, Bob Dylan? Fairport? That sort of thing?

Colin – er, no, no – Donovan, I think. Julie Felix was another . . .

Jack (*puzzled*) Julie Felix? (*Shaking his head*) No . . .

Colin (*helpfully singing rather badly*)

'We're going to the zoo, zoo, zoo –
You can come too, too, too . . .'

Jack No, I can't say I remember dancing to that.

*Jack sets the carton down on the table. They stand
watching the scene in the garden.*

Look at Tilly dancing with George there, she's a picture,
isn't she? You could paint that, you know? Pre-Raphaelite?
With her hair done like that, in that dress? Wouldn't you
say so? Pre-Raphaelite?

Colin Yes, I suppose so.

Jack Do I mean Pre-Raphaelite? Or maybe Post-
Impressionist? I don't know, don't ask me, I was never
into art. I leave that to the women. And George. He can
spout on about art and all that for ever, George can.
Anyway, sixteen years old today and she looks stunning.

Colin She certainly does.

*Tamsin comes from the garden with a couple of bin
bags of dirty rubbish. She seems under pressure.*

Tamsin Jack, for the tenth time can you please bring those
extra glasses down, we've now completely run out . . .

Jack Will do, love, just doing it . . .

Tamsin . . . and tell Tilly to dance with someone other
than George for a change. Someone her own age . . .

Tamsin goes off into the house.

Jack (*after her*) You tell her! It's her party, she can dance
with who she likes, love . . . Nothing to do with me.
(*To Colin*) Tam's a bit tense. Between you and me, Col,
confidentially, she's been hitting the bottle lately.

Colin Tamsin?

Jack On the sly. Secret drinking.

Colin Tamsin as well?

Jack As well as what?

Colin As well as everything else? That's a worry for you, Jack –

Jack It's alright. No problem. As soon as all this is over, once George has – I'm arranging for her to see someone. Sort her out. Oh, I meant to ask you earlier, mate, how's – how's all that business with George and Kathryn? Them going on holiday together? Resolved all that, have you?

Colin Hardly.

Jack They still going?

Colin As far as I know.

Jack You don't mind?

Colin No. (*Slight pause*) Well, yes, I suppose I do mind. I mind very much, Jack. If I'm truthful. I mean, how's it going to look? To other people? My wife going off on holiday on her own with another man?

Jack Quite.

Colin How's that going to reflect on me? Whatever spin Kathryn puts on it, going as his unpaid nurse and so on, people are going to jump to conclusions, aren't they?

Jack I would. I wonder how his wife feels about it?

Colin Monica? I've no idea.

Jack I mean, she's left this other bloke of hers to come home to be with George, hasn't she? How's she going to feel if he buggers off in a couple of weeks with somebody else?

456

Colin Perhaps he's planning to take them both?

Jack A threesome? I doubt it. George might fancy one but I doubt if those two would.

Colin No, Kathryn would never put up with a – no, no. I don't quite know what to do, Jack, I really don't.

Jack You should have a quiet word with Monica, that's what you should do.

Colin You think so?

Jack Have it out with her. You should have it out with Monica, mate.

Colin Have it out?

Jack Out in the open.

Colin With Monica?

Jack The only way.

Colin Think so?

Jack Have it out in the open with her now. She's just down there now. See?

Colin (*losing his nerve*) No, I couldn't possibly, Jack, I couldn't possibly have it out, not with Monica. I mean, I'm a person who loathes having things out with anyone. I go to any lengths sometimes simply to avoid having it out.

Jack Well, if you won't, then I will.

Colin You will?

Jack (*calling down the garden*) Monica! (*He waves*) I don't mind having it out with her for you. I'm a businessman, I'm used to having it out. (*Calling again*) Monica! Over here, love! (*He waves again*)

Tamsin returns from the house. She sees the carton of glasses still on the table.

Tamsin Have you still not taken them yet? I can't believe it . . . I'm being left to do everything –

Jack Listen, there's no need – I keep saying –

Tamsin – all I'm asking you to do –

Jack – I'm paying good money for people to do all this – why's it left to you –?

Tamsin – because it's quicker to do it myself, that's why –

Jack – why the hell aren't they doing it –?

Tamsin – they're worse than useless –

Jack – they're professional caterers, love, being paid to help you –

Tamsin – they're a load of bloody college students – most of them stoned out of their . . . Are you going to take those fucking glasses down there or not?

Jack – no, I'm fucking not, Tam, will you fucking calm down, woman –?

Colin (*picking up the carton, nervously*) I'll take them, I'll take them!

Tamsin/Jack (*together, fiercely*) LEAVE THEM!

Colin scurries off down the garden.
Jack and Tamsin breathe heavily for a moment trying to regain their composure.

Jack (*recovering*) Now, calm down, love. Calm down. People are staring.

Tamsin Let them stare. I don't care, any more. I just don't care . . . our marriage is a bloody shipwreck . . . a car crash . . .

Jack It's Tilly's party, love. We've got to think of Tilly . . .

Tamsin Oh, bugger Tilly . . . Bugger her!

Jack What are you saying? She's our daughter, Tam . . .

Tamsin (*going off into the house*) No, she's your daughter. And she's a spoilt, pampered, self-centred brat! Which is entirely your fault!

Jack Bloody hell, Tam! How much have you had, love?

Jack stands shocked.

(*To himself*) She's totally rat-arsed.

Monica comes from the garden.

Monica Anything wrong, Jack?

Jack Ah, Monica!

Monica Tam alright, is she?

Jack Yes, she just – she just had a little crisis.

Monica Does she need a hand in there?

Jack No, no. Please! Leave her! Honestly. She's perfectly fine.

Monica Sure?

Jack You came with George, I see.

Monica Yes, we both came on the bus.

Jack Nice to see you together again. If only for . . . the time being.

Monica Yes, it is. For the time being. Sim's picking me up later. He needed the car today. He'll drive me home.

Jack Oh, right.

Pause.

Monica Great party. You've done her proud. She's a popular girl, your Tilly, isn't she? Loads of friends.

Jack Oh, yes. I'm not sure how many of this lot she knows personally, mind you, but who's counting? Probably climbing over the back wall there, some of them . . .

They laugh.

Monica George is showing off his dancing skills. As usual. I've not had a single dance with him. Fine way to treat your date, I must say.

Jack You want to dance with George?

Monica No . . .

Jack Because I can always tell Tilly to . . .

Monica No, no, no! Really. Leave them be. It's her birthday. Not my thing, this type of music. George was more into this sort of thing, of course. Constantly. God, she looks great. You must be so proud of her, Jack.

Jack (*modestly*) Well . . . Can't claim all the credit for that. Like her mum. When Tam was . . .

Monica Yes. Did you want me for something? You were waving me over . . .

Jack Yes. I really needed a quiet word, Monica . . .

Monica No chance of a quiet word, not down there.

Jack Yes, yes, yes. (*Gathering his thoughts*) It's a wee bit of a problem. Colin asked me to – talk to you about it – it's – I don't know if you're aware but it's this business of George and Kathryn . . .

Monica (*blankly*) George and Kathryn.

Jack About them going off on holiday together.

460

Monica Holiday?

Jack To Tenerife, apparently.

Monica George and Kathryn?

Jack You didn't know?

Monica To Tenerife? Who told you that?

Jack Colin.

Monica Who told Colin?

Jack Well, Kathryn, apparently.

Monica That she was going off on holiday with George?

Jack She says that George asked her.

Monica Kathryn's not going off on holiday with George.

Jack She's not?

Monica Certainly not.

Jack How do you know?

Monica Because I'm going off on holiday with George.

Jack Oh, I see. He's going with you, then?

Monica Obviously.

Jack So it wouldn't be like – that you'd both be going? You and Kathryn?

Monica Certainly not! I'm his wife, for God's sake. Despite everything, he's still my husband! He's certainly not going off with Kathryn, for God's sake. *Kathryn?* She's got her own bloody husband. Why isn't she going with him?

Jack Yes, I think that was what Colin was wondering.

Monica What's he got to say about it?

Jack He's not very happy, obviously.

Monica Well, then, he should stop her, the wimp! I mean, what's it going to look like if George goes off with Colin's wife? What am I going to look like?

Jack That's what I'm saying. Maybe George wants both of you to go along? Kathryn for the nursing and you, you know, for the – other stuff . . . Maybe George was thinking of that perhaps?

Monica (*growing steadily angrier*) Yes, that's perhaps what George wants but I can assure you, that isn't what George is going to get. George and me and *Kathryn*? The three of us? That is so gross! That is obscene. You have to be joking, for God's sake . . . Excuse me – (*Calling*) George! George!

> *Monica stamps off down the garden.*
> *Jack anxiously watches her go.*
> *Tamsin comes from the house and catches the end of this.*

Jack Oh, bloody hell . . .

Tamsin Who have you upset now? What have you been saying to Monica?

Jack We may have a problem here, Tam. George has double-booked.

Tamsin What?

Jack Apparently he's asked Monica to go on holiday with him.

Tamsin Yes, I know. To Tenerife.

Jack Yes, but did you also know he'd apparently asked Kathryn as well?

Tamsin Kathryn?

Jack I mean, it's not in a sense our problem . . .

Tamsin He's not taking Kathryn.

Jack No. That's exactly what Monica said –

Tamsin He's not taking Monica either.

Jack He isn't?

Tamsin Certainly not. She doesn't even want to go.

Jack She seemed to want to go just now.

Tamsin Well, she can't, even if she wants to.

Jack Why's that?

Tamsin Because George's already asked me. He's taking me. I've agreed to go.

Jack (*a little bemused*) You? He's asked all three of you? You're all of you going?

Tamsin What? All of us? Me, Monica and Kathryn? All three of us? You're joking! God, even by your chauvinistic standards, Jack, that is obscene! Obscene!

> *Tamsin goes into the house angrily.*
> *Jack stands, a troubled man.*

Jack Oh, my God!

> *Colin appears from the garden, tentatively.*

Colin OK, Jack? Had it out with her, did you?

Jack Yes, I had it out. Yes. We had it out . . .

> *Jack moves indoors still stunned by the news. Colin follows him.*

Colin Jack . . . Jack . . .

> *As they both go indoors, the sounds of the party fade and the lights cross-fade to the farm. Kathryn enters*

from the house, picking her way rather gingerly across the yard. Monica follows. They stand separately at a distance in silence.

In a moment, from the direction of the house, the sound of a small sports car pulling up, revving its engine ostentatiously and then silence. A second later, Tamsin joins them.

A silence.

Kathryn We need to sort this out.

Monica I've already said, there's nothing to sort out. He's coming with me. You two have no right to him –

Kathryn We have just as much right as you –

Monica I'm his wife.

Tamsin Who walked out on him. Left George all on his own so you could move in with – this farmer. I mean, I'm sorry, I'm sure he's a very nice farmer but –

Monica He is. He's particularly nice. Simeon's a very, very nice farmer indeed.

Tamsin Well, there you are then –

Monica As, by the same token, I'm sure your own husband is very nice.

Kathryn He'd be nicer still if she wasn't having an affair with George behind his back –

Tamsin How many more times, I am not having an affair with George!

Kathryn Well, dear, I don't know what else you'd call it. Mauling and pawing, fiddling and fumbling with each other during rehearsal when you think the rest of us aren't looking. Right in the middle of my scene last week –

Tamsin We were rehearsing –

Kathryn Well, bully for you! Practice makes perfect, dear!

Tamsin Jealous?

Kathryn Listen to me, I have known George far longer than either of you. We had a closeness, an intimacy, an understanding –

Monica Till you walked out on him and married Colin –

Kathryn (*emotionally*) I was there at the start of George's life, on the threshold of my own life . . . At overture and beginners . . . I really believe I'm owed it to be there with him at his final curtain . . .

> *She is quite moved by her own oratory.*
> *A short pause*

Tamsin I can't believe you said that. That is such – such sentimental bullshit, Kathryn . . .

Kathryn Oh, what would you know, you little girl . . . with your ugly little pink convertible car and your nasty vulgar nail extensions –

Tamsin – God! You're a spiteful, unpleasant woman, you really are –

Kathryn – and your badly dyed hair, you spoilt, tight-arsed little trollop –

Tamsin – you're a jealous, sexually frustrated, dried-up old bag, aren't you, without a shred of –

Monica (*sharply, over this*) Will you stop this, please? At once! This is getting us nowhere!

> *Slight pause.*

Kathryn Good mind to slap your face, cheeky little minx.

Tamsin Try it! I go to the gym twice a week, darling. I promise you, you'll finish up in the cow shit.

Monica Oh, I'm going for a walk. You two can sort this out between you, you stupid pair of schoolgirls. George is going with me and that's final.

Monica goes off across the fields.
Kathryn and Tamsin regain their composure.

Tamsin Sorry.

Kathryn No. I'm sorry.

Pause.

Has it occurred to anyone to ask George exactly what he wants?

Tamsin I think he wants precisely this.

Kathryn Really? And what is that? Precisely?

Tamsin I mean, what a way to go, eh? A load of women fighting over you? Threatening to cover each other in cow shit? Bloke's dream, isn't it?

Kathryn No, that doesn't sound like George. That might be the dream of lots of men, but that's not George. That's all rather petty. He's more of a man than that.

Tamsin Then what is he trying to do?

Kathryn You can never be sure with George. I think he might just be trying to put things right. Bring us all to our senses. Before he goes.

Pause.

But we can't be sure. I must call for my taxi. I'd have asked the man to wait but I wasn't sure how long all this was going to take.

Tamsin I'll give you a lift if you like.

Kathryn Oh, thank you.

Tamsin If you don't mind squeezing into my ugly little pink car . . .

Kathryn No, I think this dried-up old bag could just about manage that . . .

Kathryn and Tamsin go off towards the house. As they do so, the lights cross-fade to Colin and Kathryn's at night. Colin enters, returning from the end-of-show party. He stands outside taking in the night air.

Then lights up on Jack and Tamsin's, also at night. Jack, glass in hand, steps outside and stands. Like Colin he has been to the party. All, in their various ways, show signs they have been drinking.

Finally, at the farm, the sound of a car engine as headlights momentarily rake the yard. These die along with the elderly engine.

Simeon enters. He has been to the party, too. He is dressed in an unaccustomed suit. He stands in the darkness, staring out over the fields. Monica enters the farmyard.

Monica Yes, he's fine. Both fast asleep on the sofa. Him and Mother. Looked as if they've been playing Scrabble . . .

Simeon is silent. There is evidently an atmosphere between them.

Great party, wasn't it? Show was good, too, didn't you think? I thought it was. Colin was surprisingly good. Didn't think he had it in him. I thought Tamsin was a bit – well, I thought she was trying a bit too hard occasionally. And Kathryn was – well – she's always Kathryn, isn't she? She was good, I mean, don't get me wrong but – And George, of course, he was . . . good. Did you enjoy it, then? You haven't said.

Simeon Prefer movies.

Monica We can go to the cinema next time, can't we? Soon as I get back. Together. You and me. Mum'll babysit. Why not? Soon as I'm back.

Simeon Still going, then? Tomorrow morning?

Monica First thing. Early flight.

Simeon Not changed your mind then?

Monica I have to, Sim. For –

Simeon For him? For George?

Monica For me.

> *They stand.*
> *At Colin and Kathryn's, Kathryn comes out of the house to join Colin. A similar post-show tension between them.*

Kathryn It's still very mild. For September. Unbelievably mellow.

Colin Mmmm.

Kathryn Well, that was a good party. I mean, whatever her production's like, Peggy can always give a good party at the end of the run. You can't fault her parties. (*Smiling nostalgically*) Her final show, this. Her swan song. Passing of an era. I've done, God, it must be over twenty shows with her now. Dear old Peggy, she's no Peter Hall, but she's a reliable old workhorse. Gets the job done. Pretty smooth tonight, wasn't it? Third time lucky. (*Pause*) Oh, by the way, I'm sorry. I nearly ruined that first scene of ours, didn't I? My mind went totally blank. It must have been on . . . other things. Thank you for rescuing me. You were brilliant.

Colin I wondered whether to come in or not. But then there was such a long silence, even by your standards. I thought for a moment you might have been pausing. You know, for laughs. But seeing no one was laughing, I just came in with my next line, willy-nilly.

Kathryn No, quite right, you did right. As I say, my mind must have wandered on to . . .

Colin Other things. Like tomorrow morning?

Kathryn Partly.

Colin You still set on going?

Kathryn Yes. You'll be perfectly fine, I've left everything for you . . . don't worry, I've stocked up . . .

Colin Even if I asked you not to? You're still going?

Kathryn Yes, I am. But then you haven't asked me not to, have you?

Colin (*shrugging*) It's your own life, after all.

Kathryn No, it's our life, Colin. Yours and mine. It used to be, anyway.

Silence between them as they sit together in the darkness.
At Jack and Tamsin's, Tamsin comes out to join Jack.

Tamsin Tilly's gone straight up to bed. She was dead on her feet. One party too many, I guess. Enjoy the show, then, did you? Glad you both waited till the last night to see it. We more or less got it right tonight. More or less. Tilly enjoyed it. She said she did.

Jack Yes, she was having a great time. I was watching her, sitting next to me. Laughing away there.

Tamsin How about you? Did you laugh?

Jack Yeah, yeah. I laughed a bit.

Tamsin A bit?

Jack Well, you know, I couldn't take those scenes you had with George, I'm afraid. Couldn't keep your hands off each other, could you?

Tamsin We were acting. George is very good. At acting.

Jack Yes. Fooled me. Both of you. Look, don't go tomorrow, Tam. This is stupid, I'm asking you again not to go. I'm begging you. Please don't go. If you go, I will fucking fall apart, girl. I mean it. I will.

Tamsin is silent.

Listen, I'm sorry. I've ballsed everything up, I know that. And I don't deserve you, I know that. But I do love you, Tam. I love you very much.

Jack embraces her. He is crying. Tamsin responds and holds him.

You know that, you know that, don't you?

Tamsin Yes, I know that.

Jack You know that.

Tamsin It's alright, I'm not leaving.

Jack You're not leaving?

Tamsin (*kissing him on the head*) What, and leave you all alone with little Miss Midnight Caller? She's not having you. You belong to me, you bugger. Come on, it's chilly. Come inside.

Jack Yes.

Tamsin and Jack go into the house together.

Simeon Look, don't, for God's sake, go. Why do you have to go? You don't love him, do you? You said that. You love me, don't you?

Monica Two weeks. I'll be back. Promise. Then I'll be here. As long as you want me to stay. You mean the world to me, Sim. You know that.

Simeon (*walking away, resigned*) Yes.

Simeon goes off to the house.

Monica (*calling after him*) Sim, trust me. Please. (*To herself, in sudden panic*) Oh, God, I'm going to lose him, I know I am. What am I going to do? What am I going to do?

Monica follows Simeon off.
The lights fade on the farm area.
At Colin and Kathryn's the pair continue to sit in silence. One of the clocks strikes two.

Colin (*suddenly and, for him, quite forcefully*) Listen, I – I'd really rather prefer it if you didn't go, Kathryn. I really would be far happier, on the whole, if you stayed here.

Kathryn What?

Colin I insist you stay. With me. I insist!

Kathryn is silent. The other clock strikes three.

Do you hear me? (*Pause*) Kathryn? (*Pause*) Did you hear what I said?

Kathryn Yes, I was just pausing –

Colin For laughs?

Kathryn In amazement. You haven't said anything to me as forcefully as that for years. Not since I damaged the up-and-over door. My God, you were almost involved.

Colin So what's your answer? Are you staying or going?

Kathryn (*a slight pause*) In that case. Staying.

Colin (*a bit surprised*) What?

Kathryn Staying. Since you insist.

Colin Staying?

Kathryn Staying! Do listen, Colin. You never listen half the time, do you?

Colin Ah. My turn for amazement, then.

Kathryn Why's that?

Colin I could have sworn you'd have said 'going'.

Kathryn Well, there you are. Them that don't ask, don't get, as my grandmother used to say.

Colin George meant a lot to you, didn't he?

Kathryn Yes. He did. Once. But that was – back in the dark ages. We've all moved on. Grown up. Well, I'm not sure whether George has – he doesn't seem to have aged a jot – a sort of hippy Peter Pan. No, I could never have given him what he wanted. Not in the long term.

Colin You mean sex and things?

Kathryn No, not sex! I'm not talking about sex. I meant endless youthful fun.

Colin Fun?

Kathryn You probably won't believe this, Colin, but in those days I was quite a – jolly girl.

Colin Jolly?

Kathryn George and I laughed an awful lot in those days. We never seemed to stop, even when we were . . .

But the problem was he wanted to stay young for ever. Whereas I – as women tend to. Have to. In the end, someone has to be responsible.

Colin Glad you did. Grow up. I don't think I'd want to live with somebody jolly. A jolly Wendy. Well, not for long. No, on the whole you suit me fine. You tick the right boxes as far as I'm concerned.

Kathryn (*rising*) Thank you, Colin. Such a way with words, dear.

Colin (*rising*) I don't think I was ever that jolly even when I was young, you know.

Kathryn No, you weren't. That was one of the reasons I married you.

Colin Was it? What was the other one?

Kathryn You were never really young either, Colin.

Kathryn and Colin go indoors.
    The lights fade on their area.
    Jack comes out of the house.

Jack (*calling*) Tilly! Tilly!

Tamsin comes out.

Tamsin She's nowhere in the house, Jack. She's gone.

Jack Hang on, she may be in the tree house –

Tamsin No, Jack! I'm telling you, she's gone. She's left a note on her bed. Tilly's gone.

Jack Where?

Tamsin Where do you think? With George. She's gone off with George!

Jack George?

Tamsin She's taken her passport!

Jack She's gone off with George? (*Rushing into the house*) Oh, my God. My little girl! He's taken my little princess!

Jack rushes back into the house.

(*Yelling*) Tilly! Tilly!

Tamsin (*to herself*) Oh, dear God. (*Following*) Jack! Jack!

Jack (*off, despairingly*) GEORGE, YOU BASTARD!

Tamsin and Jack rush off. As they do so the lights on the area fade to:

Blackout.

SCENE TWO
(EPILOGUE)

November.
Cold and overcast.
At Colin and Kathryn's. Kathryn comes out of the house. She is dressed in funeral black.
She stands and takes a deep breath.
In a moment, Colin, similarly dressed, comes out to join her.

Colin You alright?

Kathryn nods.

Sure? (*Pause*) Rain's holding off. I thought I'd take the brolly just in case, though.

Kathryn I'm going to start making my way there, you know.

Colin What, now? We're in hours of time. It's only eighteen and a half minutes past.

Kathryn I'd like to get to the church a little bit early.

Colin Oh, alright. I'll get the car out, then, shall I?

Kathryn No, I'll walk.

Colin Walk?

Kathryn On my own. You follow in the car later. I'd like a few moments to myself.

Colin You sure? You don't need me along with you?

Kathryn No, not today, Colin. I'll be fine. Honestly.

Kathryn goes indoors.
  Colin stands alone. If he's at all hurt, he doesn't show it.

Colin Suits me. It's one hell of a walk, anyway. All uphill.

Colin slowly goes indoors.
  The lights cross-fade to George's house.
  In a moment, a blast of familiar rock music.
  After a second, Monica, also dressed for the funeral, comes outside. The music plays on as she fumbles in her bag for a cigarette. She is about to light it when the music stops abruptly. She hurriedly replaces the cigarette in its packet.
  Simeon comes out.

Simeon Sorry. Were you listening to that?

Monica Not really.

Simeon Not your sort of music, was it? A bit loud.

Monica Yes.

Simeon Seen everything you want to see, have you? I mean, take your time, I'm not rushing you . . .

Monica Yes, I just wanted a last look, you know . . .

Simeon Yes. In that case, I think we should . . . probably be . . .

Monica Yes . . .

Simeon . . . on our way. Whenever you're ready.

Simeon makes to return indoors.

Monica Sim . . .

Simeon Yes?

Monica Thanks for coming. I appreciate it.

Simeon (*shrugging awkwardly*) Well . . .

Simeon goes indoors.
   In a moment, Monica follows him.
   The lights cross-fade to Jack and Tamsin's.
   Jack comes outside. He is also dressed in dark clothes.
   He wanders a little restlessly. Looks at his watch.

Jack (*calling*) Tam! Tam!

Tamsin (*off*) Just a minute! Just a minute!

Jack (*calling*) We're going to be late at this rate.

Tamsin (*off*) Wait!

Jack (*impatiently*) Women!

He paces up and down anxiously. He checks his watch.
   Tamsin comes out, also dressed for the funeral.

Tamsin Sorry, I couldn't find these shoes anywhere. I looked in every single wardrobe. I knew I had them, I knew I hadn't thrown them out . . . Then I hadn't got the right tights . . . Tilly's on her way down . . . She's finishing getting ready.

476

Jack For God's sake. What's she playing at? Look at the time.

Tamsin She overslept. You know what she's like.

Jack I thought she'd decided she wasn't coming anyway? She said last night she didn't believe in funerals . . . ?

Tamsin Till you told her she had to come. Both of you, screaming and shouting.

Jack Well, she has to come. Out of respect for George.

Tamsin She hardly knew him. He was your friend.

Jack Hardly knew him? Shacked up in a hotel with him in the Canary Islands? How close did they have to get?

Tamsin It wasn't like that.

Jack And you believe her? (*Yelling through the door*) Tilly! TILLY! You come down this minute, do you hear me!

Tamsin I'll get her, I'll get her. Don't yell at her, Jack, not today . . . She's probably just as upset as we are. She doesn't show it. It's not cool to cry, apparently . . .

Tamsin goes indoors.

Jack (*calling after her*) I still can't take it in, you know. What the hell was George doing paragliding in the first place? A man in his condition, paragliding? It's classed as an extreme sport, isn't it? Why didn't that Spanish lot stop him from flying out to sea? Don't they have any bloody regulations over there?

Tamsin returns.

Jack Is she coming, then?

Tamsin No. She's changed her mind. She doesn't want to come.

477

Jack Doesn't want to –? (*Walking away frustratedly*)
I don't believe this . . .

Tamsin Jack. Please. Keep calm today. Come on.

Jack He was my friend, Tam. Why? Why? Why did he
do it? She was my little daughter.

Tamsin She's sixteen years old and a grown woman and
I promise you nothing happened between them.

Jack How do you know that?

Tamsin I'm her mother.

Jack Then why the hell did she go with him if it wasn't
for that? Why?

Tamsin She said it sounded like – like a bit of fun.

Jack (*incredulously*) A bit of fun? *Fun?*

Tamsin Yeah, fun. You know, fun. Like we used to have.

They go off through the garden to the garage.
  *The lights cross-fade to a new location. Separate and
yet overlapping with the other areas, this one is abstract,
perhaps indicated by lighting alone. It is an exterior
graveyard.*
  *The mourners gather around the invisible grave,
Kathryn and Colin, Monica and Simeon and finally
Jack and Tamsin.*
  *Jack has brought along a portable CD player which
he starts and sets down on the ground. Music starts.
George-style rock music which plays softly at first and
steadily builds.*
  *A seventh figure joins them, a late arrival, also
dressed in dark clothes. It is Tilly. She stands a little
apart from the other mourners.*
  Everyone, except Tilly, holds single white stem roses.

They stand, respectfully, heads bowed, saying a final goodbye to their friend.

A clergyman's voice, mingling with the music, begins to pay a kindly meant, if inaccurate, tribute to the late George Riley.

Voice We are all of us gathered here today, to say our final farewell to George Riley. Although, sadly, I didn't have the pleasure of ever meeting George personally, I do sense that he was a person greatly loved by all those who were fortunate enough to know him.

Under the next, Jack's mobile starts to ring its inappropriately cheerful ring. Jack hurriedly cancels the call. Tamsin glares at him.

George, so I'm told, was someone with an overwhelming passion for life and an infectious sense of fun. To sum him up, he was a joyous man in an often sadly joyless world. You know, learning more about George as I have been doing recently, sharing fond memories of him with his loving wife Veronica, with his friends, Jack and Tamara, Kathryn and Colin and, of course, with Tilly, whom I understand was with George during his final moments . . .

At the mention of his daughter's name, Jack starts to cry.

Tamsin, affected by this, starts crying too. Monica soon starts crying as well.

Kathryn joins in, a little louder.

Simeon, moved by Monica's grief, joins in.

Colin stands bravely holding it all in, his body convulsing silently.

Tilly, alone, stands motionless watching them expressionlessly. The voice continues.

. . . learning more about George as I have done recently, put me in mind of something our Lord once said long ago to the woman taken in adultery. 'Woman, where are they? Did no one condemn you?' She replied, 'No one, Lord.' And Jesus said, 'I do not condemn you either. Go, and from now on do not sin any more.'

As the music swells, the voice fades.

The display of grief grows louder still. After the roses are tossed into the grave, one by one, the party moves off, the exhibition of grief reaching a near crescendo, a little for George but a lot, we suspect, out of self-pity.

Tilly stares at them all, reluctant to join in such a public and, in her view, excessive display of emotion.

The others leave. Tilly shakes her head. With a last look towards where George lies, she gives a little wave and follows them out. As she does so, the music builds further and the lights fade to:

Blackout.

End of Play.